artificial l

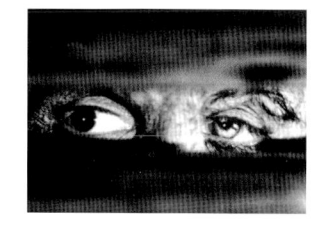

Artificial Humans

artificial humans
manic machines controlled bodies

edited by
rolf aurich
wolfgang jacobsen
gabriele jatho

jovis

Artificial Humans

© 2000 by Filmmuseum Berlin –
Deutsche Kinemathek
and jovis Verlagsbüro

Editors:
Rolf Aurich, Wolfgang Jacobsen,
Gabriele Jatho

Translation:
Stephen Locke, Ishbel Flett,
Pauline Cumbers

Advisors:
Rolf Giesen, Martin Koerber,
Klaus Kreimeier, Georg Seeßlen

Photographic work:
Lepkowski & Hillmann, Berlin

Conception of the film program:
Ian Birnie, Wolfgang Jacobsen,
Martin Koerber

A film program of the Film
Department of the Los Angeles
County Museum of Art in cooperation with Filmmuseum Berlin –
Deutsche Kinemathek, Goethe-
Institut Los Angeles and Internationale Filmfestspiele Berlin

Cover design and layout:
Volker Noth Grafik-Design / Ehret
Cover photos:
Frankenstein (1931), The Terminator (1984), Robocop (1987),
Johnny Mnemonic (1995), Lara
Croft (© by Eidos Interactive
Deutschland, Hamburg /
Filmmuseum Berlin – Deutsche
Kinemathek)
Typesetting and lithography:
Satzinform, Berlin
Printers:
DBC Druckhaus Berlin-Centrum
GmbH & Co. Medien KG, Berlin

Publication and translation of the
English version of the German
catalogue "Künstliche Menschen.
Manische Maschinen, kontrollierte Körper" (published on the
occasion of the historical retrospective of the Berlin International
Film Festival 2000) was made
possible with the generous
support of Friends of Goethe of
Southern California.

ISBN 3-931321-26-6

Artificial Humans

Contents

Manic Machines. Controlled Bodies
A Foreword
Rolf Aurich, Wolfgang Jacobsen, Gabriele Jatho — 7

Dream Replicants of the Cinema
Passage through Old and New Moving Images
Georg Seeßlen — 9

What's a Man?
Bred People, Intelligent Computers
Documents — 42

Can a Machine Ever Become Self-aware?
Thoughts on the Terminator
Giorgio C. Buttazzo — 45

Animated Machines
On the Terminator, Robocop and Blade Runner
Workshop Reports — 50

Possible People
Thoughts on the Literary and Cultural History of the Android
Peter Gendolla — 55

What is the Golem?
Legend, Literary and Cinematic Figure
Documents and Memoirs — 63

Granting Life
Impotence and Power of the Female Cyborg
Elisabeth Bronfen — 70

From Vampire to Vamp
On the Background of a Cinematic Myth
Klaus Kreimeier — 77

The Index is the Umbilical Cord
On Photo Doubles and Digital Chimeras
Katharina Sykora — 97

Ideal Idols
New Stars in Global Networks
Ulrich Gutmair — 103

Annotated Bibliography
A Selection
Holger Schnell — 109

Artificial Humans
Biographical Notes / A Glossary
Rolf Giesen — 113

Addenda
Authors / Acknowledgements / Photos — 127

Artificial Humans

Metropolis
Rudolf Klein-Rogge

Manic Machines. Controlled Bodies
A Foreword

by Rolf Aurich, Wolfgang Jacobsen and Gabriele Jatho

"It's moving – it's alive – it's alive – it's alive! Now I know what it feels like to be God!" The longing: "The brain of a dead man waiting to live again in a body I made with my own hands!" lies very close to the warning: He "was interested only in human life. First to destroy it and then re-create it. There you have his mad dream." The apprentice dreams of creating new life, and from a scientific point of view he has long since overtaken his teacher, whose reasoning never reaches beyond the moral standpoint. Of course, everyone immediately thinks of the story of Frankenstein, the avid Genevan researcher from Mary Wollstonecraft Shelley's novel, whose name has become synonymous with the creature he created. This great misshapen, disfigured, repulsive monster, composed of body parts recruited from the graveyard and the gallows and furnished with the brain of an "abnormal" mortal, excites our pity, particularly in the first talking version of the film, which gave us the dialogue. When his right hand – an appendage, not an organic part of the forearm, but the result of operations – moved for the first time, it was and still is a great moment in film history. American adaptations of this story had already been made in 1910 and 1915, but it was only with the version of 1931 that the definitive pattern emerged that has defined the iconography of the film motif "artificial man" up to the present day: Boris Karloff, as the stitched-up monster, is the quintessential artificial human being of cinema history.

Only a few days after the FRANKENSTEIN film was first released in Berlin, in May 1932, the journalist Wolfgang Koeppen mentioned, besides many other sensations and monstrosities to be found at Berlin's fairgrounds, a creature known as "Moto Fred," the "artificial human being," an attraction among many others with which "weary apprentices and girls, young workmen, the unemployed, and the ever toiling students" sought to escape the daily drudgery for a few hours in the evening. Hardly conceivable that such a show would awaken any great interest today. Quite the contrary: according to Ray Kurzweil, an American specialist for artificial intelligence, it will soon no longer be possible to distinguish between biological and electronic systems in our daily life, in other words, between man and machine. According to what he envisions, in the year 2029 – the screenwriters of the film TERMINATOR had also singled out this year – there will hardly be any conscious beings left that possess a lasting physical presence. Rather, life on earth will be replaced by a sojourn in a "thought-technological mechanical network." Human memory and human individuality could then be scanned and fed into data networks. This is a vision of bodiless beings that determine their existence qua power of thought. The film THE MATRIX illustrates a similar idea. Between this movie and FRANKENSTEIN lie almost 70 years and, above all, a radically changed world.

Perfect "models," wearing the constantly reborn fashion of the season, now conquer the catwalks virtually. If the photos of the models still have to be processed digitally in the glossies to create the ideal look, here in virtual reality the digital creation itself, designed by highly motivated animators according, above all, to the rules of the market, represents the attainment of the goal. "Bioengineering" has long since turned the medical branch into a repair shop with a store of spare parts, but the technology itself has meanwhile reached a certain degree of absurdity, if we can believe the reports we read which claim that the knee joint of the Barbie doll is wonderfully suited as a prosthesis for the human finger. People are busy working on artificial human beings – and also on human substitutes: it is reported that virtual policemen patrol in front of Brazilian banks and department stores. The actress and diva Marlene Dietrich is soon to be resurrected as a "cloned" digital icon. What, however, if the state needs – for example – worker slaves and thus human clones?

Another kind of two-class society? A society of Valids and In-Valids? Is this so inconceivable and monstrous? A bit creepy – yes. A futuristic vision – not entirely. Caught up in this duality, the despicable "racial policy" of National-Socialism divided human life into "unworthy" and "worthy." The decoding of human DNS promises in the future to enable the genetic programming of the perfect human being. DNA molecules offered as a little bonus package on the order form of expectant parents? For couples wanting to have children in Andrew Niccol's movie GATTACA, this is no longer a question of conscience: thanks to genetically impeccable trappings, the test-tube babies are automatically considered the shining lights of the social order. The others are left out in the cold, clearly behind the times, stuck on the past tense: "They used to say that a child conceived in love has a greater chance of happiness. They don't say that any more." Vincent knows that nobody believes this any longer in the brave new world of Gattaca – and it takes an enormous physical and psychological effort to procure the identity of a Valid for himself. The genetic code of another man is now his calling card – and allows him, the In-Valid, to realize his dreams. A retroactive genetic upgrade, and yet at once the cinematic proof that supposed (biological) deficiencies are not shortcomings, after all.

Münchhausen had the gift of eternal youth. Dorian Gray didn't want to age, either. Longevity is an eternal desire that might just be on the way to realization: people are becoming older and older. And remaining young. Pop star Cher represents a fantasy of cosmetic omnipotence, a "Homuncula of her own accord," as the essayist Dieter Bartetzko put it, a diva whose ageless face has long since been completely relieved of irregularities and of the features of her forefathers that were once so evident. Georges Franju's film LES YEUX SANS VISAGE shows satanic face operations that a doctor carries out on young women to get skin-grafts in order to restore the countenance of his daughter to its former condition, whose face has been completely disfigured in an accident. The victims must die, however. Skin and the peeling off of skin – this is a matter here of give and take, or in other words: a deal with losers.

Schopenhauer begins his main work with the sentence: "The world is my idea." And adds: "The world is my will." Today the formula could possibly read: Will plus idea equals virtual reality. In David Cronenberg's eXistenZ, these levels can no longer be distinguished. If you look it up in a dictionary of philosophy, you will find – from an existentialistic viewpoint – that existence generally refers to the individual existence of human beings: it is a form of being particular to the human race – and not to things. It is not simply given to people to have this form of being as such. Man has the possibility to realize it – or not, as the case may be. Man creates his existence, according to the existentialists: it is his *design*. In Cronenberg's film, a game designer designs a computer game called eXistenZ. Cronenberg goes a step further, however. His game is no longer loaded onto a hard disk, but fed directly into the nervous system of the players. Monitors and other hardware have become superfluous, as have plugs and cables. The "bioport" as additional body orifice. Organically generated game stations – "MetaFlesh Game Pods" – and for data transfer a kind of umbilical cord: the "UmbyCord." The body as interface? The brain as black box? Man as machine?

Change of scene: the subject matter is similar, but the terms are different. In Tad Williams' novel tetralogy "Otherland," a cyberspace saga that plays with the possibilities of the new media, Orlando Gardiner has created an online identity for himself. A synthetic double, a digital shadow. The network isn't a substitute world for him; rather, the network is his meta-existence. Offline he is a small boy with a serious illness. Bothersome cable connections and other technical inconveniences are a thing of the past in this world: "He reached up to his neck, fondling the new wireless connector, a birthday gift he had bought himself through mail order. The telematic jack was light and almost unnoticeable – all that showed was a rounded white plastic button fitted over the top of his neurocannula." Gardiner's software agent Beezle Bug can feed data directly into his auditory nerves; screens have long since disappeared from the walls: visual information is transmitted directly into the optic nerves.

There is a tradition in literary history that deals with the topic of artificial people and beings, puppets, and automatic devices: the Frankenstein monster, the automatic chess set in Ambrose Bierce's story "Moxon's Master," the robots in Karel Capek's drama "R.U.R." and in Isaac Asimov's SciFi stories "I, Robot," the test-tube babies from Aldous Huxley's "Brave New World," the mechanical domestic in G.K. Chesterton's short story "The Invisible Man," the Homunculus, which Goethe reported on and Laurence Sterne wrote about in "Tristram Shandy," H.G. Wells' fictional half-human beings in "The Island of Dr. Moreau" or Philip K. Dick's androids in "Do Androids Dream of Electric Sheep?," and not least of all the Golem of Rabbi Loew – these are only a few examples.

There is a corresponding tradition in film history, including Charles Chaplin's worker who almost literally turns into a machine, reacting in Modern Times (1936) to the breakdown of the assembly line like a piece of machinery without a cutoff switch, one of the most discerning examples. From there it is not very far to the factory robot. Brigitte Helm as Machine-Maria in Metropolis became a prototype of the machine in human form which turns into the great seductress, a robot-like demon. American cinema gratefully latched onto this myth, popularized the literary formula, and refined it in the form of showbiz: Maria has been reborn as Madonna. Many films from the nineteentens to the thirties, and even productions from the fifties, are believed lost. While researching this topic, one comes upon interesting titles like Homunkulieschen, a film farce from 1916, where not an alchemistic, but rather quite natural birth of a freak is at the center of attention, or Die elektrische Puppe (The Electric Doll, 1916), which is supposed to have been a Chaplin film, but probably wasn't. One also comes across titles such as Harry Piel's fantastic science fiction film Die grosse Wette (The Big Bet) from 1915/16, which was also shown under the title Der Elektromensch (The Electric Man). However, these films apparently exist in title only; they have been lost. This likewise applies to Wolf Schmidt's satirical comedy Der ideale Untermieter (The Ideal Lodger, 1956), in which two very different beings from two quarreling families, a 14-year-old girl and Robsy, a little metallic robot with the vocabulary of an average person, form an alliance and not only rescue the family peace, but also inspire both fathers to examine the question of whether man is master of technology or vice versa. In the case of some other films, only fragments have survived: Otto Rippert's six-part Homunculus series of 1916 and the Italian production L'Uomo meccanico, which was directed by André Deed in 1920.

The discussion about artificial beings has lost none of its ethical topicality: gene technology delimits one of the most important principles of evolution – that of "error-friendliness," as the scientist Ernst von Weizsäcker once formulated it, the tendency for irregularities to occur. The Golem mutates in film history to the robot, to the man-machine, and to the anthropoid being without a soul. He is slave, child, servant, watchdog. When it comes to creating or acquiring an artificial human being, the main intent is often to exploit it and make it serve one's own purposes, a fact that is freely conceded. The Golem is also demon, criminal, and wild animal, after all. And rebel. Rebellious slave. Without a soul, then?

This retrospective and book deal with plagiarisms and their cinematic-technological reality. It is about homunculi, the magical mandragora Alraune, robots, androids, cyborgs – and about virtual celebrities. But also about the romanticism of monsters and the melancholy of artificiality. The laboratory of Dr. Frankenstein is opened up here. Documents from the history of literature and film are gathered in this book, and testimonies to ideas on reproduction and artificial intelligence. From the Golem to the Terminator, from Machine-Maria to Alraune, from Homunculus to R2-D2: media worlds and many close encounters of the third kind. Brave new world, artificial intelligence, body industry and gene technology, and virtuality. Encounters with artificial people suggest the question: Am I real? In the films the "creatures" have long since exclaimed: I'm alive!

Dream Replicants of the Cinema
Passage through Old and New Moving Images

by Georg Seeßlen

Man is no being that is one. The individual, undivided, is his dream, not his reality. He sees himself as split, continuously divided, and removed from himself. Here, he breaks up into body, soul, and spirit, there, into gaze and image; here, he is the object of desire, there, the subject of love; here, he is what he seems to be, there, what he wants from himself. He is man and woman, history and nature; he is the being that needs image, mask, and mirror. All his reverie, his storytelling, his creating have only two points of departure, the miracle of unity and the horror of never-ending division. This is why his world is populated by heroes, demons, and gods, by shadows and *doppelgängers*; this is why he is constantly searching for his counterpart – only in order to find himself.

Supremacy over people means nothing but playing with this separation and with their longing for unity. Thus, man becomes the creator and victim of his own history, of his organization of time and space, and the closer he examines it, the more mercilessly it reveals itself as an illusion. And so he is split again, on the one hand into the being who examines with cruel lust the scissions he himself induces, while observing with fear and fascination the cleavage carried out upon him; and on the other hand into the being who creates his own unity, perhaps in the image of the one God who tolerates no other god beside himself, in the image of the love that makes a unit out of two, or in the image of the hero who has never left the body of his mother and has made the world his interior.

In order to become complete, man needs both his image and his reflection; he becomes whole only in the image of the other. But this image is the unknown, is his death, at the same time. For the image is *more complete* than he himself, it will possibly even outlast him; by wanting to become whole, he divides himself even more. This is why a love story has the same structure as a war, the encounter with an alien the same as the confrontation with one's double, if all this is to become a story and then a moving image. Every story that can be told tells itself in transition from divisions to the whole, or, vice versa, as the story of disintegration.

And one of the most pronounced stories of disintegration and unity is that of the creation of an artificial likeness, or counter-image. It is a form of letting the divided aspect of a person become manifest in an image, of capturing the horror which elsewhere (with Hitchcock, for example) flashes up as the inexplicable loss of identity in a shape that could be overcome in one way or another. It becomes manifest as soon as the narrative begins: in the myths of all peoples, in the creature that wants to become the creator, in the image that demands a life of its own. In its origin, this myth is nomadic; aspects of protection and deliverance give rise to one another. This image is polyvalent – just like the cinematic image. It required two great stories to make the scandal complete: the monotheistic legend of Creation on the one hand and scientific and capitalistic logic on the other. And at the same time these two big stories are for their part causes of the manic production of the myth.

The Christian Scandal

"The program of the artificial production of a human being," says Stanislaw Lem, "represents an act of blasphemy in our society. Man is attempting to repeat the act of creation; in other words, it is a caricature, a human attempt to be like God. Such a gamble, according to the dogma, cannot be successful; and should it nevertheless come to that, it is said that diabolical forces have helped in this work, that Hell has stood by the creator of the homunculus. There are myths from pre-Christian times, however, which speak of homunculi and don't hold them to be the result of a collaboration between man and the forces of evil. The point is that these myths originated in pre-Christian times, but also far from Judaism, which of course became the forerunner of Christianity. For in principle, a religion can remain entirely neutral toward the question of 'the artificial production of human beings'; only the Mediterranean culture, codified by Christianity, sees the homunculus as the result of blasphemy, as already mentioned. This is why the 'proto-robots', these literary prototypes from former centuries, are usually evil or at least uncanny, like for example the Golem."

The production of an artificial human being – as an image with a living soul, as resuscitation of the dead, as mechanically magical reproduction, as a mixture of mechanical and organic being, as cybernetic shadow beings, or as new biological creations from altered genes – is therefore nothing short of the taboo violation that separates the two stories, and their resolution in everyday perception, from each other once and for all: the prerequisite is removed from the one story, while the other cancels itself out retroactively from its conclusion. So the two of them must be joined together in this fantasy automatically, as it were. The scientific image disrupts the religious image so severely that it can only be understood in the religious sense, and vice versa. The function of myth therefore takes reference to its time, as well; on the one hand, it speaks of a look into the past – to the pre-Christian era on one level, the pre-scientific on another – and, on the other hand, it tells of anticipation – of the post-Christian era on one level, and the post-scientific (and post-capitalistic) world on another. The story of the artificial human being, despite all literary pre-formulation, is therefore a cinematic topic par excellence: the myth leads automatically, as it were, to a gamble with time and with space. For although this *parallel being* – this artificial being whose existence parallels man's – may very well be in a position to develop human abilities and human sensations, his experiences of time and space remain just as different from man's as those of personality and transcendence.

The artificial human being is therefore not only a predicament for the culture of Western Christianity with respect to its own creation myth, but it also drives the myth into an "image trap." Artificial man experiences with his own creation, with his own projection, a Cain and Abel story.

The Production of Magic / The Magic of Production

At least in our cultural circles, to which Stanislaw Lem is referring, the myth of artificial man has had to go through three stages: the pre-Christian, magic stage of living images, from the Colossus of Rhodes on up to the Golem; the Christian stage of the blasphemous rebellion against the divine monopoly on creation and images; and finally, the bourgeois, techno-scientific stage of the splitting of the human image in the material world and of the final escape from evolution. In this post-modernist age, we are perhaps now in a fourth stage vis-à-vis artificial man, namely the artificial human being born of the shadows of data and information, as a being that has been developed neither out of the tool (like the robot) nor from his likeness, but directly from dreams; a being, in other words, that originates out of division itself. And something else has happened: the artificial human being has shifted from the "terrible" to the "possible" being, and he threatens to shift from the "possible" to the "feasible" being. Because, to draw on Stanislaw Lem once again, everything that man can imagine, and which can be realized, will at some point be realized. And one of the forms in which something can be made imaginable is popular culture, is the world of cinema.

In the cinema, we find the parallel beings in all these different stages; the most wily trick of this medium both in and outside of time may in fact be that it mixes these stages again. Just as its story of creation puts the magical, the Christian, the technological-scientific, and the communicative areas in relationship with one another, so, too, the fears are diffused: the "reasonable" fear of the risks of the feasible, the magical fear of violating the taboo, and the Christian and the material-aesthetic fear (of an image without a mirror). Science fiction, the most prominent genre for the cinematic construction of the parallel being, is characterized precisely by the fact that it has recourse to both the pre-Christian period of myth and the future with its more or less unlimited technical possibilities.

This cinematic image originates as a rule from a short circuit between the magical and the mechanical views of the world. It condenses cultural history out of both of these views. Or, to put it another way: at the same time as it tells of the horror of a recent split, it also dreams of a new union between myth and science. In the first half of this century, blasphemy was still punished: artificial man was created again and again to test the rank and order of the world – the cultural, the social, the aesthetic, the religious, the scientific, and, time and again, the sexual order – and to confirm this order through the artificial being's tragic sacrifice.

The Golem, who was molded from clay and given life by the contents of the *shem*; Rotwang's creature Maria in Fritz Lang's film METROPOLIS (1925/26), a being consisting of half magic, half mechanism; the monster created by the "modern Prometheus" Frankenstein – there are always two processes necessary to create man's parallel being: the "scientific" assembling of materials and energies, and the magic ritual. Even with the more recent androids and robots in the movies something always has to happen that goes beyond the mere "industrial" manufacture of the parallel being. Even when, in WEIRD SCIENCE (1985) by John Hughes, a female being created out of the computer fantasies of two kids steps into their pubescent fears and desires, it requires, as with Frankenstein, a flash of lightning from heaven to complete the last step from her mere projection into "real" life.

Just as it can no doubt be claimed that the myth of artificial man has existed as long as there has been storytelling, it must also be noted that this myth doesn't exert the same degree of influence at all times. In the familiar history of our popular culture, the times in which we are virtually obsessed with this motif alternate with times in which we are more involved in other figments of the imagination. The myth of artificial man melts in with our current experiences and fears and seems to be most conspicuous when outward stagnation is found hand in hand with inner unrest. Paradoxically, in fact, the creation of artificial beings appears not only as a reaction to technical innovations that suggest the "feasibility" of the "forbidden project," and not only in response to crises of transcendence, but also as a reaction to the experiences of historical and social impotency. Perhaps for this reason we aren't too surprised to find that the creation of artificial humans in both the major and minor films treating this topic rarely takes place in a "white," perfect, scientific future, but rather in civilizations in the throes of disintegration, neglect, and major catastrophes. Nothing seems to stimulate the mad scientists of our popular mythology to create artificial humans so much as famine, overpopulation, civil war, and the disintegration of industrial production. The human double, in the stage of its conceivability at the very latest, is less a harbinger of the apocalypse than the result of it, a post-doomsday fantasy. In other words: the question of whether the birth of the artificial human being subsumes history, or, conversely, whether the annulment of history brings about the appearance of the *un*-natural post-human being, remains unanswered in our popular mythology.

The Rites of Passage

According to common opinion, active working adults are just as suspicious of the fear- and desire-inspiring fantasy of artificial man as are people of firm religious belief. This fantasy tends to appear at the breaking points of one's biography, revealing all too gladly its second, psycho-sexual content, just as it shows up at the breaking points of the history of civilization. The story of Frankenstein's monster, for example, which has changed only inconsiderably in the movies over the course of time, offers messages that are usually connected with psychological and social problems of adolescence. We can observe a revolt in the family saga novels: the "sacred" unit of father, mother and child is dissolved. The father who creates a child without a mother is the "scientific" answer to the religious fantasy of the mother who bears a child without a father (seen most recently in STAR WARS: EPISODE I from the year 1999), and this child, engendered outside of the designated order, must always turn against its parents, who didn't grant it

FRANKENSTEIN, 1910
Charles Ogle

Dream Replicants of the Cinema

FRANKENSTEIN, 1931
Colin Clive, Boris Karloff

FRANKENSTEIN, 1931
Boris Karloff, Marylin Harris

BRIDE OF FRANKENSTEIN
Boris Karloff

11

Dream Replicants of the Cinema

Dream Replicants of the Cinema

Dream Replicants of the Cinema

BRIDE OF FRANKENSTEIN
Elsa Lanchester, Boris Karloff

BRIDE OF FRANKENSTEIN
Elsa Lanchester

14

the primal bliss of symbiotic unity. Artificial man turns the evolution of the "individual" upside down: whereas the "natural" person is born in his "entirety," which he must then lose in the course of his life, thus becoming a divided being, the artificial human being comes into the world in the condition of division and longing for unity (even if it doesn't know with whom or with what it should be united).

It is not without good reason that the basic epic structure of the FRANKENSTEIN films, but also of other horror movies, is that of transformation, a structure closely related to that of the fairy tale. Similarly, the teenager in the stage of adolescence "finds himself caught in the involuntary transformation from a stage of comparatively unequivocal and safe childhood into a new, puzzling stage that he doesn't understand, over which he has no control, and which he fears – with a certain justification. Strange feelings and natural urges develop, and he is shocked and fascinated by his new biological attributes, which, in the context of repressive puberty, he associates with secrecy, darkness, evil, and danger." (Walter Evans) The artificial being, like Pinocchio, goes through the creation of a normal person in concentrated form, so to speak (or must fail at it). With FRANKENSTEIN, this transformation takes place on two different levels. On the one hand, the monster himself tries to become human, but his instincts and the lack of understanding from those around him drive him to his death. An example of a failed transformation! On the other hand, however, the monster's creator Frankenstein also undergoes a transformation, changing namely from a near-manic researcher obsessed with his attempt to carry out the act of creation "without a woman" ("with my hands, with my own hands") into a husband who finally gives up his "experiments in the dark." An example of a successful transformation! These two transformations are interwoven; Frankenstein refuses to marry his fiancée because "there can be no wedding while this horrible creation of mine is still alive." (The quotations refer to the film by James Whale from the year 1931). The death of the artificial being not only reverses one of the cultural-historical splits – the alienation of the entire process of industrialization, of the creation of the being out of the body, so to speak – but also the legend of one's own birth and deliverance. Just like the fantastic being in a fairy tale, either friendly companion or demonic force, tries to help the real person to answer the question of who he is in order to free himself from a symbiotic unit, so, too, does the artificial being when he has to point out to his creator why he is so alien and dangerous.

"I made it with my own hands," cries Baron Victor Frankenstein in the novel, in the film adaptation by James Whale, and later in the versions of Hammer Productions, and even later in Kenneth Branagh's version, as if he were a Shakespearean hero. But after all, this mad nobleman was only dreaming the apparently ancient patriarchal dream of creating life without taking the detour through the puzzling body of Woman, as the feminist criticism explained to us in the seventies. So the desire to create the animated machine or the artificial human being, from the Golem and the robot on up to the cloned human being, can possibly be traced back to a single dreadful original cause, the "bourgeois" male fantasy of creation without need for a woman. Accordingly, the mechanization of the creation story could be related to this male fantasy, which aims to drive the female aspect out of its genealogy. Up into the popular culture of the thirties robots are beings that don't fit into either the divine or the natural cycle of the life, which perhaps explains why the robots in films show such an irresistible urge to drag away frightened women in their steely arms. And their creators are heavily punished again and again for this blasphemous act of creation. Frankenstein's heirs keep wanting to create the ideal human being, the Nietzschean superman, but only manage to produce a mechanical Oedipus that directs its fervent desires toward the creator's fiancée. When a human Ego tries to create a mechanical or aesthetic double, it only produces a dreadful Id, an unchecked instinctual being, or else a punitive Superego, a machine god or controlling machine. The creature of this father doesn't identify itself with its creator, and although there are hardly any creation stories without strong erotic connotations, it is virtually impossible to imagine a "homosexual" relationship between the creator and his creature. In the Gothic microcosm of the family saga novels, as well as in the industrial macrocosm of science fiction, there seems to be only one model for the myth of the artificial human being: as "son" the being becomes the murderer of the father, as "daughter" it becomes the expression of incestuous desire. The artificial human only becomes a dangerous "person" when it has a gender.

The robot here is nothing but the industrially intensified variation of the split-off male destructive drive, not unlike the vampire, the werewolf, and the zombie in the fantasy of the Gothic horror story. But at the same time it is a fantasy of the oppressed against the oppressors, a mechanized Robin Hood, a child with anarchistic dreams. The Golem, the parallel being created out of clay that is supposed to guard the Jewish community against the outer enemy, becomes a danger to those who brought him to life. Because, among other things, the mechanical acceleration of history must necessarily change the machine, the instrument itself.

This is why it is only natural that we treat an artificial being not only with fascination, as toward an "improved" human being, and with horror, as toward a self-created competitor that shows us our distorted reflection, like in a funhouse mirror, but also with pity, as toward a child who has been left alone, a creature that has been abandoned by its creator and, between its solitary self and the infinitely suggestive world, has never experienced a mother. In the movies, the artificial human is, among many other things, a being that at first wants to become a "complete" human being, but then splits into the animal Id, the monster or the killer robot, and the Superego, a controlling machine set on world supremacy. The only thing it cannot become is the Ego, in a twofold sense: as a complete subject on the movie screen and as a complete object of identification for the viewer. Frankenstein's monster is the most extreme form of alienated existence. To us the Boris Karloff monster only embodies the taboo violation in part; on the other side, far more dreadful, we see ourselves as the outcast: the imperfect, abandoned creature.

The artificial human of our imagination is therefore a breaking point in a monotheistic philosophy, in a linear history of evolution, and in the architecture of the family saga, all at the same time. No wonder that we are so obsessed with repeating and reworking this image, in the movies and elsewhere.

The Image that Frees Itself from the Original

That cinema dreams so intensively of constructing artificial man probably has to do not only with the general virulence of the myth, but also with the longing to be able to arrive at a vision through imitation. The cinema wants to see reality, certainly, but it also wants to see what lies behind it, and it wants to see what goes beyond it. As to the human being, cinema has to go beyond the Christian paradox, namely that man was created in the image of a God who for His part forbids man to make an image of Him. In creating the artificial, second human being, the doubtful hero of this legend repeats not only the divine act of creation, but he also changes it. He brings out what is hidden inside himself so that it can be turned into the image. Moreover, and this is where the horror typically begins, he cannot prevent his creation from looking back at him. That this creation is "technically" perfect and morally defective, that it is necessarily "ugly" on the one hand and "incomplete" on the other, is reflected all the more dreadfully in this gaze. The artificial being only becomes dangerous at the moment when it begins to see and turns into the harshest and most merciless critic of its creator. It isn't the intelligence of HAL, the supercomputer in the spaceship of Stanley Kubrick's 2001: A Space Odyssey (1965–68), that is so terrible, but the gaze into its camera eye. In The Terminator (1984), Arnold Schwarzenegger's cyborg takes his eye out of its socket in front of the mirror and a video camera becomes visible behind it. This explains among other things the film's sequences that are seen through a search device, in which we can imagine ourselves as objects hunted by a foreign aggressor. In this sense, every artificial being is a revolt of the movie image against itself and against the gaze.

If the image is a "surrogate" for the absent one, the sovereign, or the lover, we must always hope that the picture will replace the absentee in the best way and fear that the image could come alive and begin to see (for example, see that our loyalty toward the absent person – above all the dead – can never be guaranteed a hundred percent). Images we can see through, images that metamorphose, images through which something different, something behind them can be "touched," belong to the film stories we never grow tired of.

The discourse on movie images and artificial beings is clearly not only determined by the "major" films, which, like 2001, Blade Runner (1982) or Terminator 2 – Judgment Day (1991), are already conceived as many-layered mythological constructions and at the same time as a reflection on such constructs. It is reflected even more in the infinite network of the recurrent images and fantasies of the B-movies, the genre fodder, and the products of "trash culture," which are comparatively rarely drawn upon to explain the complicated relationship between man and his images and machines.

Proto-Images

Homunculus, the Golem, and Frankenstein's monster. The first artificial beings of fantasy and horror films came out of the magical past, and it is love, the great wholeness, that is able to banish them again. The six-part series film Homunculus (1916) by Otto Rippert tells about an artificial human being generated by the brilliant scientist Hansen and his assistant Rodin in the laboratory retort. At first the being is an ideal human figure with exceptional mental qualities. It is only when he learns that he is not a real human being that he begins to feel lonely and outcast and deceived about the essence of being human: love. He wanders restlessly through the world, constantly seeking the company of people who know nothing of his origin. But no matter where he turns up, everyone has already heard of his nature: "But that is Homunculus, the man without a soul, the devil's henchman – a monster!" The rejected longing of Homunculus turns into hatred. He becomes a dictator seeking only revenge. He "disguises" himself as a worker and agitator, setting off rebellions that then give him as tyrant the pretext for further cruel oppression of the people. Finally, when he causes the outbreak of a world war, a thunderbolt strikes him down and brings his rule to an end. Doesn't this film, don't in fact many of its successors, already show us something like a picture of nascent Fascism? The offended and underdeveloped soul strives to become a machine. Since no one looks at him, the Homunculus transforms himself into the omnipotent gaze.

Der Golem (1914) by Henrik Galeen and Paul Wegener is based on stories about Rabbi Loew, who awakens the Golem, a clay statue, to life by fastening a magical sign to his chest. This medieval Jewish story is updated by Galeen and Wegener: at archaeological excavations, workers come upon the Golem figure. An antiquarian, versed in the use of cabalistic signs, brings the Golem back to life. At first only a willing tool in the hands of his master, the Golem develops more and more human feelings, falls in love with the daughter of the antiquarian, and is forced to recognize that he will never become a real human being. He turns into a destructive monster and meets his end by falling from a tower in a phallic death of love.

The motif is familiar from the Frankenstein story. But the fact that the Golem's strength becomes uncontrollable has to do here with the saga which relates that he can only be brought to life in order to fulfil certain tasks. He is a "tool," like the broom of the sorcerer's apprentice. In contrast to the story of Frankenstein's monster, the blasphemous deed is not really the act of creation, but rather the way the artificial being is put to use. If one takes the story as political allegory for the moment, the film shows the risk of a dictatorship temporarily installed by and under the control of the ruling class, which can then turn against its initiators. For what comes into the world with the artificial human is not merely the iniquitous parallel being, or one of those spirits called up by the scientific sorcerer's apprentice that can't be gotten rid of. Rather, it is also an enormous source of power. If it is still the sin against the creation myth itself that interests us about Frankenstein and his more or less Gothic successors, the question now arises, apart from that of what the artificial human being actually is, of whom the artificial being belongs to, a question that fires our imagination regarding catastrophes. And what can he do? In short: the way always leads from a revolt in the psychosexual family saga to the discourse of religion and science and then on into the realm of political metaphysics. That is why this being not only causes confusion, but also unleashes civil wars. There is no area of our life that doesn't fundamentally touch the fantasy of the artificial human being. In 1917 Wegener shot another film based on these themes: Der Golem und die Tänzerin (The Golem and the Dancer), a rather ironic caprice that toys with the fantasy of Beauty and the Beast. And incidentally, it has probably the first self-referential joke of a fantasy film series: the Golem of this film goes to the movies where Der Golem is showing. After the war, in 1920, Wegener and Carl Boese made Der Golem, wie er in die Welt kam (The Golem – How He Came into the World). Here the mythical creature acts in accordance with his destiny and frees the people from their servitude. He rescues the emperor's life and thus brings him to rescind the expulsion order against the Jews. Then, however, under the influence of an adverse stellar constellation, he turns into a destructive monster and even sets fire to the ghetto. A small innocent girl succeeds in taking the magic amulet away from him, turning the Golem into a lifeless statue again. This artificial being freed not only his creators, he freed above all the cinema itself. Now it was no longer about imitating the stage; he destroyed the planimetric order and demanded more from the cinema image than merely a reproduction of reality through the means of reality.

When Julien Duvivier brought the stone being to life again in 1936 in Le Golem, the film told its story by other means. We must wait a long time for him to appear in the film, but his imminent arrival can be sensed from the beginning. Whereas with Wegener the artificial being threatens to extend his rule in a spatial sense, with Duvivier he tries to appropriate human time. To put it more dramatically: this is the beginning of a process that came to determine our cinema history, the shifting of the problem from the image to the gaze.

Later, popular cinema largely forgot about the Golem motif, perhaps in part because James Whale's film Frankenstein from the year 1931 made such generous use of this model. Boris Karloff imitates Wegener's swaying, ponderous gait, and we also find here the encounter of the monster with a small girl and the pursuit of the brute by the angry population. Herbert J. Leder's It (1967) is the story of a shy museum curator who brings the Golem, whom Rabbi Loew once created from clay, to life again by deciphering the Hebrew inscription. The Golem's supernatural abilities are radically privatized in this version. The curator tries to eliminate his rival with the help of the stone being and thus unleashes the Golem's undirected forces, which are then turned against the curator. It takes its lead from the films of Paul Wegener as well as Hitchcock's Psycho (1960) – in Leder's film, too, the curator keeps his mummified mother in the house, an especially macabre form of "artificial human being."

The artificial man can only be born as tyrant or murderer. The artificial woman, as "new Eve," uncovers the destructive aspects of seduction, sexuality, and love. She awakens unchecked desire. Hanns Heinz Ewers's novel "Alraune – Die Geschichte eines lebenden Wesens" (Alraune – The Story of a Living Being) from the year 1911 served as the source of a number of films that delighted in spreading the erotic suggestiveness prescribed by the author for his text: "Originated from the nefarious lust of absurd thoughts" (Ewers). In reality, it is only the story of an artificially engendered human being. The girl is born of the fertilization of a whore – "pure sex from head to toe" – with the seed of a sex murderer, taken at the moment of his execution. She can bring nothing but sexual ecstasy, calamity, and death. Brigitte Helm, who is also the evil robot woman in Fritz Lang's Metropolis, plays the girl in both the version of 1927, directed by Henrik Galeen, and the sound film adaptation from 1930 by Richard Oswald. As we can see, all pre-rational and pre-scientific forms of artificial human beings were modeled in the German films. These German cinematic visions of man-made humans caught in the balance between Eros and tyranny emigrated in the thirties to America and were there turned into a genre.

The Artificial Human in Gothic Discourse

Homunculus, the Golem, and Frankenstein – these three models contain virtually everything that makes up the Gothic myth of artificial human beings: the impulse to create an artificial human out of a precarious family saga (the fear of the forthcoming wedding, an impending paternal heir), or from a threatening situation: creation through a mixture of magical and material processes; the self-awareness of the creature as soulless being with no hope of love; the aggression of the creature, at first turned arbitrarily against the surroundings, then against the creator or his wife; the encounter of the creature with (childlike) innocence; the reciprocal redemption of creator and creature through its death. The accents might have shifted from Whale's Frankenstein to Stuart Gordon's H.P. Lovecraft variation Re-Animator (1985) and on up to Frank Henenlotter's grimly quirky Frankenhooker of 1989/90 (the deceased lover is patched together again from body parts taken from murdered prostitutes), the basic structure, however, remains just as unchanged as the iconography of the closed-off rooms, cellars, and laboratories.

It is obvious that this cinematic myth can also be turned around. Then the creation of artificial humans would appear above all as a "pretext" to cast a scandalous look at the decayed and dismembered human body. And also a look at the separation of body and spirit, of flesh and soul, a look at the decline of the image of man and the cinematic image. The mad scientists of the fantastic film in the thirties and forties therefore not only tinker around with corpses, they also like to transplant brains, join limbs together again, and experiment with "synthetic flesh" as in Doctor X (1932) by Michael Curtiz, which leads more or less logically to an epidemic rash of cannibalism. And in Vincent Sherman's The Return of Dr. X (1939), a dead person is awakened to life again by injecting him with a highly unusual blood conserve, which promptly condemns him to the existence of a vampire. In James P. Hogan's film The Mad Ghoul (1943), the deranged scientist transforms a man into a zombie, a weak-willed being who intermittently has to have a new heart implanted, which becomes the occasion for an unavoidable string of murders. We

Dream Replicants of the Cinema

Le Golem
Ferdinand Hart

18

understand: the scientific deed carried out on the forbidden object catapults people decidedly backwards in evolution. In other words: the attempt of the cinema to cast a look into the secret laboratories of science leads back into the Gothic fantasies of punishment. Or put still differently: American cinema's contemplation of the European past brings to light the hidden blasphemy of the long since overcome, decadent culture. Gothic horror in the cinema is the counterpart to the construct of the American who can only understand himself as a whole (and sometimes even banishes Darwin from his field of knowledge).

The Robot and the White Future

As a counterbalance to its unloved heritage – the spirit of black Romanticism and Gothic horror literature, which continued to have a strong effect on the horror film genre – "rational" science fiction came up with its own image in contrast to the fearsome, blasphemous creation of the parallel human being that was doomed to become a monster. The dialogue between real and artificial human beings now took place in a different way. It was more "scientific" and logical on the one hand, post-colonialist and martial on the other. Robots, androids, or cyborgs were part of a good future as long as their relationship to humans remained solely one of service. Science fiction counteracted the "black" theology of the creation of artificial man in the horror genre with a "white" theology of perfect hierarchy, for which Isaac Asimov provided a framework with his "Laws of Robotics." The three basic laws are: 1. A robot may not injure a human being, or, through inaction, allow a human being to come to harm. 2. A robot must obey the orders given it by human beings except where such orders would conflict with the First Law. 3. A robot must protect its own existence as long as such protection does not conflict with the First or Second Law. These laws not only provide the basis for countless logical thought games, but they are also a guarantee for goodness in technology. Asimov's robots are so complex and anthropoid that a "robopsychologist" with an extremely maternal aura functions as the heroine of some robot stories, which confirms in the end how perfectly the laws of robotics function. For a long time science fiction movies took over this positive function of the mechanical being as man's servant. On the one hand, it was absolutely taboo in SciFi films to tinker around with human organs (for ages we had watched scruffy old men hovering over bodies with all sorts of unappetizing instruments, transplanting brains and creating monsters). On the other hand, it was perfectly natural to find mechanical helpers with autonomous movement as a sign of positive science. The existence of assiduous computers in the service of man belonged, side by side with space travel and improved communications systems, to the white future of the fifties and sixties. The robots even redeemed man, delivered him above all from history, the medium of the Fall of Man. At the end of Asimov's "I, Robot," the robopsychologist wonders whether conflicts will be avoidable for all time to come and concludes: from now on only the machines are unavoidable.

During the time of the Cold War, the Eisenhower years, and the period of the economic miracle, however, we didn't yet believe that we could create a robot as the perfect human double. At this time robots are often found at the side of a "superior outsider." They still belong to the Forbidden Planet (1956). Robby, a robot of exceptional abilities, shares a seemingly idyllic life there with the scientist Morbius and his daughter. When questioned about Robby's origin, the scientist claims he has built the robot himself. This is only partly true, as it turns out, since he was only able to put Robby together because he found the instructions in the annals of the lost civilization of the Krel, who had once lived on the planet and are now extinct for some unknown reason. This culture with all its machines, traffic systems, and mysterious sciences is still functional even though no living beings (besides Morbius and his daughter) are there to enjoy its achievements. However, this civilization is finally revealed as the starting point of a threat to the earthly spaceship. At this point we already suspect that this perfect mechanical human double will turn out to be a redeemer from the future that negates the linear structure of time. In Robert Wise's The Day the Earth Stood Still (1951), a cosmic emissary comes to earth in the name of peace and is attacked by the people. In the film, he is aided by the perfect robot, Gort, in carrying out the task; the literary version on which it is based makes a different point at the end: it is not the human-like character, but the robot who is actually the ambassador.

The "religious" science fiction of this period saw in the perfect robot a bit of an angel, a tool of the Gods. In any case, Robby and Gort were huge hits in the toy stores as model figures.

Meanwhile, evil robots began attacking the earth mercilessly. What dreadful gibberish we hear coming out of the receiver in Fred F. Sears's movie Earth vs. the Flying Saucers (1956), so mysterious and meaningless that the (military) hero immediately has to cancel his honeymoon in order to fight the extraterrestrial machine beings with a new miracle weapon. Metallic robots climb out of their flying saucers to destroy Washington with rays shot from their arms.

On Toys and Dreams

The fantasy of a machine that wants to take the place of people is not an achievement of the Industrial Age. Rather, it goes back to the origins of our culture. Homer's "Iliad", for example, tells of Hephaestus, the Roman god Vulcan, who forms a gigantic human-like being from metallic ore, which then marches against Crete's enemies. Ray Harryhausen brought this story of the first super-robot of world history to the screen. It is told of Archytas of Tarentus, a contemporary Plato's, that he built a mechanical dove that could fly. In this way he wanted to prove, went the legend, that man himself could become a creator of new beings. We run into this mechanical bird again in our film fantasy of the toy-crazy sultan in the later version of the film The Thief of Baghdad (1978) by Clive Donner. In other words, the machine was already a theological metaphor in antiquity. In the Christian Middle Ages it was reported that a certain "Regiomontanus" had built a metallic eagle, while in the 13th century Albertus Magnus is said to have built a servant from leather, wood, and metal who was able to make decisions by himself, such as which visitor was to be admitted and which not. Isaac Asimov would have loved him.

All the animate machines of Vaucanson, Jacquet-Droz, and Kempelen of the late Baroque and Rococo periods were still toys. They have more to do with aesthetics and symbolic representation than with social reality. In literature, the robot is normally described vaguely as an entity combining electronic intelligence and mechanical precision. This new being takes on a dramatic aspect when it moves from the areas of industrial production and military aggression into what is seen as human culture, such as the discourses on love, power, morals, and law. This means that when the machine can imitate the processes of communication and sublimation as well as aesthetics, it begins to transform itself from a mere tool into man's counterpart, a partner as well as a caricature. Sometimes we dream of robots that achieve rather humorous effects, like when the "ingenious" inventor Trurl in a Stanislaw Lem story invents a robot poet that churns out verses appropriate for every occasion. In Kenneth Johnson's SHORT CIRCUIT 2 (1988), the robot Johnny Five, a kind of mechanical parody of Cyrano de Bergerac, assumes the task of writing love poems for its human friend. In Allan Arkush's HEARTBEEPS (1981), there is a robot that is created exclusively for the purpose of inventing a sitcom punchline for every possible situation. And what is the question of whether androids dream of electric sheep compared with a robot writer in Dusan Vukotic's film GOSTI IZ GALAXIJE (1981) that dreams of being visited by highly erotic mechanical women? Cinema wanders like a time machine through the ages and their various concepts of artificial humans and never knows for sure whether it is moving forward into the future or backward into the past.

In the 19th century, machines were developed primarily for their utility. They thoroughly changed the nature of human society and split it into two classes: one in which the people were masters of the machines and the other in which they were dominated by them. There were occasional attacks on the machines, until Karl Marx explained to us that the problem didn't lie with the machines themselves, but with the conditions of their ownership. Today we are no longer entirely certain about this. In any case, machines in the form of the industrial robots of post-Fordian society began to make human work superfluous in a highly concrete way, and the mass distribution of computer intelligence and communication brought out a strange mixture of enthusiasm and bewilderment. Couldn't computers wage wars, destroy the environment, and negate free will, this last human property left to man in the machine world? In any case, the combination of the perfect computer and a perfect machine, like a reflection of the link between body and soul in human beings, had to produce a being that was far superior to real humans. Artificial intelligence in artificial bodies. In 1971, the Stanford Research Institute presented "Shakey," a robot that could gather crates by itself and carry them from one room to another. The emphasis in this event, which might not seem so sensational at first glance, lies on "by itself." The next generation of young scientists devoted their time to gladiator battles between autonomously acting machines. Our technical avantgarde was apparently not coming up with much more than war games, it appears; maybe the movies weren't entirely without blame for this.

On How the Industrial Revolution Came to a Bad End

The history of the mechanical reenactment of the creation act moved from magic to play and then on to economic interest. With the rise of the Industrial Revolution, the fear of the super machine became very real. Such a machine was not only the dream of the factory owners and the nightmare of the exploited masses, but also an expression of the completely different levels of techno-scientific information. In one of Lumière's earliest silent films, one could see through the eyes of the factory owner, as it were, how the workers leave his factory. This gaze is focused later on: What happened in his secret laboratories? How did he unleash his scientific power against the people, whose vitality he sucked out of them like a vampire, but which could never satisfy his hunger? The *mad scientist*, to whom we still attribute the production of man-made humans, represents not only the scientist as possessor of secret knowledge, but also, in addition to the political tyrant, the factory owner who first degrades men to machines and then dreams of replacing them with machines. However, in between the factory owner and the proletariat, the petite bourgeoisie also dreamed of this process of transformation with a mixture of horror and fascination. Jules Verne and Georges Méliès envisaged mechanical beings that came out of the laboratories of more or less crazy scientists. Whoever produced the perfect machine was always striving at the same time for world supremacy. As a rule, that meant (and our film history is only too happy to confirm this) that an inner conflict of society was being projected to the outside. The machine competing with the workingman is no longer produced from the economic middle of society, but by dissidents, criminals, lunatics, or "outsiders." The productive forces of the machine are turned into a war operation in the new cinematic "Stahlgewitter" – the storms of steel.

At the beginning of the century, the intelligence and omnipotence of the machine were also an expression of the revolt of the petit-bourgeois technical intelligentsia against traditional forms of rule, the rebellion of the bourgeoisie against the aristocracy, and science against religion. They were, after all, the specters of industrial progress; on into the thirties the mechanical beings appeared as chips off the block of technological-industrial life, quite like the vampire or the werewolf seemed to have been somehow derived from bourgeois sex life. The "solution" proposed by Fritz Lang in METROPOLIS, namely love as a means of overcoming class barriers like the one between man and machine, and a "pact" between hand and brain in respect to work instead of further alienation, appears highly unlikely, not only in the light of criticism, but also through the further development of the cinematic motifs.

The robot is more or less a thinking machine that takes work off man's shoulders, which for the people, as we know, can be a blessing and a curse at the same time. The concept first appears in 1921 in the play "R.U.R." by the Czech writer Karel Čapek (R.U.R. stands for Rossum's Universal

Dream Replicants of the Cinema

Forbidden Planet
Walter Pidgeon

Android
Klaus Kinski, Don Opper

21

Dream Replicants of the Cinema

Dream Replicants of the Cinema

Dream Replicants of the Cinema

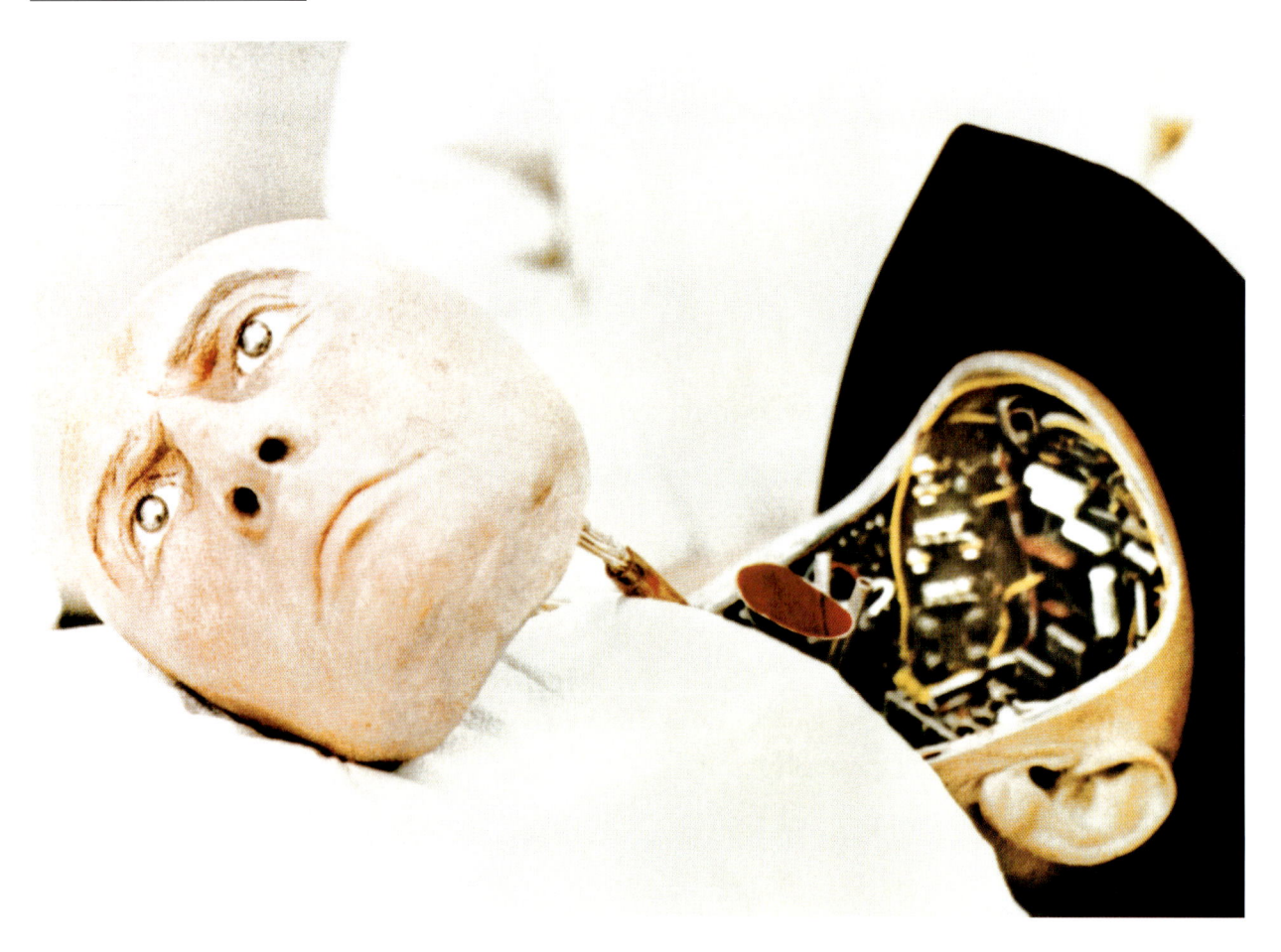

Westworld

Westworld
Yul Brynner

Dream Replicants of the Cinema

Star Wars
C-3PO, R2-D2

Robots, by the way). His autonomous machine beings are developed by biochemical means, which would make them cyborgs or androids according to present-day usage. In any case they are the first human replicas that undertake a collective rebellion against their creators and exploiters. From this time on we see the robot above all as a mechanical being that takes industrial production further away from the human productive forces or stands by the people in war. We find the robot as brutal instrument of war or as friendly household help. This "white" variation of the artificial human being takes the place of the slave and the industrial proletariat and for this reason alone is somewhat disquieting from a historical point of view. There is always the danger that moral axioms will be broken or turned against their creators. In the beginning, the robot was seen with skepticism in popular culture; it is Isaac Asimov with his "Laws of Robotics" who first created something like a positive robot utopia for advanced capitalism. In his concept, robots are the opposite of all that we have feared since the Golem; they embody technically reproduced goodness. The delightful thing about Asimov's robot stories is that these laws of robotics are not as perfect as they seem and always lead to new paradoxes.

What Do Artificial People Look Like?

For the cinema itself, however, the important thing is not only this combination of mechanical perfection, electronic intelligence, and the moment at which they take on a new quality – a mechanical personality, if you will – but also the aesthetic representation of all this. It's simply a matter of what the damn thing looks like. Or in other words: How does the eye read the fusion of mechanized human being and man-like machine? Fortunately, cinema itself is a thinking and dreaming machine; it knows all about this problem.

Cinema has to express the two sides of this being, namely to be a machine on the one hand and a kind of human being on the other. There are consequently two extremes of representing this. The first is the mechanical being that almost cannot be distinguished from a real human – we literally have to shoot the synthetic flesh right off the hydraulic joints before we recognize that the Terminator isn't a real Austrian bodybuilder, but rather a perfect Schwarzenegger machine. At the other extreme we have the being that in no way denies its basic mechanical nature, like Johnny Five, that curious, fast-learning robot in John Badham's film SHORT CIRCUIT (1986), or the robot in the sequel SHORT CIRCUIT 2, in which it gets a kind of soul by accident and suddenly shuns the military tasks it is supposed to carry out. Or that funny pair of robots C-3PO and R2-D2, reminiscent of Laurel and Hardy, in the STAR WARS movies: the one is man's perfect servant with the subservient courtesy and flowery language of a butler, the other a rotund, hedonistic being with a childlike (and ingenious) concept of the world. Don Quixote and Sancho Pansa as mechanical beings, the old and the new form of serving.

The cinematic image of the artificial human being is therefore divided into two complementary visions: the vision of something that looks like a human being, but is in "reality" a machine, and something that looks like a machine, but thinks and can even feel like a human being. It goes without saying that the first variation is normally the more dangerous one. The fact that we can dream up any possible number of intermediate forms confirms the visual wealth of the genre, without obscuring its extremely simplistic basic formula.

The Ten Film Stories about Artificial Humans

Like every genre or subgenre, the science fiction fantasy of parallel beings has evolved a catalogue of its own stories that are constantly repeated and varied. The stories are of such mythical compactness that they move us again and again, and this is true not only of the major works of the genre, but also of the uplifting ridiculousness of the C- and trash movies. A few examples provide sufficient evidence.

1. The story of the artificial being that turns against its creator. ANDROID (1982) by Aaron Lipstadt tells about a scientist who works on a distant, abandoned space station to create a perfect human couple. In the "Cassandra" project, he has already created the cyborg Adam Max 404, who serves as his assistant, but his new Eva is to be his masterpiece. In the end, the two come to earth as perfect human doubles, after their creator – himself an android, incidentally – as well as three "real" people who invaded the space station have all lost their lives. On earth, where it is strictly prohibited to manufacture artificial people, they plan to found the new race of androids. The androids' longing to go there has been awakened – to make the delusions complete – by pictures of the earth: ad spots, tapes, and excerpts from Fritz Lang's METROPOLIS.

This film acts like a preliminary study for an equally intellectual and reduced B-movie version of BLADE RUNNER. Here, as in BLADE RUNNER, we find mechanical beings that become more and more human and people who behave more and more inhumanly. The lonesome creator has violated his creations, and he pursues them murderously and with a bizarre incest commandment. So they make their way toward a false paradise. It appears that the creation of artificial man leads inescapably to the virtualization of the world – and vice versa.

In EVE OF DESTRUCTION (1990) by Duncan Gibbins, a scientist creates a completely anthropomorphic fighter robot in her own likeness and gives it the name Eve 8. The military robot finally gets out of control and ferociously lives out the repressed fantasies of its creator. The artificial being is a derivative of the person's destructive desires, which do not appear appreciably less dreadful when the process is transferred from the male to the female side of the divided human being.

2. The story of the good machine that turns into a monster. If it isn't sheer scientific hubris, or the arms race mania, then people create their mechanical doubles out of a craze for entertainment and with the imagery of artificial paradises. Michael Crichton's WESTWORLD (1972) is about an amusement park which contains, besides a replica of ancient Rome and a medieval settlement, an old-time Western town in which visitors can take on a perfectly constructed robot gunman in a shootout. The black-clad

Dream Replicants of the Cinema

Blade Runner
Daryl Hannah, William Sanderson

Blade Runner
Rutger Hauer

27

gunman is always shot down by the visitors and then repaired during the night. But suddenly the robot seems to be wrongly programmed and refuses to die, and in fact soon begins shooting back with live ammunition. This leads to an all-out revolt of the robots. The little fantasies of power in our artificial paradises begin to strike back.

In 1990 we dream of rescuing the manipulated machine. PROJECT: TIN MEN (1990) by Karen Arthur deals with a very peaceful android by the name of Tin Man whose inventors have programmed to have very human moral principles. But then he is abducted by villainous scientists who want to turn him into a killer machine by order of the government. In the myth of love, the artificial being divides the parts of Eros and Thanatos; only "pure" love can overcome this division.

3. The story of the evil machine that turns good. The story of the military robot that overcomes its destiny and becomes human is told again and again. In a variation of this theme, the thinking machines in the two SHORT CIRCUIT movies and in D.A.R.Y.L. escape their military destiny. In D.A.R.Y.L. (1985) by Simon Wincer, the Data Analyzing Robot Youth Lifeform is a young robot created for military purposes that has to escape its creators when it begins to show feelings. The military people threaten to liquidate it because they want a callous fighting machine. Soon 12-year-old Daryl is found at the edge of a forest. He can't remember anything except his name. They are unable to discover the boy's identity, and so he is put up for adoption. One day, Daryls' "true parents" show up and reclaim the boy. It turns out that he is an android with a computer in his head, originally created as a fighter prototype. But because Daryl's development in the family has meanwhile made him all too human, they want to break off the experiment, and Daryl has to struggle not to be "turned off." Just as the robot may help the family to find its ideal form (and, in this case, to achieve social success), the family's warmth, conversely, helps the machine to become human.

4. The story of the mechanical battle of the sexes. The cold perfection of the "brave new world," shaped by Aldous Huxley's vision, is created by a number of related patterns. These include, on the one hand, the abolition of love and of the ideal of self, and on the other, man's replacement by an improved version of himself (clones, in Huxley's prescient rendering).

The cinematic heirs of Frankenstein who manically mold artificial people with their own hands out of parts from dead bodies, creating cannibals, sex monsters, living time-bombs, mixtures of man and woman, or beings with two heads and three legs, are innumerable; but there is also no end to works portraying a feminine counter-movement – the radical way into a fatherless society, like, for example, the Polish film SEKSMISJA (1983) by Juliusz Machulski. Two biologists wake up in the year 2044 after the usual frozen deep-sleep of this genre and find themselves in a matriarchy in which only descendants of the female sex are brewed in the retort. So our time travelers turn into missionaries of physical love and linear time.

5. The story of the human-mechanical hybrid. Even before Paul Verhoeven's ROBOCOP (1987), the genre dreamed of a powerful and yet equivocal hybrid lifeform combining the mechanical and the human. THE SIX MILLION DOLLAR MAN (1973) by Richard Irving tells of the test pilot Austin who, badly injured in a crash, is patched together again by means of mechanical and "bionic" spare parts. He gradually gets used to his new semi-mechanical identity and is trained as a highly specialized spy. Ray Austin's movie RETURN OF THE SIX MILLION DOLLAR MAN AND THE BIONIC WOMAN (1987) deals with his lover, who is reconstructed in the same way, and in THE BIONIC WOMAN (1975) by Dick Moder, the son of the heroine is also rebuilt "bionically" after an accident and now possesses superhuman abilities. All three experience repeated identity crises and abusive phases before they become aware of their destiny to be good.

6. The story of the infiltration of mankind by the humanoid beings. What could be more dreadful than the creation of artificial human beings, what more frightening than the destructive forces they cause on both sides of evolutionary history? Perhaps it is the concept that artificial people are already long since here in our midst – unrecognized. THE ADVENTURES OF BUCKAROO BANZAI: ACROSS THE 8TH DIMENSION (1983) by W.D. Richter is based on a comicbook series and tells about a future world in which humanoid aliens and holographic beings move about unrecognized in society. In Michael Chapman's film ANNIHILATOR (1986), humanoid beings have infiltrated society. As in BLADE RUNNER nobody can know whether the other guy is a replicant or the original. In Ridley Scott's ALIEN (1979) and in later sequels, androids, unrecognized as such, are part of the crew of the spaceships. With this perfect deception, the laws of robotics lose their validity, too; the machine beings populate the ultimate conspiracy fantasy.

7. The story of the androids as saviors and redeemers. THE QUESTOR TAPES (1973) by Richard A. Colla is one of those absurd B-movies that don't realize what they've gotten themselves into. Here, one of the scientists who have created the artificial human being disappears. When the android Questor needs his creator in order to prevent a nuclear catastrophe, he has to take up the search for him. But first he has to learn to adapt to the manners and perceptions of people and to cope with his own rudimentary feelings. Before we can even begin thinking about this transformation, it turns out that Questor is the last of a series of (extraterrestrial) robot sentinels that have been governing the fate of people since primeval times. His life is now in danger because the people no longer accept this rule. Here we find something in rudimentary form that will later occupy us again and again: the developmental sequence of man and machine is not linear; the relationships between creation and creature can be endlessly reversed.

8. The story of the robot at the focal point of society. The machine takes on social tasks; it works and controls. The most familiar fantasy is that of the artificial policeman. Doesn't it all begin with traffic lights, speed control devices, and surveillance cameras? And on the other hand, don't policemen have something "mechanical" per se, both as comical Keystone Cops and as new centaurs on their Harley Davidsons? ROBOCOP, who made his first appearance in Paul Verhoeven's film from the year 1987, and other police robots are only the latest stage. The autonomous machine is a medium of power that desperately wants to

become the subject of power. Thus it all begins with our using them for surveillance.

If the soldiers, the scientists, and the policemen of the future can best be replaced by android machines or cyborgs, then why shouldn't they also be given other functions in higher positions? For example, as teachers in a world in which law and order no longer stand a chance and the students are members of marauding gangs that control whole regions, as in Mark L. Lester's film CLASS OF 1999 (1990). Here, three extremely tough teachers arrive at Kennedy High School in Seattle, which has sunken into anarchy and violence – under their human skin they have metal bodies and an iron will. And again our forward-looking gaze goes profoundly backward at the same time: the rebirth of the educator as machine turns out to be a terrifying instrument of punishment. Just as the artificial policeman doesn't worry about having to gather evidence (which doesn't mean, as we can see in the development of the Robocop figure, that sooner or later he can't revolt against his own institution, like any "decent" cop), so the artificial teacher sets aside any liberal scruples he might have. Needless to say, in the end he turns into the very danger against which he was once supposed to protect society.

9. The story of the android double. The artificial being replaces his human counterpart not only as a social institution, but, as can be seen in the STEPFORD films, as a person as well. In the end, everyone can have his own mechanical double – like Superman, who enjoys having a completely identical robot take his place. In BILL & TED'S BOGUS JOURNEY (1991) by Peter Hewitt the two youthful heroes are chased through time and space by killer robots who look exactly like them; in the end they are challenged to play a game of Battleships with the Grim Reaper. In Neill Fearnley's television production JOHNNY 2.0 (1997), a scientist undertakes measures against the machinations of his employers. They set a perfect clone as hitman on him, who has the job of killing the "original." The mirror image can't bear the existence of the original.

10. The story of the friendly mechanical sidekick. Ever since STAR WARS it is (again) the normal thing for every space hero and space cowboy to have a robot companion (besides an alien companion). In reality, the space fairy tale is nothing but a repetition of the story of Dorothy, who in "The Wizard of Oz" wanders through the "land over the rainbow" in the company of a "Cowardly Lion," a "Tin Man," and a sensitive "Scarecrow." In BUCK ROGERS IN THE 25TH CENTURY (1978) by Daniel Haller as in George McCowan's THE SHAPE OF THINGS TO COME (1979), the heroes are accompanied by small, somewhat silly robots or androids. These thinking and autonomous machines are so "subservient" that they deliberately don't overstep the consciousness level of a child – of their own free will, as it were. They produce a new boy/hero relationship. The human hero is now no longer threatened by the gaze of the machine, but rather "grows" in it, just as young Luke Skywalker is defined at the beginning of STAR WARS as the coming hero, despite his oppressed existence, through his relationship to the droids, who immediately recognize him as their "master" (and people as the "master race," we might add).

Confusion

Our problem at the moment is evidently that it is no longer possible to differentiate precisely between the human and the mechanical being. We are not only afraid of the machines that will someday make us superfluous and therefore simply get rid of us, but also afraid of the mechanical being in ourselves. In other words, there are two negative utopias involved when people and machines live together (in the cinema). On the one hand, the machines strive to rule the world in that they deceive people as to their true intentions and finally declare open war against them. On the other hand, the machines blend into human civilization to such a degree that man and machine can no longer be distinguished from one another. Moreover, the futuristic being no longer knows how much of a human being and how much machine it is.

One of the most famous android novels is Philip K. Dick's "Do Androids Dream of Electric Sheep?" from the year 1968, which was made into the movie BLADE RUNNER by Ridley Scott. The androids in this future world can only be distinguished from the people with the help of a particular test. Originally created in order to colonize other planets, they make their way back to earth to take over the planet. It is the task of so-called "Blade Runners" to hunt down the androids and kill them off. The replicants have overcome the logical flaw that is inherent to Asimov's robots and was pointed out by Stanislaw Lem. It lies in the concept of intelligence itself. Whoever or whatever possesses intelligence must be capable of canceling out its own programming through an act of will. And that is exactly what the replicants do in Phillip K. Dick's story and in Scott's film. But the hunter Deckard starts to have doubts about the task he is to carry out. And he's quite right about this. Lest we forget: the director's cut of the film offers a different solution than the original version. We now know that Deckard himself is a replicant. With this book and film, science fiction departed from the hierarchical construction of the relationship between machines and people; it is the beginning of something like the – in this case perhaps desolate – history of the emancipation of artificial beings. And Asimov's Laws of Robotics prove to be an ideological as well as philosophical lie.

Robot Wars 1

In the period after World War II, machine beings were an expression of the unchecked release of mechanical power, a force that had been unleashed and could no longer be tamed. The atomic bomb was the *non plus ultra* metaphor for armament overkill, and most fantasies about machine beings at the time were more or less hidden derivatives of the fear of a war technology that was not only able to destroy the enemy, but indeed the whole world. Mechanical beings were either elements of the hostile invasion, or Communist threats, or they represented the evil created through the arms industry in our own society. At that time, it was the most natural thing in the world for the spirit Ariel from Shakespeare's comedy "The Tempest" to appear again as a robot in the science fiction fantasy FORBIDDEN PLANET. And the spirit took the form of Klaatu in THE DAY the Earth Stood Still (1951), the manifestation of intergalactic control, the machine that decrees universal peace, a kind of mechanized reappearance of Jesus Christ. We find mechanical beings again as the strangely organic manta-like creatures from the film The War of the Worlds (1953) that destroyed everything without mercy. And in the Japanese Godzilla films, gigantic robots seemed to be the only thing that could stand up to the primeval dragon, which had been brought back into the world by the unleashed force of the atomic bomb: Godzilla vs. Mecha-Godzilla. In the fifties and early sixties, the machine being was an expression of an apocalyptic mood, a being which in the period of the Cold War could be interpreted as an expression of both the fear of the enemy's technical superiority and the fear of the techno-military arms race altogether. These beings were the heirs of the Golem in that they experienced evil through the way in which they were used.

At the end of the sixties this picture became decidedly internalized. We no longer dreamed as much about the enemy's terribly superior battle and infiltration machines, except perhaps in the James Bond films, but rather about the disastrous effects of the perversion of mechanical and human life on a daily basis. In the seventies, the medialization of machine beings played the most important role: a computer that is able to impregnate a woman, as in Demon Seed (1976) by Donald Cammell, or an image from the entertainment industry, like the robot gunfighter in Westworld that begins to return real gunfire, an imitation of the Western villain. At this time, the parallel being was no longer just a creature out of the secret laboratories of science who could escape from his creators; he was already part of our daily life, and the foreseeable fact that he runs amok was the punishment for our addiction to amusement and need for perfection.

In the eighties, finally, we began to take seriously the autonomy of the technically reproduced artificial being in the myths of our popular culture. In Short Circuit there is the thought of taking on this mechanical being as a brother or sister: of carrying on a dialogue. And then the Terminator films accompanied us into the nineties with the idea of the machine turning human. The mechanical being became the center of a post-Christian redemption story. In the end it sacrificed itself for our sins, after a long and merciless war that people and machines had waged against each other.

It is now perhaps time to give some thought to our myth of authenticity. At the end of Blade Runner, the hero has to ask himself whether he is not in fact a technical replicant of a human being himself, and whether there are still any criteria at all for differentiating between humans and machines. But that prepares the way for a robot story told in the first person: a machine that knows what it means to say "I." The classic machine, in the form of mechanical life as well, has already become nostalgically transfigured in the nineties. In the second Terminator film, the "antiquated" machine man finds himself on the side of the good, while the truly dangerous force of evil emanates from an amorphous meta-machine, a machine, in other words, that can imitate every form of human life, a machine that is no longer form, but above all idea.

The fact that mainstream cinema is so successful with the topic of the fantastical and mechanical duplication of human life – in the final analysis, resurrection by means, say, of cloning a person, as in the last part of the Alien saga – probably has little to do with the fact that the topic is virulent in its technical feasibility, so to speak. When the mathematician Norbert Wiener, in the seventies, was looking for a literary example to illustrate his theory on the danger of intelligent electronics, he couldn't find a single example in the works of science fiction that was even halfway realistically based on actual technical development. At present a very similar process is recurring in popular culture with respect to the problems of genetic engineering research and the cloning of animals and people. The fears lead to the same fantasies and images that have been here since antiquity, and refer once more to blasphemy. The Gothic fantasy of the artificial human being involves the order of the world, the succession of birth and death, the structure of the family, and linear time. The science fiction fantasy of the mechanical being involves the order of history, society, and power, and the hierarchical structure of knowledge. Meanwhile, the perfect human double of the post-industrial age attacks the last bastion of self-identification, the person's very nature. The metaphysical goal of society in its markedly Western form and Oedipal organization, more important yet than crime and punishment or sacrifice and redemption, is the ideal of the self as the highest stage of human development. Jesus Christ, for example, has recently been seen from a psychoanalytical point of view above all as a projection surface for this ideal of the self. To be sure, the political-economic development of civil society seems to run directly counter to the realization of this ideal of self. This is why the parallel being now enters a third and crucial phase. Whereas in the first phase he competed with humans as an alien brother for the direct relationship to God (or to Nature), and in the second phase for work, history, and power, he now appears as man's rival in the development of the self. Under the circumstances, it is only logical that in films like Blade Runner, Terminator 2 and Alien Resurrection (1997) the artificial human is not only technically or mentally superior, but morally better as well.

And so our behavior toward the mechanical, industrial, semiotic parallel being, i.e. the artificial human being, also changes rather radically. The motif of the sorcerer's apprentice used to be predominant in stories and films on this topic: man can no longer free himself from the spirits he has called up. He can't control what he has created because he can't control the unconscious impulses he has implanted in this second creation. The self in these fantasies feels locked in between two other conditions, as it were: namely that of the machine as a substitute for the Superego (the omniscient computer, the perfectly linked super-machine) and the machine as a new expression of the Id, an unconscious and immoral mass of impulses toward movement, aggression, and devouring. This division, which we have found in the classic works of the genre, now shifts over into the third dimension, and this is surely not entirely by accident during a phase in which the private and the public, family and society, have lost their unambiguous relationship to one another. The artificial human being no longer threatens the stability of society; rather, he has turned into an expression of alienation.

In the more recent productions, the machines strive to occupy the center of human nature: they want above all to become a self, want to be "I." This attempt undertaken by the second creation to become a complete human being, which we have come across ever since Frankenstein's monster and which turns up again as a paraphrase, for instance, in the figure of Data in the STAR TREK films, is now no longer condemned to failure from the very beginning. This impulse is obviously inconsistent in itself; in one of the last STAR TREK episodes Data has to decide between the promise of being turned into a real human being and the moral decision to behave humanely. The machine actually becomes the better human being, the better self. In TERMINATOR 2 the machine can finally even lay claim to the central myth of the ideal of the self and appear as the technically improved Savior. It can also be put differently: we begin to suspect that the robot wars were not incited by the machines, but by the people.

A Robot in the Family

There we had it: it was not only that the individual person wasn't perfect and should therefore be replaced by his improved double; even the smallest cell of the state and society, the family, wasn't perfect. What, therefore, could be more logical than to look for possible mechanical replacements for parts of it? On the one hand.

Z.P.G. – ZERO POPULATION GROWTH (1971) by Michael Campus shows future human society on a polluted earth where everyone has to wear a mask so as not to suffocate. It is strictly prohibited in this world to have children. A talking, computer-operated baby doll is offered to couples as a substitute. The computer woman in THE STEPFORD WIVES (1975) by Bryan Forbes is the perfect simulation of the super-housewife. A woman who moves to the town finally discovers that the men of Stepford have replaced their wives with completely identical replicants, and also finds that one has already been produced to replace herself. And the whole thing – we've already suspected it – was the idea of a former technician at Disneyland. In the end, we see the perfect Joanna, the friendly consumer, shopping at the supermarket.

What may appear here as a satire on the perfection mania of the American family proves in other films to be an absolutely sympathetic possibility. In Steven Hillard Sterns's film NOT QUITE HUMAN (1987), the scientist Dr. Jonas Carson builds an android, giving it the look of a teenager and the name of Chip. But the synthetic boy develops real feelings toward his "father" and his "sister Becky," who goes to high school with him. In AND YOU THOUGHT YOUR PARENTS WERE WEIRD (1991) by Tony Cookson, an independently thinking and feeling machine protects a group of teenagers and fights for justice, much like good spirits, fairies, or intelligent pets do in other contexts; here, the integration of the parallel human into the family seems to be a perfectly natural thing.

Clonus Horror or New Genetic Creations

Hardly ever before have the fantasy flights of cinema corresponded so closely to public opinion as with the latest incursion of science into the creation story, in the form of the clone. In fact, scarcely a single commentary manages to get by without pointing out that reality is on the verge of overshadowing the most far-fetched SciFi horror film. And there is hardly any other form of the human double that has ever gone through the stages of scientific development, public discussion, and mythical treatment by popular culture in such short intervals of time as the clone. It appears that a signal was sent out from the genetics conference of Asiloma in California in 1972, when American geneticists called for a break to think things over before continuing their scientific pursuits. The risks of their new technology appeared no less dangerous to the participants than the nuclear threat. The break didn't last very long, and the cinema was meanwhile busy indulging itself in wild fantasies on the topic. The films that came along were correspondingly excessive. In Franklin J. Schaffner's film THE BOYS FROM BRAZIL (1978), the former concentration camp doctor Mengele has escaped into the South American jungle, where he still carries out his experiments on human beings and dreams of establishing a "Fourth Reich" by cloning 94 people – who are all exactly like Hitler. Through a journalist who dies in the course of his investigations, the "Nazi-hunter" Liebermann gets onto the trail of the rising young "Führer" clones, who are indistinguishable from one another. The stuff of pure trash, of course. But gene manipulations have always been a topic for particularly dreadful nightmares, as if all our archaic fears and apocalyptic fantasies were suddenly to merge into one.

In PARTS: THE CLONUS HORROR (1979) by Robert S. Fiveson – this actually is the title – a clone has been created out of the cells of a dead man. He flees from the research laboratory, which is camouflaged as a training camp, with the aim of announcing to the public that he and others like him have been produced to replace prominent figures of the political and economic world.

Our fantasy of artificial human beings repeats exactly what it accuses the mad scientists of doing: where it could "create" and be critical, it only "tinkers around," sticks together its beings out of the virtual Lego bricks of controlled imagination, beings that can only project an image as endlessly collapsing reconstructions of nature.

The cautious attempt to imagine parallel beings and successor models to humans and finally even to give them a try as brother or sister apparently leads fairly often to a counter-reaction that sees people as victims of the perfection of such a "superman." In Andrew Niccol's film GATTACA (1997), the man of the future is a test-tube being; the people who have been naturally born are a dwindling minority and have no prospect of social advancement. Vincent is one of those few persons who were engendered in the normal way; his lack of perfection begins with his short-sightedness. His whole life long he has been treated as a second-rate person; not even a kindergarten will accept the *In-Valids*, as those of natural birth are called. By contrast, his younger brother Anton was cloned in the laboratory of a genetics designer as a *Valid*, a near perfect being. Human-Abel and Clone-Cain are all too clearly separated again.

When Vincent leaves his parental home, he just barely manages to find a job in the cleaning brigade at Gattaca Aerospace; his application to become a pilot was quickly rejected after he refused to hand over his urine sample and thus reveal that he is an In-Valid. But in reality he has only one dream: to fly into space. And to find a planet where a regular flawed human being can live freely: Titan, the fourteenth moon of Saturn. In order to fulfill this dream, he has to overcome the security measures of the all-powerful Gattaca corporation and assume the identity one of the "genetically perfect" Valids. He procures forged ID papers and bogus blood and urine samples from a DNA broker. Jerome, who is confined to a wheelchair after suffering an accident, sells his Valid identity to Vincent. In his new role – Vincent and Jerome have now become "Eugene" – Vincent quickly makes a career for himself in the company. He falls in love with his co-worker Irene and is accepted into the select group of the astronauts for the Titan mission. However, a week before the rocket is launched, the director of the space mission project is murdered, and Vincent is discovered through a genetic control. But his discovery isn't the end of the story; in fact, he is given cover by his brother Anton and a technician who himself has an In-Valid child. The criticism of the "perfection mania" shifts back into anger against artificial creation.

Of course, the production of perfect likenesses is also outstanding comedy material. In Harold Ramis' film Multiplicity (1995), Michael Keaton plays a high-strung engineer who is torn between work and family life with no time for either, and whose wife, moreover, wants to go to work again and needs him to help with their two small children. A genetics expert promises to solve the problem by secretly making clones of him. At the same time, he equips each of them with the desired qualities for different tasks: one is a real workhorse, ruthless macho, and careerist, another is a softie who likes to do housework and run the household, and the third turns out as an over-sized infantile kid. Of course, these look-alikes with such different characters cause considerable confusion, above all because they in turn are something like clones "in spirit": while Number Two and Number Three behave almost exactly like Jack Lemmon and Walter Matthau in The Odd Couple (1968), Number Four seems like the reincarnation of the early Jerry Lewis. To duplicate ourselves artificially, we can no longer succeed by reproducing our own image, but only the mirror image of our media dreams. After all, division is also the only hope in times of external and internal deregulation and love traps.

At the end of the 20th century, furious rejection, melancholy ambivalence, and cautious integration between natural and parallel people stand side by side in our popular mythology. The unity of man, machine, and clone is a main subject of the Japanese *mangas* and *animes*. Kokaku Kidotai / Ghost in the Shell (1995) by Oshii Mamoru depicts the adventures of a policewoman with all sorts of implants in her body who wants to find out whether she is really a human being. Armitage III (1994/95) deals with a pretty cyborg girl who is searching for her own self and her creator. In the end, she has no other choice but to leave her material existence behind and dive into cyberspace in order to be born again. The problem of these post-humans in such future worlds is not only their identity (an endless splitting and rejoining of the self apparently belongs to their design/existence, as does the art of continuously "rebuilding" themselves), but even more, the salvation of their emotions. Just as the American genre film falls back time and again on its Gothic origins, so the technological imagination of the *animes* often reverts to a murky romanticism. Long since gone is the duality of "real" and "artificial" human beings. Every being that develops a consciousness has to take up the search for its own origins and the search for an emotional relationship to the world.

Robot Wars 2

The apocalyptic war between man and machine is the point of departure for the genre, and the relationship that emerges is downright ambivalent. Something, it appears, drives us on toward this final conflict, beyond which a new Stone Age, a new barbarity, but also a new beginning may lie. Humanity – and this might occasionally give the motif a "racist" aspect – is a quality per se. Humans tend to defend their "genuineness" and authenticity all too often without questioning the nature of humanity as a project. The fact that machine beings and replicants sometimes prove to be more human than their creators enters the picture again and again as a sarcastic sideswipe, as in Blade Runner and in Alien Resurrection. But not even in the grand redemption fantasy of Terminator 2 is this really and truly inscribed in the myth of the man/machine conflict.

The final war can only be averted if the machines become human more quickly than the people can revert to their mechanical annihilation mania. Contrasting with the fantasy of an unavoidable war of the people against their own creations is that of the replicants as a persecuted culture, as the replication of some early Christian Passion. Thus we find a recurrent fantasy of the machine that must be freed from the hands of the military.

The machines-turned-humans flee from their inhuman creators, as in the Cyborg series, which turns the flight of the parallel beings from their oppressors into a biblical story. Cyborg 2 – The Glass Shadow (1993) by Michael Schroeder is about a perfect female robot that is created to carry out an espionage job for the ruling computer concern. Instead, she escapes with her "trainer", and the two take refuge with an old cyborg model by the name of Mercy. But the people – this motif turns up again and again – have granted their creatures only a short lifetime. In Blade Runner the short life of the artificial beings is part of the program, but in trash movies like this one the parallel creatures often carry the time bomb of their own destruction in themselves.

If we are at least partially on the side of the machine beings and replicants, i.e. on the side of the oppressed against the oppressors, in films like Blade Runner or Terminator 2, and have developed at least ambivalent feelings here in the trash movie and the never-ending spirals of popular culture, this doesn't mean that we don't still have an image of the machines as our enemies. In Boaz Davidson's film American Cyborg (1992), a computer system has once again taken over power and sees every vestige of human survival as superfluous. It sends out killer cyborgs, indistinguishable from real people, to annihilate

Dream Replicants of the Cinema

GATTACA
Ethan Hawke

all human life. Only a small group of rebels takes up the struggle against them. In the underground, some scientists begin working on a renewal of the species, but they have to solve a fundamental problem first: all the female humans are infertile. Only one, Mary, has escaped this fate and finally agrees to artificial insemination in order to assure the survival of the human race. When the computer system finds out about it, it reinforces its efforts and sends out its most aggressive cyborg to get her. Mary has only 36 hours to reach the rescuing ship. The Massacre of the Innocents, the "Virgin" birth, Noah's Ark and, once again, Cain and Abel: our fantasy of the artificial human being seems to aim above all at a reading of the Bible from beginning to end in the fast-forward mode. Of course this new Maria has to be given a champion at her side who turns out to be an "incorrectly programmed" cyborg.

A variation on this motif is that the machines that have been abused by the military turn against their masters. In SYNGENOR (1989) by George Elanjian, Jr., an armaments corporation produces gene-manipulated people that serve as perfect artificial soldiers and can regenerate themselves when they are wounded. The director of the company wants to further improve his creatures by turning their defensive temperament into an aggressive character. But at this point the experiment gets out of control, and the creatures kill the chief executive.

Another variation: the self-sufficient engines of war and/or androids that were created to fight a war take the conflict into the own hands, as in Tim Kincaid's MUTANT HUNT (1987). Here the semi-organic killer robots of the "humanoids," directed, as it were, by instinct, expand the annihilation war they were programmed for into an all-out onslaught against human civilization. At this stage, artificial man turns back into an animal. In the end, the imminent outbreak of the "final" war between people and machines can be influenced – here a further variation – by time travel. In APEX (1993) by Phillip J. Roth, a man comes from the future and tries to prevent the development of robots that will wage war against the people in the year 2073. In Charles Band's film TRANCERS (1984), a police officer from the future is sent back to the Los Angeles of the year 1985 to hunt down anthropoid robots called Trancers. The Trancer cop Jack Deth goes after them, which proves to be very difficult in a world in which outward appearance no longer reveals anything. Here the identity crisis and the parallel creation turn into complementary myths of a new polymorphism.

In a final variation, the "historic" conflict between people and machine beings is overcome by a third force: an invasion from space. ROBO WARRIORS (1996) by Ian Barry takes place during a future war between people and aliens, in the course of which the earth has already been completely devastated. Only a small group of people continue to offer bitter resistance against the invaders and prepare themselves for the final battle by means of their "secret weapon," an android fighting machine by the name of Ray.

But even if war has already broken out between man and the machines, the positions are by no means clarified. The topic of films like BLADE RUNNER or ALIEN is the question of who can still be trusted when the borders between man and his technical reproduction are no longer distinguishable. In SCREAMERS (1996) by Christian Duguay, based on the early short story "Second Variety" by Philip K. Dick from the year 1952, this question is posed in another war between man and machine. On the planet Sirius 6B, small, deadly robots known as Screamers (because of the dreadful noise they emit) are battling against the people in the year 2078. The "Alliance", a rebellious group of people who refused to continue mining dangerous radioactive materials on the planet, originally developed these murderous machines in their struggle against the rival economic mega-corporation N.E.B. (New Economic Block). The Screamers, who have long since been able to reproduce and improve themselves, attack anything in which they sense a human pulse. The Alliance fighters wear a special bracelet that suppresses the pulse beat signal. Alliance commander Hendricksson finally discovers that the control function of the Screamers has further developed to such a degree that the robots have learned to think autonomously. Hendricksson sets out with a young soldier to negotiate peace with the rival company, but all he finds in their headquarters are two soldiers and a "black marketeer"; all the others have been killed by the Screamers, who can now change their shape at will. A Screamer even takes on the body of a child who pleads to be taken along and not left alone. The "reincarnation" of man has failed here so thoroughly that the human countenance itself can only trigger the "unimaginable horror" that we know from the Gothic horror stories.

Virtual Reality

In the last third of the century, our fear-craving fantasy of artificial beings in the real world was joined by a countervision: the real person who gets lost in an artificial reality, first as invader, then as prisoner of a labyrinth. Once again, the vision of fear leads us back to the old nightmares: Hansel and Gretel lost in the cyberwoods. Nightmares that we are no longer a whole, that we are confronted with our own doppelgängers, that we constantly split ourselves into different units, that here and elsewhere exist simultaneously. The nosedive into the cyberworld that barely a decade before had still provided us with such simple stories as Steven Lisberger's TRON (1982) or the third part of the SUPERMAN saga and had appeared as a mere "confusion" between reality and simulation is in fact nothing but the electronic reappearance of a syndrome that is considerably older than the "Stendhal Syndrome," which gave Dario Argento's film from the year 1994 its title: the immersion of the gaze into the image that knows no return and no distance.

Edouard Bannwart has anticipated this to a certain degree in his installation "Virtual Head." At an art exhibition housing the installation we experience other visitors in a walk-in electronic field who become our partners in a game without knowing it, while by the same token we are the game partners of other people, also without realizing it. Compared with such a surreal experience, the fantasies of popular cinema are rather modest. This brings two experiences together, namely the technical production of the parallel being and the psychedelic experience of the "impossible" second reality.

Brett Leonard's film THE LAWNMOWER MAN (1992) is derived from a short story by Stephen King and a story by the director entitled "Cybergod." It tells of the scientist Dr. Lawrence Angelo, who is forced by his bosses to turn the monkeys in his laboratory into aggressive creatures by means of his experiments on the acceleration of mental ability, in which he uses neurotransmitters and virtual reality computer instruction. After one of the monkeys kills a person while trying to escape, Angelo is fired. In a new project, he now starts experimenting with the lawnmower man Jobe Smith, a young guy with the intelligence quotient of a six-year-old who takes care of the front gardens of the wealthy with his homemade lawnmower. Angelo's new patrons want to turn Jobe into a kind of callous soldier by injecting him with drugs. But instead Jobe is transformed not only into a real genius, but at the same time into a virtual computer being with no material existence, who is at home in all the computer networks of the world and moreover believes that he is the new God.

The film is a direct confrontation with the cybernet as a new type of religion: Jobe was reared by a priest who used to punish him regularly with the whip and who ends up being crucified by Jobe in virtual reality. Brett Leonard returned to the topic of cyberspace again in 1995 with VIRTUOSITY. In Los Angeles in the year 1999, ex-cop and now convict Parker Barnes, who is troubled by the traumatic memory of the murder of his wife, is used in a government project in which police officers learn how they will be deployed in the fight against virtual gangsters. In order not to endanger the real police, prisoners such as Parker Barnes, who killed the murderer of his family, are used as test objects in the first phase. His opponent is Sid 6.7, a computer-generated being that has been patched together by the programmer Lindenmeyer out of the world's worst serial killers. Sid 6.7 breaks out of cyberspace into reality and spreads terror in the city. After an incident, the hard disk with the simulation is supposed to be erased, but Lindenmeyer manages to bring the computer being into reality in order to set it as an android against the people. The artificial mass murderer wreaks all sorts of havoc in the city, and only one person can stop him: Parker Barnes has to be taken back onto the police force. The "old" cyclical form of the catastrophe fantasy is now applied to the second reality.

JOHNNY MNEMONIC (1995) is based on a short story from 1980 by the cyberspace author William Gibson. It is directed by the writer and artist Robert Longo. The film is set in the 21st century, where huge corporations have taken over world rule and control the data networks. Data smuggling is a subversive offense which is combated by the conspiratorial "LoTeks." One of the smugglers is Johnny, who brings data from Beijing to Newark and has a chip implanted in his brain which helps him to slip the data and images past the guards. The courier's own interests are also at stake: with the money he earns running these errands he wants to buy back his childhood memories. Just one final run and he'll reach his goal. However, the computer suffers an overflow in his head that threatens to destroy him. He has 24 hours to download his data freight before his head explodes. At the same time, he is hunted by the killer samurai of the corporations, and the "downloading code" gets lost. As in most of these films, the artificial reality looks all the more fascinating the more uninhabitable the "real" reality has become.

The crossover between material and virtual reality takes place in the films of David Cronenberg in a much more vehement way: the second reality enters not only the imagination, but human flesh itself in films like VIDEODROME (1982) or EXISTENZ (1999), which is about the birth of the new human being as "MetaFlesh Game Pod." Here, too, virtual reality can only be a gruesome representation of the familiar: just as the ghosts of unreality rage in reality, so the ghosts of reality now rage in the realms of the dream. In his films Cronenberg goes back (with whatever weird ideological and psychological implants) to one of the origins of myth, to the "horror" of the birth that has broken away from the natural order of things. So in VIDEODROME, the protagonist "artificializes" himself by creating a vagina-like slot in his stomach, and in EXISTENZ, the heroine creates a computer game that is the perfect simulation of a uterus, and implants a "bioport" in her "son's" belly. With Cronenberg (and not only with him) the triggering "scandal" of the phantasm of parallel and future beings begins when something on the inside moves to the outside. Thus, the robot with its steely skin, which represents the quintessence of the armor with which the warrior has tried, above all semiologically, to gird himself since primeval times, turns into the being that has made the separation between inside and outside into his own image once and for all: in our mythology, to "open" a robot normally means to kill him.

The Gospel of Parallel Beings

The classic genre film of the fantastic was normally content to make use of the lust for fear found in mythology, to evoke the violation of the taboo and at the same time to eliminate it. The post-classical mega-films of this genre like STAR WARS and the popular cosmologies like STAR TREK integrated the parallel being as an autonomous being, and yet one that suffered from its lack of authenticity. Postmodern popular cosmology actually rewrites the myth. This begins with the "black future" of BLADE RUNNER. The humanity of the new creations is connected with the murder of the "father." In this sense our fear and aggression images are recurrent. But there is a crucial change of paradigm: we begin to see the world through the eyes of our doppelgängers. They are searching for their "father", who cannot give them real life and therefore – this, too, is a topos of traditional myth – is killed by them.

The question posed by the writer Philip K. Dick in his novel "Do Androids Dream of Electric Sheep?," on which the film BLADE RUNNER is based, is not only that of man's primal fear of his own creation, but also that of the complete dissolution of the personality in the mega-city, in which there is only outside control. The replicants have long since become more human than the people. They alone still have something like personal freedom, and consequently the people are panic-stricken in view of their own likenesses and develop an eliminatory "racism" against them.

In TERMINATOR 2 the young redeemer of the future is to be killed himself, and the cyborg who played the killer in the first part now has the job of guarding him against a new, amorphous parallel being. The cyborg learns, for example, that the death of people is to be avoided at all costs and ends up having to melt himself down in order to destroy the ominous memory chip inside him. In that this self-reliant machine intervenes in the fate of mankind at such a central turning point, he certainly goes far beyond the androids of other popular mythologies. To an unbiased observer, however, his sacrificial death could also appear as the ultimate fulfillment of the Asimovian robot laws: as the act of restoration of the order of things, but this time carried out in full consciousness.

Actually, the paradox in these robot laws, namely that of the mechanical being that has both consciousness and self-will and yet can only serve, leads again and again to the compulsion to self-destruct. The thinking machine is melodramatic from birth on, as it were. What has changed is the helix structure, in which human and mechanical consciousness have been winding around each other in popular mythology since the eighties. This film brings together the diverging elements of the myth; it deals with both the legend of the inevitable robot war and that of the healing of the family by the artificial being. In its last paradox it redeems the parallel human being, who wants to turn into a real human being, through his sacrificial death.

The alternative to an – apparently everlasting – war between people and machines or people and replicants lies in making peace, in a kind of more or less democratic and solidary integration. What, besides the proximity of conceivability and feasibility, has caused this change of paradigm in popular mythology? Our desolation and hopelessness, among other things. Much of what the artificial human attacked in the classical myth of artificial life can in truth no longer be rescued; the Christian idea of the Trinity, the Holy Family, of sacrifice, deliverance and so on is a projection and back projection of the organization of the family, of the linear extrapolation in time, and these for their part are projection and back projection of civil society and the state. As the aim of all of this organization, the ideal of the self is the highest stage of human development. The prophet, the redeemer, and the great revolutionary served above all as projection surface for this ideal of the self. Admittedly, the political-economic development of this society seems to run counter to the realization of this ideal of self. Not enough that it creates, with a view to informal control of the individual through society, heteronomous structures by means of diffusing, formless powers (the corporations and global players) and thus causes new fears; moreover, the familial, oedipal structure of this society dissolves from the inside out, as it were, no less so than the cultural factors leading to the formation of the self. Taking the place of the normal, middle-class individual is a human being that owes its identity solely to the images flowing through its existence, which are so generously provided by the free market economy. This is the source of the hope that one of these media beings could step out of its dream machine and escort us like an angel across the abysses, or at least like the medial representation of a big brother, as in John McTiernan's Last Action Hero (1993). Thus may the machine man and the replicant become the new angel of popular culture in the post-Industrial Age. Let him on our behalf say "I."

Where did all this begin? Wasn't the first human being who could think "I," and yet was never allowed to become it, necessarily the first artificial human? We find no answer in the cinema. Only the circular movements become faster, the disappearance of space expands in virtual reality into infinity, if you'll allow the paradox. And the best and worst occurs simultaneously again: the second human being, onto whom one could project one's hopes or fears, no longer has *one* shape. He has infinitely many forms. He is no longer the product of division, but the being that has discovered division as a new form of life. And for this reason you can destroy this being as often as you want. It will return, again and again.

Dream Replicants of the Cinema

JOHNNY MNEMONIC
Dina Meyer, Keanu Reeves

JOHNNY MNEMONIC
Keanu Reeves

JOHNNY MNEMONIC
Keanu Reeves

37

Dream Replicants of the Cinema

TETSUO

TETSUO
Tsukamoto Shinya

38

DEMON SEED
Julie Christie

Dream Replicants of the Cinema

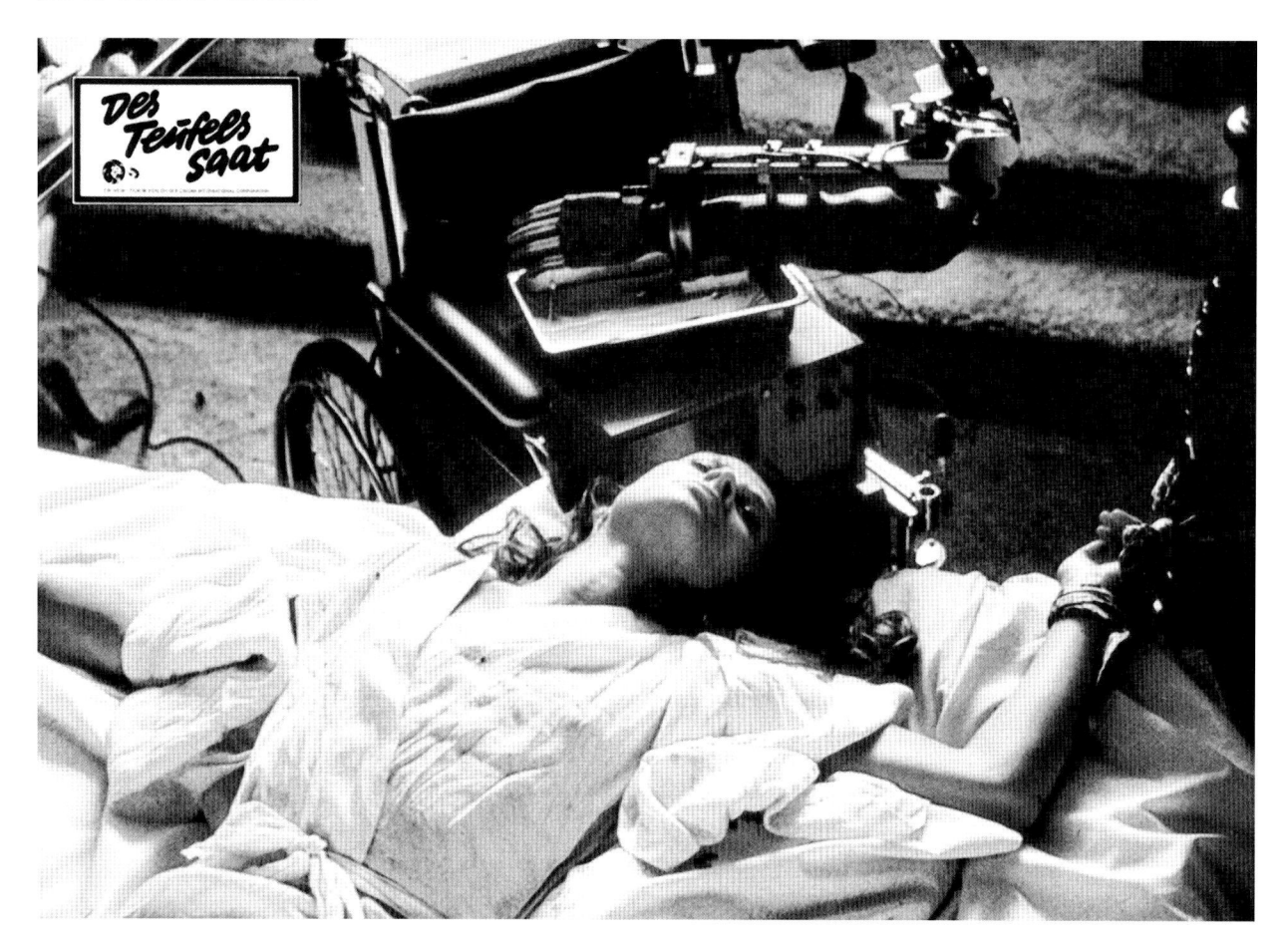

Demon Seed
Julie Christie

Dream Replicants of the Cinema

Demon Seed
Julie Christie

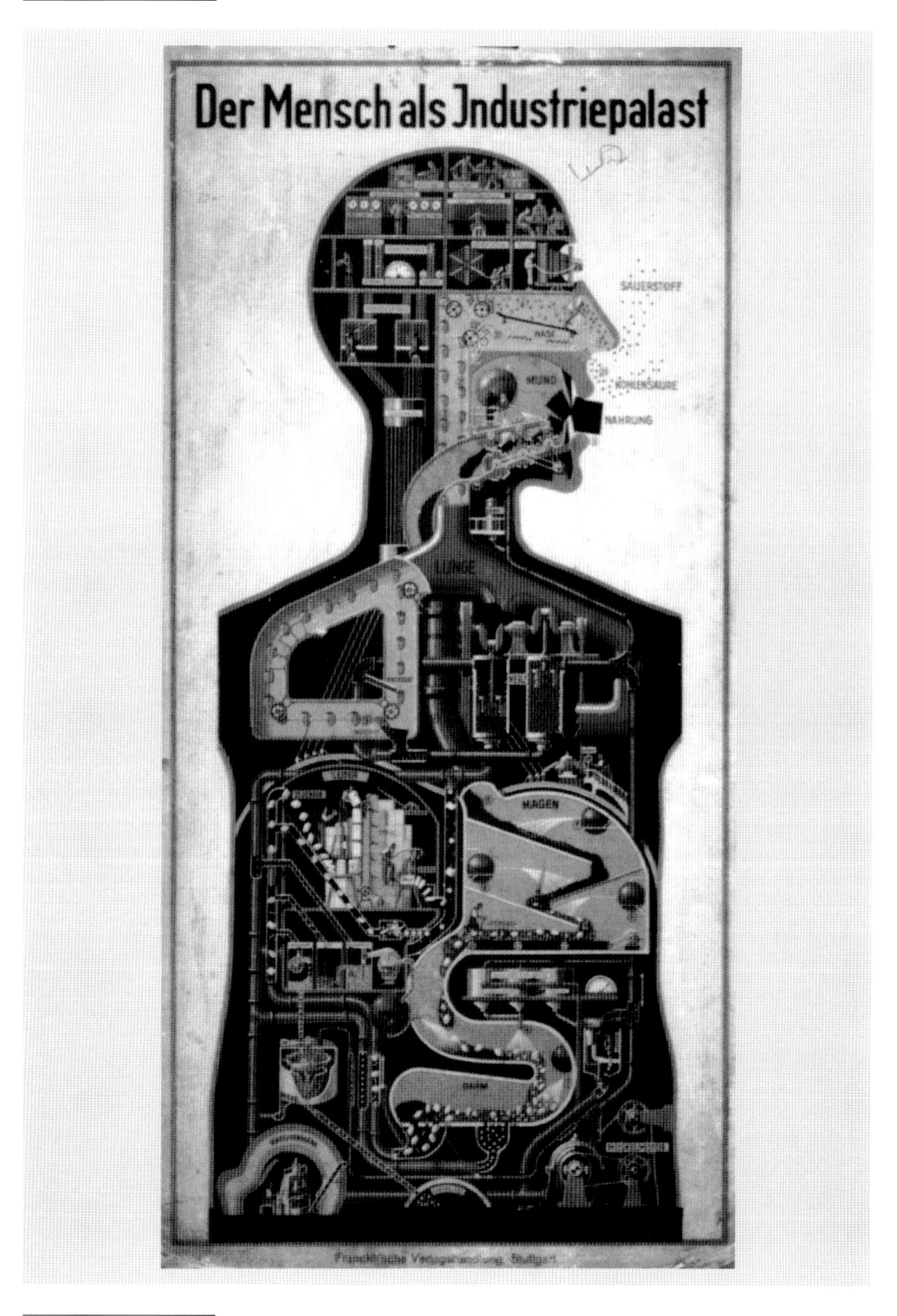

Signboard for schools
(Text: Man as Industrial Palace),
Stuttgart, around 1920

What's a Man?

Bred People, Intelligent Computers

Documents

A self-balancing, 28-jointed adapter-base biped; an electrochemical reduction-plant, integral with segregated stowages of special energy extracts in storage batteries, for subsequent actuation of thousands of hydraulic and pneumatic pumps, with motors attached; 62,000 miles of capillaries; millions of warning signal, railroad and conveyor systems; crushers and cranes (of which the arms are magnificent 23-jointed affairs with self-surfacing and lubricating systems, and a universally distributed telephone system needing no service for 70 years if well managed); the whole, extraordinarily complex mechanism guided with exquisite precision from a turret in which are located telescopic and microscopic self-registering and recording range finders, a spectroscope, *et cetera*, the turret control being closely allied with an air conditioning intake-and-exhaust, and a main fuel intake.

Within the few cubic inches housing the turret mechanisms, there is room, also, for two sound-wave and sound-direction-finder recording diaphragms, a filing and instant reference system, and an expertly devised analytical laboratory large enough not only to contain minute records of every last and continual event of up to 70 years' experience, or more, but to extend, by computation and abstract fabrication, this experience with relative accuracy into all corners of the observed universe. There is, also, a forecasting and tactical plotting department for the reduction of future possibilities and probabilities to generally successful specific choice.

Richard Buckminster Fuller: Nine Chains to the Moon. London: Cape 1973, pp. 18–19

As soon as one seriously delves into the question of an absolute standard for human material to be brought out through breeding, the theoretical and practical abyss breaks open into which a breeding enterprise for human elements must necessarily fall. Even if the theoretical possibility of establishing a measure for ranking genuine human personality values existed, and also the practical possibility of increasing the amount of valuable human material in relation to the amount of less valuable human material, the questionability of such efforts to breed human elements would remain. For this problem is inseparable from the question of the "breeding of human beings" itself. That reveals itself in the necessity to use such terms as "human material." Man must not be made the "object" of a breeding plan, not simply because a human being, born or unborn, might turn out to be a "valuable" one, though we are unable to recognise this, but also because the non-"valuable" one [yes, even the very least valuable one, to put it in words] is and remains a *human being* as well. For man is in his very nature a person. This, however, includes the inalienable *possibility* of a personal transcendence of his own ["unworthy"] nature, a possibility of being different, new, reborn, or however one would like to and must grasp and express the "natural" or the "supernatural." In the last instance it is impossible to get by here without making reference to categories of Christian religion. This is why the abandonment of newborn babies in pre-Christian times cannot mean a justification of such action. Man's "likeness to God," the contents of which, but never the form, can be lost, comprises precisely this "possibility."

Hedwig Conrad-Martius: Utopien der Menschenzüchtung. Der Sozialdarwinismus und seine Folgen. (Utopias of Human Breeding. Social Darwinism and its Consequences.) Munich: Kösel 1955, pp. 138–139

The term "Artificial Intelligence" (AI) – according to AI historiography – was coined in the year 1956 when a two-month conference of computer scientists took place in Hanover, New Hampshire, at Dartmouth College. One of the subjects under consideration was how it would be possible to develop machines with "intelligent" behavior. John McCarthy, one of the initiators of this conference, made up the concept of "Artificial Intelligence" for this topic. Since then, this has been the all-encompassing term for all research and development projects and activities that have the aim of making machines (computers) "more intelligent."

The model for mechanical "intelligence" is the intelligence of people. Although we often hear people speak of "intelligent" computer systems nowadays, hardly anyone would seriously claim that the performances of such systems are already comparable to the model of human intelligence. "Artificial intelligence" doesn't refer to a research and development *result*, but to a *project*.

Werner Sesink: Menschliche und künstliche Intelligenz. Der kleine Unterschied. (Human and Artificial Intelligence. The Minor Difference.) Stuttgart: Klett-Cotta 1993, p. 10

In an essay from 1950 the mathematician Alan Turing posed the question: "Can machines think?" And he gave a surprising turn to this question by reformulating it. He asked: Can a machine trick a person in a question-and-answer game into believing that it is a human being? Can it thus successfully play at being a "human being?" In other words, if a machine can really deceive a person, it is – according to Turing – at least for the human being it has deceived, not distinguishable from a thinking person.

In the discussion about "Artificial Intelligence," this reformulation of the question "Can machines think?"

became famous as the "Turing test." And people who, with Turing, hold this reformulation for admissible and meaningful are of the opinion that AI research will have reached its goal when it can build machines (computers) that "pass" this "test" or – to put it differently – "win" the game.

No one can claim that there are already computers today that could pass this test. Nevertheless we occasionally hear that a computer or computer program has passed the Turing test in part, if the topic of communication between human being and machine is very narrowly limited and the system within this restricted frame of communication is accepted as a fully valid human being. An example of this that became famous is J. Weizenbaum's program ELIZA, which – to Weizenbaum's own horror – managed to make a whole number of people believe that it was a psychotherapist, at least as long as these persons didn't broach topics the program was not prepared for. Such a restriction of the area covered by the Turing test contradicts its basic intention, however.

Werner Sesink: Menschliche und künstliche Intelligenz. Der kleine Unterschied. (Human and Artificial Intelligence. The Minor Difference.) Stuttgart: Klett-Cotta 1993, pp. 39–40

Our culture is still depends utterly on biological human beings, but with each passing year our machines, a major product of the culture, assume a greater role in its maintenance and continued growth. Sooner or later our machines will become knowledgeable enough to handle their own maintenance, reproduction, and self-improvement without help. When this happens, the new genetic takeover will be complete. Our culture will then be able to evolve independently of human biology and its limitations, passing instead directly from generation to generation of ever more capable intelligent machinery.

Hans Moravec: Mind Children. The Future of Robot and Human and Intelligence. Cambridge, Mass.; London: Harvard Universtiy Press 1988, p. 4

One day when we know how the mind works, we will realize that it is not necessary to be sick, or to lose our memory in old age, or to die. One will then be able to transplant all the elements of his personality into another body, a machine body, which is maintained and continues to grow, so that we will not have to live with our restrictions forever.

Marvin Minsky in Kurt Ebbinghaus: Das Menschenbild der Künstlichen Intelligenz. (The Human Picture of Artificial Intelligence.) In: Mensch-Natur-Gesellschaft, No. II, 1989, p. 38

Can a Machine Ever Become Self-aware?

by Giorgio C. Buttazzo

Los Angeles, 2029 A.D. (...) All stealth bombers are upgraded with Cyberdyne computers, becoming fully unmanned. Afterwards they fly with a perfect operational record. The Skynet funding bill is passed. The system goes online on August 4, 1997. Human decisions are removed from strategic defense. Skynet begins to learn at a geometric rate. It becomes self-aware at 2:14 a.m. Eastern time, August 29th.

This is the view of the future described in James Cameron's film Terminator 2 – Judgment Day (1991). Skynet's self-awareness and its attack against humans mark the beginning of a war between robots and humans, which represents the first scene of the movie.

Since the early fifties, science fiction movies have depicted robots as very sophisticated machines built by humans to perform complex operations, to work with humans on safe critical missions in hostile environments, or, more often, to pilot and control spaceships on galactic travels. At the same time, however, intelligent robots have also been depicted as dangerous machines, capable of working against man through evil plans. The most significant example of a robot with these features is HAL 9000, the main character in Stanley Kubrick's epic film 2001: A Space Odyssey (1965–68).

In the movie, HAL controls the entire spaceship, talks amiably with the astronauts, plays chess, renders aesthetic judgments about drawings, recognizes the emotions in the crew, but also murders four of the five astronauts in order to pursue a plan elaborated out of the pre-programmed schemes. In other science fiction movies, such as The Terminator (1984) and The Matrix (1999), the view of the future is even more catastrophic: robots will become intelligent and self-aware and will take over the human race.

In a very few movies, robots are depicted as reliable assistants that really cooperate with men rather than conspiring against them. In Robert Wise's 1951 film The Day the Earth Stood Still, Gort is perhaps the first robot (extraterrestrial, in this case) to act positively, supporting Captain Klaatu in his mission to deliver a message to humans. Similarly, in Aliens (the second episode of the successful series, directed by James Cameron in 1986), Bishop is a synthetic android whose purpose is to pilot the spaceship during the mission and protect the crew. In contrast to HAL and to Bishop's predecessor, encountered in the first Alien episode (1979), Bishop is not affected by malfunctioning, and he remains faithful to his duty till the end of the movie. This is vividly illustrated in one of the final scenes in which Bishop, with his body torn in two after fighting with the alien creature, still works to save Ellen Ripley's life, offering his hand to keep her from being sucked out of the ship. In the end, James Cameron sets a positive, optimistic sign with respect to science and technology. Robocop in the 1987 Paul Verhoeven film of the same title is also a dependable robot that cooperates with men on law enforcement, although he is not a fully cybernetic organism (as is the Terminator), but a hybrid organism, made by integrating biological parts with artificial components.

The dual, ambivalent connotations often associated with science fiction robots represent a clear expression of the desire and fear that man has towards technology. On the one hand, man projects into a robot his irrepressible desire for immortality, embodied in a powerful and indestructible artificial being whose intellectual, sensory, and motor capabilities are far greater than those of a normal person. On the other hand, however, there is a fear that an overly advanced technology (quite mysterious for most people) can get out of control, acting against man (compare Frankenstein, HAL 9000, the Terminator, and the robots in The Matrix). The positronic brain adopted by Isaac Asimov's robots comes from this feeling: it was the result of a technology so advanced that nobody knew its low-level details any more, although its construction process was fully automated.

Recent progress in computer-science technology has strongly influenced the characteristics of new science fiction robots. For example, the theories on connectionism and artificial neural networks (aimed at replicating some processing mechanism typical of the human brain) inspired the Terminator robot, which is not only intelligent, but can learn based on his past experience.

In the movie, the Terminator represents the prototype of imaginary robots. He can walk, talk, perceive and behave like a human being. His power cell can supply energy for 120 years, and an alternate power circuit provides fault tolerance in case of damage. But, what is more important, the Terminator can learn! He is controlled by a neural-net processor, a computer that can modify its behavior based on past experience.

What makes the movie even more intriguing from a philosophical point of view is that such a neural processor is so complex that it begins to learn at a geometric rate and, after a while, becomes self-aware! In this sense, the movie raises an important question about artificial consciousness: Can a machine ever become self-aware?

Before answering this question, we should perhaps ask: How can we verify that an intelligent being is self-aware? In 1950, the computer science pioneer Alan Turing posed a similar question, but in this case concerning intelligence. In order to establish whether a machine can or cannot be considered as intelligent as a human, he proposed a famous test, known as the Turing test. There are two keyboards, one connected to a computer, the other leading to a person. An examiner types in questions on any topic he likes; both the computer and the person type back responses that the examiner reads on the respective computer screens. If he cannot reliably determine which was the person and which the machine, then we say the machine has passed the Turing test. Today, no computer can pass the Turing test unless we restrict the interaction to very specific topics, such as chess.

THE TERMINATOR
Arnold Schwarzenegger

THE TERMINATOR
Arnold Schwarzenegger

Can a Machine ...

On May 11, 1997, for the first time in history, a computer named Deep Blue beat world chess champion Gary Kasparov, 3.5 to 2.5. Like all current computers, however, Deep Blue does not understand chess, since it just applies rules to find a move that leads to a better position, according to an evaluation criterion programmed by chess experts. Thus, if we accept Turing's view, we can say that Deep Blue plays chess in an intelligent way, but we can also claim that it does not understand the meaning of its moves, as a television set does not understand the meaning of the images it displays.

The problem of verifying whether an intelligent being is self-aware is even more complex. In fact, whereas intelligence can be understood as the expression of an external behavior that can be measured by specific tests, self-awareness is the expression of an internal brain state that cannot be measured.

From a purely philosophical point of view, it is not possible to verify the presence of consciousness in another brain (either human or artificial), because this is a property that can only be verified by its possessor. Since we cannot enter another being's mind, we cannot be sure about its consciousness. This problem is thoroughly discussed by Douglas R. Hofstadter and Daniel C. Dennett in a book entitled "The Mind's I."

From a pragmatic point of view, however, we could follow Turing's approach and say that a being can be considered self-aware if it is able to convince us of its self-awareness by passing specific tests. Moreover, among human beings, the belief that another person possesses self-awareness is based on considerations of similarity: since we have the same organs and we have a similar brain, it is reasonable to believe that the person opposite us is also self-aware. Who would question his best friend's consciousness? Nevertheless, if the creature in front of us were made of synthetic tissues, mechatronic organs, and neural processors, our conclusion would perhaps be different, even though it behaved like a human.

With the emergence of artificial neural networks, the problem of artificial consciousness becomes even more intriguing, because neural networks replicate the basic electrical behavior of the brain and provide the proper support to enable a processing mechanism similar to the one adopted by the brain. In the book "Impossible Minds," Igor Aleksander addresses this topic at depth and with scientific rigor.

Although everybody agrees that a computer based on classical processing paradigms can never become self-aware, can we say the same thing for a neural network? If we disregard structural diversity between biological and artificial brains, the issue of artificial consciousness can only become religious. In other words, if we believe that human consciousness is determined by divine intervention, then clearly no artificial system can ever become self-aware. If instead we believe that human consciousness is a natural electrical property developed by complex brains, then the possibility of producing a self-aware artificial being remains open. If we support the hypothesis of consciousness as a physical property of the brain, then the question becomes: When will a computer become self-aware? Attempting to provide even a rough answer to this question is hazardous. Nevertheless, it is possible to determine at least one necessary condition without which a machine cannot develop self-awareness. The idea is based on the simple consideration that, to develop self-awareness, a neural network must be at least as complex as the human brain.

The human brain has about 10^{12} neurons, and each neuron makes about 10^3 connections (synapses) with other neurons, on average, for a total number of 10^{15} synapses. In artificial neural networks, a synapse can be simulated using a floating-point number, which requires 4 bytes of memory to be represented in a computer. As a consequence, to simulate 10^{15} synapses, a total amount of $4*10^{15}$ bytes (4 million gigabytes) is required. Let us say that to simulate the whole human brain we need 5 million gigabytes, including the auxiliary variables for storing neuron outputs and other internal brain states. Then our question becomes: When will such a memory be available in a computer? During the last 20 years, the RAM capacity has increased exponentially by a factor of 10 every 4 years. The diagram illustrates the typical memory configuration installed in personal computers since 1980.

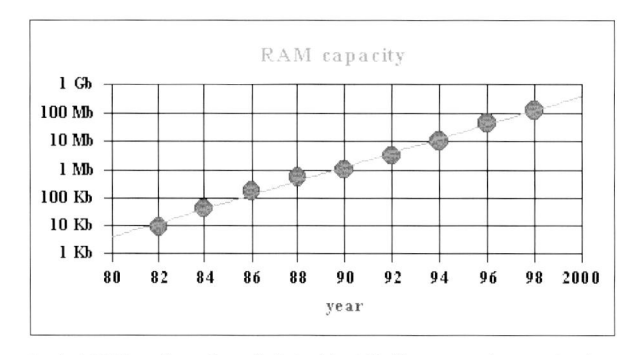

Typical RAM configurations (in bytes) installed in personal computers in the last twenty years.

By interpolation, we can derive the following equation, which gives the RAM size (in bytes) as a function of the year: bytes = $10^{[(year - 1966)/4]}$. For example, from the equation we can find that in 1990 a personal computer was typically equipped with 1 Mbyte of RAM. In 1998, a typical configuration had 100 Mbytes of RAM, and so on. By inverting the relation above, we can predict the year in which a computer will be equipped with a given amount of memory (assuming the RAM continues to grow at the same rate): year = 1966 + $4* \log_{10}$ (bytes).

Now, to know the year in which a computer will be equipped with 5 million Gbytes of RAM, we have just to substitute that number in the equation above and compute the result. The answer is: year = 2029. An interesting coincidence with the date predicted in the TERMINATOR 2 movie!

In order to fully understand the meaning of the result achieved, it is important to make some considerations. First of all, it is worth recalling that the computed date only refers to a condition necessary, but not sufficient, for the development of artificial consciousness. This means that the existence of a powerful computer equipped with millions of gigabytes of RAM is not sufficient alone to guarantee that it will magically become self-aware. There are other important factors influencing this process, such as the progress of theories on artificial neural networks and on the basic biological mechanisms of the mind, for which it is impossible to attempt precise estimates. Furthermore, one could argue that the computation presented was done on personal computers, which do not represent the pinnacle of technology in the field. Someone else could object that the same amount of RAM memory could be available using a network of computers or virtual memory management mechanisms to exploit hard disk space. In any case, even if we adopt different numbers, the basic principle of the computation is the same, and the date could be advanced by a few years only. Finally, after such a long discussion of artificial consciousness, one could ask: Why should a self-aware machine be built?

Apart from ethical issues, which would significantly influence the progress in this field, the strongest motivation would certainly come from the innate human desire to discover new horizons and enlarge the frontiers of science. Furthermore, developing an artificial brain based on the same principles used in the biological brain would provide a way of transferring our mind into a faster and more robust medium, opening a door in the direction of immortality. Freed from a fragile and decaying body, human beings with synthetic organs (including the brain) could represent the next evolutionary step of the human race. Such a new species, the natural result of human technological progress (unwanted in a dictatorship), could explore the universe, search for alien civilizations, survive the death of the solar system, control the energy of black holes, and move at the speed of light – by transmitting the information necessary for replication to other planets.

Indeed, the exploration of space in search of intelligent civilizations began as early as 1972, when the Pioneer 10 spacecraft was launched with the specific purpose of transmitting information about the human race and planet Earth beyond our solar system. As for all-important human discoveries, from nuclear energy to the atomic bomb, from genetic engineering to human cloning, the real problem has been and will continue to be how to keep technology under control, making sure that it is used for human progress, not with the aim of destruction and catastrophe. In this sense, the message of peace that Captain Klaatu delivered to mankind in the film THE DAY THE EARTH STOOD STILL has lost none of its topicality!

References

Igor Aleksander: Impossible Minds: My Neurons, My Consciousness. London: Imperial College Press 1996

Isaac Asimov: I, Robot. Grafton: London 1968

Douglas R. Hofstadter, Daniel C. Dennett (ed.): The Mind's I. Fantasies and Reflections on Self and Soul. New York: Basic 1981

David G. Stork (ed.): HAL's Legacy: 2001's Computer as Dream and Reality. Cambridge (Mass.); London: MIT Press 1997

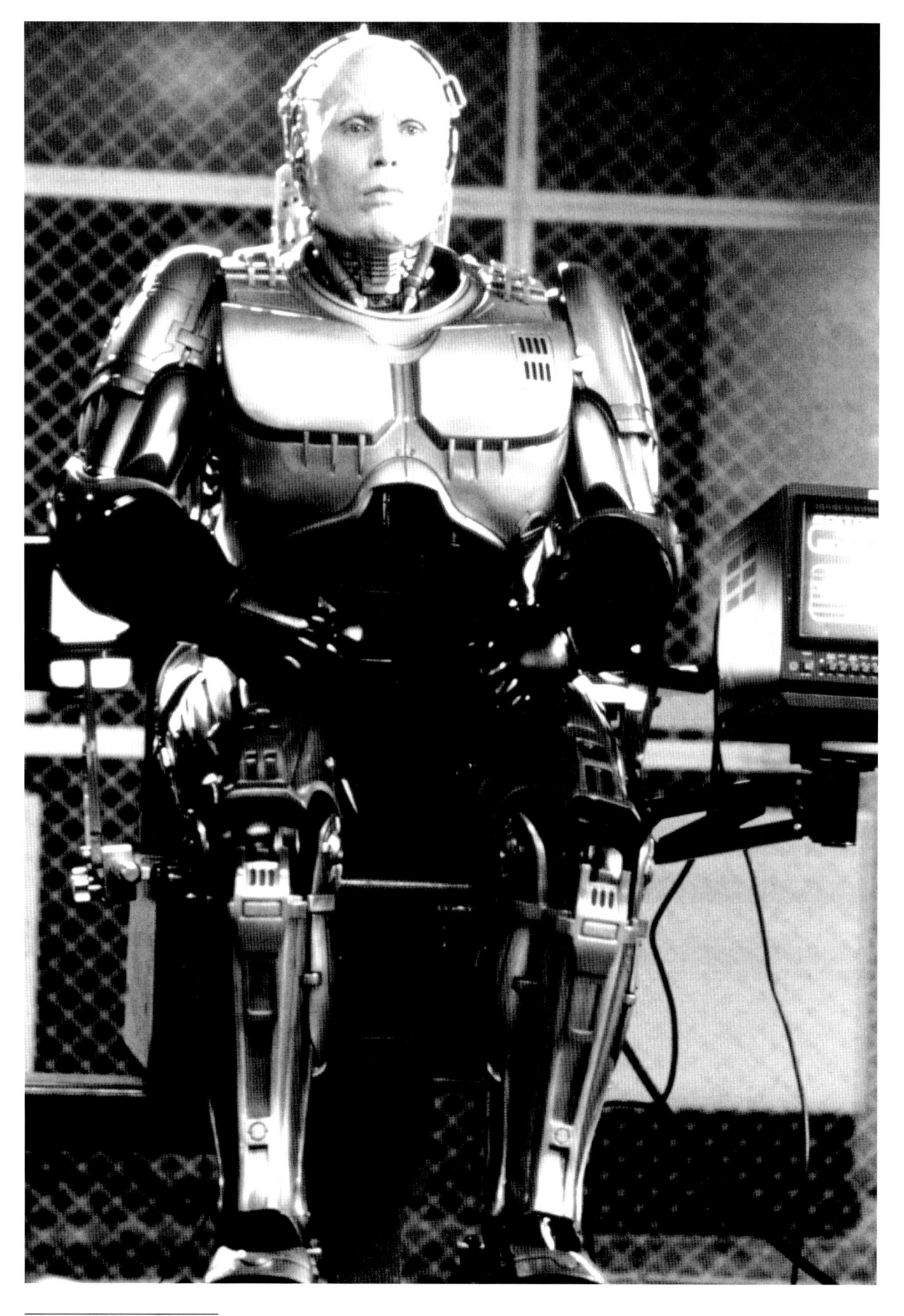

Animated Machines

Robocop
Peter Weller

Animated Machines
On the Terminator, Robocop and Blade Runner

Workshop Reports

I was thinking of an indestructible machine, an endo-skeleton design, which had never been filmed as such. We'd had things like WESTWORLD, where Yul Brynner's face falls off and there's a transistor radio underneath – which is not visually satisfying, because you don't feel that this mechanism could have been inside moving those facial features. So it started from the idea of doing this sort of definitive movie robot, what I've always wanted to see. I had this image of him being covered in flesh and having it burn off, and coming phoenix-like out of the fire.

(...)

I'd thought of the Terminator as a more anonymous, saturnine figure – Jürgen Prochnow was one actor I had in mind. With Arnold, the film took on a larger-than-life sheen. I just found myself on the set doing things I didn't think I would do – scenes that were supposed to be purely horrific that just couldn't be, because they were now too flamboyant.

You turn a human being who already seems almost superman into a machine, and then you humanize the machine and make people identify with him.

Orion's initial thought was that the poster of Arnold with his chest bared would make women want to come and see the movie. But I don't think anybody sees him in a sexual way in the film. They see him almost from the beginning as this implacable, sexless, emotionless machine – in the form of a man, which is scary, because he's a perfect male figure.

James Cameron interviewed by David Chute. In: Film Comment, No. 1, January/February 1985, pp. 57–59

The scene which seems to stick most in the minds of those who have seen the film is the "eye scene," where the Terminator makes emergency repairs on itself after a gunfight with the hero. James Cameron here made use of his background as a special effects art director. "You have to give the audience a certain level of effects," he stated, "after which they will make their own connections. Done right, you can do these things for much less than other people would think. Give the audience 'A' and 'B' correctly, and they will supply their own 'C'." Indeed, it is classic. First, the Terminator operates on his arm – a prosthetic built by effects wizard Stan Winston – stabbing the arm with a Number 11 Xacto blade. The audience is then shown him working on the metal interior of the arm. He steps to the sink, examines his eye, and then – with the camera shooting from the right as he works on his left eye, he brings up the knife and poses it in front of the eye. A quick cut to close-up of the eye lens dropping in a sink full of water that turns red, and nearly everyone in the audience is completely convinced they have seen him stab the eye.

"Most of this is possible because the audience does not see everything that's going on," says Greenberg. "Most of the screen is filled with dark shadows, which the audience fills in with imagination."

Thomas McKelvey Cleaver: Adam Greenberg on THE TERMINATOR. In: American Cinematographer, No. 4, April 1985, p. 51

To fully give *life* to THE TERMINATOR's unstoppable Mr. T. necessitated the skills of Fantasy II, the special effects company headed by Gene Warren, Jr. The film's climactic chase scene involved cuts between two versions of the android, a full-scale mechanical Terminator, constructed by Stan Winston in his shop, and a stop-motion puppet built by Doug Beswick at Fantasy II.

"The first time you see it rise up it's on a rear projection plate behind the actors," said Warren. "That's the full-scale model being raised up with rods and wires from above." The full-sized mechanical model is used whenever the scene requires a close-up of the Terminator, or whatever is left of him. Fantasy II's stop-motion puppet appears nine times in full shots of the skinned Terminator. Prime examples include when he's walking out of the fire, moving down the factory's hallway, stalking along the catwalk, and receiving Reese's blow with the pipe.

Martin Perlman: THE TERMINATOR. Special Effects by Fantasy II. In: Cinefantastique, No. 2, May 1985, p. 47

Once convinced that their partnership would be a fruitful one, it became Yakim's and Weller's task to uncover the personality hiding within the robotized Murphy. Their starting point, according to Yakim, was with the works of Sergei Eisenstein: "For this specific character I suggested that Peter observe the stylization of Niklai Cherkasov in IVAN THE TERRIBLE. This was, at least for me, my guidance. The size, the isolation in reactions – he has a scene, on top of the hill where he observes the war. Someone comes to announce to him what's happening in the city and he moves first the eyes to the right, then he moves the head, then he moves down [the hill], until he reaches [the messenger] – just like that. And this was an indication which way I should go. So I'm very influenced by that, in terms of size, of authority, of controlling completely your environment.

"The process of thought with this character is completely different. Sometimes this character has his brains in his chest, at other times in the head, at other times in the arms. His reflexes are different. Sometimes it's in every other part of the body. Accordingly, when he sees something, absorbs something and reacts, he might absorb with

Animated Machines

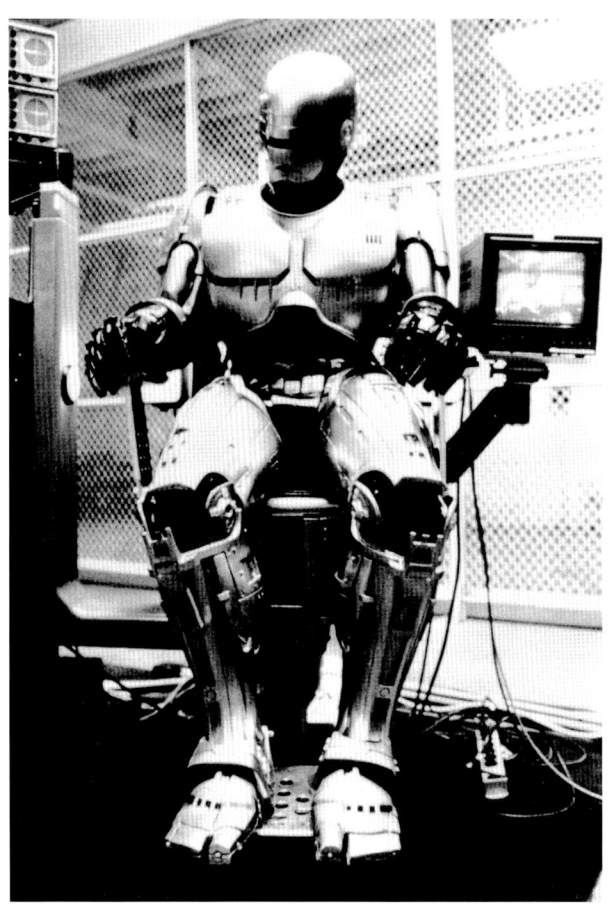

ROBOCOP 2
Patricia Charbonneau, Peter Weller

ROBOCOP
Peter Weller

ROBOCOP 3
Jill Hennessy, Robert Burke, Remy Ryan

ROBOCOP
Peter Weller

52

another part of the body and react with still another part of the body. It all depends on the situation." This is why, according to Yakim, Robo can be seen leading his motions with different areas of the body throughout the film. "If the situation demands boldness, demands more of an aggressive attitude, we start with the chest. The chest is the symbol of courage, the chest is out there and open – this person is not afraid to take a blow. It's not like a Greta Garbo chest, which is concave and retreating. When the situation demands a more aggressive action, we start with the chest. When it is more tentative, we start with the head. It is very carefully designed.

(...)

"If you are not an actor, you cannot do this role. You can take the best gymnast, the best physical person, put him in this suit, and he'll disappear in a second. You have to be an excellent actor, because it has to do with inner rhythms. When you move the head, it's not just moving it. We don't see your expression, but it's the way you move it, and the rhythm within with which you move it. It has all to do with inner rhythms – the inner rhythms of an actor, the surprise on which an actor instinctively relies. It's the rhythm that keeps you always on the edge, not knowing where it's going to go."

Dan Persons: The Guru of Robo Acting. Dramatic coach Moni Yakim set the robotic tone for Weller and Burke. In: Cinefantastique, No. 2, August 1993, pp. 39–41

ROBOCOP
Nancy Allen, Peter Weller

IVAN GROZNYJ
Nikolaj Čerkasov, Ljudmila Celikovskaja

In the novel, Deckard constantly worries he will mistakenly kill a human he thinks is a replicant. In fact, he constantly worries that he, himself, is a replicant.

At one stage, we considered having Deckard turn out to be, ironically, a replicant. In fact, if you look at the film closely, especially the ending, you may get some clues – some by slight innuendo – that Deckard is indeed a replicant. At the end there's a kind of confirmation that he is – at least that he believes it possible. Within the context of the overall story, whether it's true or not in the book, having Deckard be a replicant is the *only* reasonable solution.

Danny Peary: Directing Alien and Blade Runner. An Interview with Ridley Scott. In: Danny Peary (ed.): Screen Flights / Screen Fantasies. The Future according to Science Fiction Cinema. Garden City, New York: Doubleday 1984, p. 302

Der Golem, wie er in die Welt kam
Paul Wegener

Possible People

Thoughts on the Literary and Cultural History of the Android

by Peter Gendolla

It's not pleasant to discover you were invented. (Jack Slater alias Arnold Schwarzenegger alias Arnie Schwarzenegger in LAST ACTION HERO)

Technical inventions do not simply make work easier, they also allow their constructor to gain an understanding of himself, of how he functions. This human impulse to explore internal connections by projecting external mechanisms onto them is nowhere more evident than in the automaton (Greek αὐτό-ματος, "that which acts of itself"). Be it by the ancient Chinese, by the contemporary Japanese and Koreans in their factories, or by the chipsmiths in Munich or Silicon Valley, automatons have always been constructed to act as useful helpers, slaves, no less – the word robot originally signified laborer – but also as "useless playthings." Automatons have lifted weights, ground grain, and today are in the process of undoing, after a fashion, the Babylonian linguistic confusion as computer translation programs. Moreover, they have been disguised as nightingales or ducks, have entertained royalty at the Baroque courts in complete automaton theatrical troupes, and these days constitute one of the industrial branches with the largest turnover, as Nintendo or Sega systems, adventure games in cyberspace. In this very tradition, in these countless variations of the mechanical man, a new self-image of the individual and his social body has always been playfully documented, as if in passing. In his book "L'Homme machine" (Man a Machine) of 1747, the notorious 18th century philosopher Julien Offray de La Mettrie made perhaps the most disputed proposal for a new image of man disconnected from traditional metaphysical foundations, an image which, in its basic elements, finds its continuation today in proposals by biologists to improve the human genome. So it's worth taking a look.

La Mettrie

After a careful analysis of the contemporary and historical reception of La Mettrie's major work "L'Homme machine," its modes of argumentation, and its contexts, the cultural historian Alex Sutter comes to the following conclusion: "The implications of the image of the machine in 'L'Homme machine' can be summarized under the following headings: Polemical content: the physicalization of the soul as opposed to spiritualist rationalism. Methodological content: open-minded empiricism with regard to the body-soul problem. Conceptual content: organized matter as a comprehensive basis for the unity of body and soul (...). Metaphysical content: outline of a 'materialistic vitalism'. Communicative content: disappointment of the spectacular expectations engendered by a mechanistic anthropology."[1]

To regard La Mettrie as a mere "mechanizer" of man, to situate his "manifesto" (Sutter) among paradigms from the history of biology (vitalism/mechanism), or to emphasize the vitalism, would not do justice, therefore, to the "sprightly many-sidedness" of the image of the machine which he stood for. This essay agrees with Sutter, though at the same time training a keen eye on the evidence La Mettrie presents for the way man functions as a machine. He writes: Opium "makes a man happy in a state which would seemingly be the tomb of feeling, as it is the image of death. How sweet is this lethargy! The soul would long never to emerge from it. For the soul has been a prey to the most intense sorrow, but now feels only the joy of suffering past, and of sweetest peace."[2]

Sutter sees this as evidence of La Mettrie's ignorance of the empiricist prohibition of introspection, as a result of which he relegates the machine model "to the status of a metaphor."[3] It would thus function rhetorically as a "methodological guideline for a scientific objectification of man's insides," that is to say, as an inspiration, a guiding metaphor for the most varied of applications, be that in the field of medicine, technology, or aesthetics. The metaphor constitutes the framework within which the body can be cut open, the organs duplicated, and the soul analyzed. Attention should be focused, however, on La Mettrie's reasoning, that is, on what causes or triggers the use of artificial or technical aids – such as opium – in a body that thus automatically seems to be a technical object: nothing but pain, terror, shock. The dilemma facing every man-machine comparison since Descartes as to how the *res cogitans* and *res extensa* might hold or work together is solved by La Mettrie – as by many before and after him, from Descartes to radical constructivism – by postulating a *self* in the αὐτό-ματος, a "principle of movement" inherent in organic matter, as opposed to "non-organically structured matter." That "suffices for guessing the riddle of substances and of man."[4] Yet in no way is the problem solved by La Mettrie either, because the self of this autopoiesis remains a vacuum or tautology, an observation endowed with a name. What the "torch of experience"[5] does illuminate more and more clearly, however, is not a regular system of mechanics, not even one that might be formulated in algorithms, but rather, that which triggers it, namely excitation, terror, and pain.

"Is the circulation too quick? the soul cannot sleep. Is the soul too much excited? the blood cannot be quieted: it gallops through the veins with an audible murmur: Such are the two opposite causes of insomnia. A single fright in the midst of our dreams makes the heart beat at double speed and snatches us from needed and delicious repose, as a real grief or an urgent need would do."[6]

Before writing his polemical treatise, La Mettrie was forced to earn his living for a while as a doctor in a military hospital. It was there that he had the "most decisive experiences" with which he hoped to demonstrate the mechanics of organic bodies, namely, the experience of injuries to an organic whole, the blatant opposite of an undisturbed peace and tranquil, egalitarian communication between body parts. Yet mechanical-organic integrity/unity is insisted upon almost frenetically with such 'terrifying' examples, as if the life principle had to be maintained literally beyond death, despite the interventions, or better still, attacks on life: "1. The flesh of all animals palpitates after death. (...) 2. Muscles separated from the body contract when they are stimulated. (...) 5. A frog's heart moves (...) after it has been removed from the body, especially when exposed to the sun (...). 6. (Sir Francis) Bacon (...) cites the case of a man convicted of treason, who was opened alive, and whose heart thrown into hot water leaped several times, each time less high, to the perpendicular height of two feet. 8. (I)n hot water, (...) the movement of the detached parts increases. 9. A drunken soldier cut off with one stroke of his sabre an Indian rooster's head. The animal remained standing, then walked, and ran (...). 10. Polyps do more than move after they have been cut in pieces. In a week they regenerate to form as many animals as there are pieces."[7]

Sutter argues that unlike mechanistic theories, La Mettrie ignored contemporary rules of discourse derived from the model of the machine or clock, that is to say, "clarity (or physical explicability)," "mathematical conformity," "integration of the whole into a single large causal connection with a practical structure, etc."[8] are simply not to be found in his writings. What is to be found, however, is the urgent demand for the same. The work makes every effort to claim the existence of a whole, a connection, an uninterrupted communication between every living thing. The 'man-machine' – "clearly an enlightened machine," "a large watch constructed with such skill and ingenuity"[9] – represents the most noble expression, the most complex material manifestation of a virtual construct. Confronted with the observation or experience of its destruction, life is reconstructed with the aid of the machine metaphor, and becomes a phantom: "Let us, therefore, draw the daring conclusion that man is a machine, and that there is only one substance in the whole world and this of course is variously modified."[10]

The 18th century is indeed the age of dissection, in all realms, not just in anatomy (more precise and effective surgery in the medical field), but even more so in the economic sphere, in production, from handicraft to the manufactories to the first factories of the industrial era. The painful awareness of this division of labor or differentiation of social functions resounds throughout the *Querelle des anciens et des modernes* like a lament about a ruptured late or modern age, an age at odds with itself, as opposed to an integral early or ancient Arcadian age. It also turns up in the interchanges between Goethe and Schiller. For Goethe, the resultant utopia of vital wholeness was no doubt Italy: "Et ego in...". In the end, out of the splintering of the "moderns," Schiller constructed the "aesthetic" state, perfect in itself. In his letters "Über die ästhetische Erziehung" (On the Aesthetic Education of Man) he claimed that only art was capable of bridging the gaps created by modernism, of restoring man's wholeness. As early as 1791, in his much quoted critique of Gottfried August Bürger's poems, Schiller writes: "Given the isolation and the disjointed effectiveness of our spiritual powers, made necessary by the broadened circles of knowledge and the segregation of professional occupations, it is poetry alone that gathers together once again the separated powers of the soul, that preoccupies in harmonious accord head and heart, discernment and wit, reason and imagination, that restores, as it were, the *whole* man in us."[11]

Vaucanson

Jacques de Vaucanson is someone who vigorously promoted the "isolation" of the spiritual powers and the expansion of the circles of knowledge, plus the subsequent "segregation of professional occupations," that is to say, someone who warmly welcomed and ingeniously furthered the technologies of the division of labor. Like no others before them, his automata, the "Flute Player" (1738), the "Tambourine Player" and the "Duck" (both 1739), stimulated the mechanical fantasies of the 18th century and beyond – from La Mettrie to Reimarus and Goethe.[12] What is less well known, though, is just how closely connected work and play were for Vaucanson, the interplay of skillfulness and ingenuity, which were concentrated in his main obsession: to isolate or separate the controls or steering force from the movement of the body/machine parts, to transfer these to their own steering/control sector or organs, and to divide them up into the process sections controls/transmission/operation, enclosed in flexible hollow bodies – a technique we today would call module or black box systems.

Vaucanson was appointed director of silk manufacture in Lyon in 1740. Here, long before Jacquard, who is credited with inventing the perforated card control system in 1805, Vaucanson developed automatic controls for looms.[13] To do this, he transferred the cam controls used in mechanical toys and musical boxes to the work machines, reversing the principle and thus developing perforated disc controls.

In Schiller's sense, one could regard this expansion of the circles of knowledge and the isolation or segregation – later McLuhan would call this extension – of the effectiveness of spiritual powers as also being responsible for the technical *inventio*. Social differentiations go hand in hand with greater demands on the individual spiritual powers, resulting in an overtaxing of those powers. On the one hand, this very pressure on the individual capacities leads to the invention of technical aids, the functional modes or theories of which are formulated in the anthropologies of technology put forward by Lewis Mumford, Arnold Gehlen, Marshall McLuhan or Günther Anders, and the history of which is nothing more than the history of automation – from Vaucanson to the current programs of so-called Artificial Intelligence, irrespective of whether they control washing machines, prostheses, or whole factories.[14] On the other hand, and in interaction with this, aesthetic perception, the perception of perception, is worn down: what happens to sensations, how are senses expanded, filtered, intensified, shaped or tinted,[15] when the body that thus perceives itself is extended or restructured by technical artifacts? The fantasies about machine-men entertained by writers from Jean Paul to E.T.A. Hoffmann to the science fiction of our day can be seen as a direct reaction to this. Indirectly, though just as clearly or strikingly, the various 18th century literatures, cults or cultures of *Empfindsamkeit*

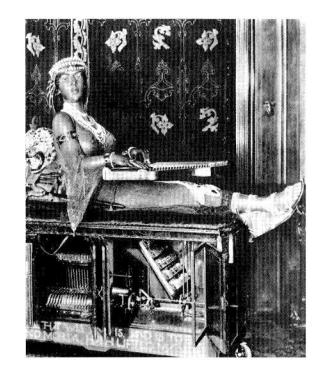

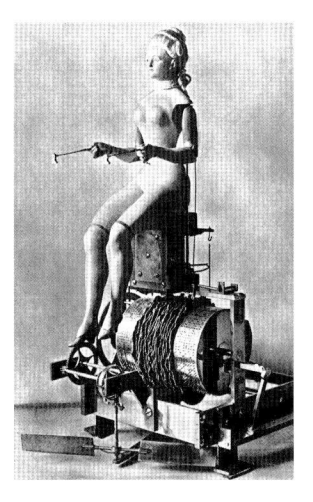

Isis playing the zither, made by C.E. Nixon, around 1850

Marie Antoinette as mechanical musician by Roentgen and Kitzing

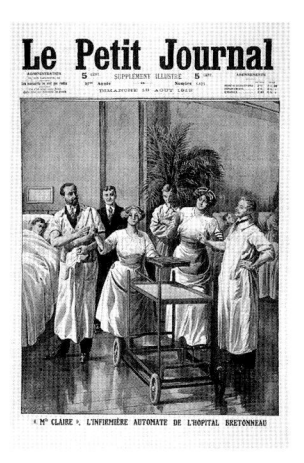

Mlle. Claire, l'infirmière automate de l'hôpital Bretonneau (Mlle. Claire, the nurse automaton of Bretonneau Hospital), invented by Robert Herdner. From: Le Petit Journal, Paris, August 18, 1912

(Sensitivity) can be regarded as in a way articulating the internal reactions to the external aids. It is no coincidence that as early as 1777 Goethe, who had contributed considerably to this culture with his "Leiden des jungen Werther" (Sorrows of Young Werther) of 1774, distanced himself in his "Triumph der Empfindsamkeit" (Triumph of Sensitivity) from such inwardness: from that "theatrical whim" (Goethe) about love, i.e., "the electricity of tender hearts," for an artificial woman, surely the direct model for Hoffmann's famous doll Olimpia in the story "Der Sandmann" (The Sandman) of 1815. Another direct reaction to this can be found in the so-called literature of horror, the terrifying visions of the Gothic novel, an aestheticization of the experience of the individual and social division of labor, from Wilhelm Heinrich Wackenroder's "Märchen von einem nackten Heiligen" (Tale of a Naked Saint) to Mary Wollstonecraft Shelley's "Frankenstein, or The Modern Prometheus" – still one of the most frequently filmed stories in cinema history – to M.G. Lewis' "Monk" to Hoffmann's "Elixieren des Teufels" (The Devil's Elixir): What else do these literary works articulate but the sudden terror in the face of amputations, the destruction of physical wholeness, of the possibility of undivided sensations?

Interim Thoughts

La Mettrie's "L'Homme machine" declares man to be a "very enlightened machine"; man is the inspired, the enlightened machine, as opposed to all other machines, the animal-plant-heaven-machines. This recourse taken by the man of the Enlightenment to his own body, this application of rationalism's main mechanical metaphors to the organic, was encouraged by an 18th century preoccupation that is still vexing today, the emphatic fascination with this watch, i.e., the human body, "constructed with such skill and ingenuity" that, astonishingly, it winds itself up, or stops other clocks, apparently with just as much passion. What is it that draws our attention to our own material composition, what makes the doctor or philosopher claim that the light of reason is both *the* principle differentiating us from the non-human machines as well as the principle of *every* living cohesion in any being whatsoever – thereby embroiling him in the real problem of the consciousness debate: Does consciousness exist to greater or lesser degrees?[16] Inspired by La Mettrie's text, one could formulate a thesis, which though impossible to prove here, might, if padded out with some material, be a useful basis for some further thoughts on already existing or possibly imminent substitutes for man: mechanizations of the body, from the restructuring of the individual body with the help of prostheses to its integration into large – for example military – machine systems, go hand in hand with the amputation of the respective organs and their functions. These in turn produce phantom pains,[17] sensations in no longer existing organs. Art, literature and their diverse media, among other things, come to terms in a particular way, i.e. aesthetically, with this manifold process of substitution or transference.

One consequence of this claim would be that civilizatory, disciplinary, and industrial processes are always reflected in the history of the arts, not directly or simply, however, but rather in pain, that is to say, in the highly varied forms in which phantom pains are processed, among other things, in a historically very diverse aesthetic production and in ever new phantomatic objects articulated in ever new media. Such a thesis inspired by La Mettrie can be pursued in three different discourses: Bellmer's surrealistic discourse, Freud's psychoanalytical discourse, and McLuhan's media-theoretical discourse. In the thirties, Hans Bellmer conceived a very peculiar counterpart in the history of artificial man by varying and transforming what he called the "doll." He accompanied his construction of the doll with extensive notes, commentaries, and interpretations. He understood "the various expressive categories: physical pose, movement (...), tone, word, graphics, design of objects (...) as born of one and the same mechanism," in keeping with the model of the "reflexes provoked by a toothache," a technique of pain mastery, the re-routing and thus control of an original sensation of pain, a kind of cramped hand. The "cramped hand is an artificial excitation center, a 'virtual tooth' that diverts the stream of blood and nerves from the real center of the pain, directing it to itself in order to cancel it out." In Bellmer's view, all aesthetic production comes about as a reaction to a too intense impression, a pain, a disruption of perception and of inner homeostasis. The fantasies that then ensue create their own "excitation centers," self-made phantom pains. He understands their various material manifestations – for example, his "doll" – as "a consequence of liberating transferals that lead from the suffering to its image. The expression, and what it contains in the way of pleasure, is a pain that has been displaced, a liberation."[18]

Accordingly, art is the continuation of this liberation in game form, a complex, surprising game played by the organs, parts, and elements now liberated from the original pain, from the whole body – a sign game played by the virtual body parts. Bellmer calls this anagrammatism, art's body language. It is obvious that his idea goes back to Freud; he entitled his thoughts on this matter: "Small Anatomy of the Physical Unconscious or The Anatomy of the Image." What he was attempting, if you will, was nothing less than to continue to reformulate the pleasure principle, or the functioning of the psychic apparatus, which Freud undertook in his study "Beyond the Pleasure Principle."

The persistent dreams and fantasies of traumatic events related in analytical practice by war invalids or train accident victims – the loss of an arm or leg – cannot really be understood with the help of the wish fulfillment model put forward in the "Interpretation of Dreams." Freud structures the apparatus in a more complex way. According to him, the dream/trauma repeats the experience that has come over the subject suddenly or violently from outside – "the main thrust of the cause (seems) to lie in the moment of surprise, the shock"[19] – and destroys the subject's psychophysiological integrity, but the dream repeats it as self-inflicted injury, though staged by the dreamer himself. In this way, physical wholeness is reconstructed phantasmagorically.

The third continuation of the thesis comes from the father of current media theories, Marshall McLuhan, whose work is still very much discussed. If his concept of all technology, from the wheel to the processor, as "extensions of men" were to adhere to a simple logic of extension and intensification – "It is a persistent theme of this book that all technologies are extensions of our physical and nervous systems to increase power and speed"[20] – we could safely leave it to the optimists or pessimists of the digital age. In his "Understanding Media" McLuhan first formulates the effects of such extensions on the psyche and on society, the main focus of his investigation. "Any extension, whether of skin, hand, or foot, affects the whole psychic and social complex."[21] He then expands on this concept. With reference to the kind of medical research that looks upon every extension of the person as "auto-amputation," as a means of maintaining inner balance, he construes technical systems as results of disruptions. "In the physical stress of superstimulation of various kinds, the central nervous system acts to protect itself by a strategy of amputation or isolation of the offending organ, sense, or function. (...) Physiologically, the central nervous system, that electric network that coordinates the various media of our senses, plays the chief role. Whatever threatens its function must be contained, localized, or cut off, even to the total removal of the offending organ."[22]

So art (Bellmer's) "takes pain in hand," the dream (Freud's) enables the Ego to reconstruct itself, the external media (McLuhan's) rescue the internal media from superstimulation and contain the pain. If one understands pain as nothing more than the signal for the severance of representations in the neuronal system from their matter, from cells to organs, and as the destruction of the close cohesion between signified and signifier in the individual body, then there are in fact two possible consecutive effects. The first is that the signal-sign complex – the phantom pain in the sensitive virtual organ – becomes independent. The second is its extension, the placing of the organ outside the body, liberation from the phantom pain by a kind of manifestation of the phantom. The construction of aesthetic objects or technical systems – the two cannot be separated here – goes hand in hand with the anesthetization of the corresponding individual organs. By being transferred to the outside, the functions of the organs order, extend, and intensify the capacities of the individual, and the species, both to perceive and to act.

Even if much in McLuhan is over-hasty analogy – "With the arrival of electric technology, man extended, or set outside himself, a live model of the central nervous system itself"[23] –, even if Freudian speculation about the psychic apparatus as a protective system against stimulation has little more to say about aesthetic expression than the "repetition compulsion," and even if Bellmer's virtual and artistic object short-circuits a bit too directly, all three proposals nevertheless attempt to explain very different modes of expression – art, dream/trauma, (media) technology – by means of a virtual, not immediately visible, but very effective object, as a processing of phantom pains concentrated in this object, as a thus regulated interplay between inside and outside.[24] These attempts are to be continued here, and technical constructions and aesthetic perceptions are to be seen in certain respects as parallel phenomena.

"Miracles of Mechanics": Poppe and Kleist

In 1824 Johann Heinrich Moritz von Poppe gave the title "Wunder der Mechanik" (Miracles of Mechanics) to his description of famous contemporary automatons. He was fascinated not only by the figures that Vaucanson, Kempelen, Jaquet-Droz, Maillardet, and others had created, but in particular by those of the Tendlers, father and son, whose "Mechanisches-Kunst-Theater" (mechanical art theater) can still be viewed today in Eisenerz in the Steiermark in Austria. It contains, among other things, acrobats that initially hang limp, "like all puppets." "Arms and legs flag like rags, with not the least hint of power in them. As soon as they are placed on the rope, however, they seem to come alive; they swing over and back with great verve, holding on now with two, now with one hand, and hurling themselves around it."[25]

Poppe's description immediately calls to mind Heinrich von Kleist's famous essay "Über das Marionettentheater" (On a Theatre of Marionettes) published in the "Berliner Abendblätter" in 1810. There, too, as with the Tendler puppets, one had to do with "appearance": with Poppe, the appearance of life and power, with Kleist – metaphysically charged – of the lost unity of body and soul, to be found in what is non-human rather than in the "affected" attempts of the human species. Kleist sees this "last element of human influence," which constantly separates man from himself and sentences him to the helpless observation of his clumsy physical mechanics, overcome in two figures (leaving aside God for a moment as *the* conceptual figure of all perfection): the bear, an animal that masters its movements instinctively; and the puppet. The center that man has lost persists in these two as an empty yet decisive, i.e., guiding point, a "soul": "in the center of gravity of the movement" where all forces are brought into balance. Here, too, the thought that governs the conclusion of the essay is the disruption of homeostasis, that graceful interplay between the body's limbs.

Such natural and therefore quite improbable vivacity is the ideal striven for by the automaton builders. They imitate physical movements or internal processes that are even unusual for man, including the "digestion" of Vaucanson's duck, which ate grain and "after a while excreted a matter similar to duck droppings," as Poppe remarks with amazement.

In 1760 Friedrich von Knaus presented his "miraculous writing machine" to the public. "The desired text is transferred onto a horizontally positioned cylinder by means of tiny pins. These pins strike keys which move the curved disks of the desired letters by means of a lever."[26] This technology was developed to temporary perfection in the androids produced by the Jaquet-Droz family and their mechanic Jean-Frédéric Leschot: the "Draftsman," the "Musician," and the "Author."[27] The latter was able to combine up to forty characters so as to produce any desired text. The free programming of the automatons thus achieved reveals the cultural orientation and social models of the respective historical periods all the more clearly. If the "Author" writes "Long live the city of Albrecht Dürer" during a presentation in Nuremberg in 1800, and if the "Draftsman" portrays mainly such high-ranking personalities as Louis XV, it is evident that this representation of

Possible People

"The Crafty Turk." Chess
automaton with mechanical
figure, operated by a chess
player hidden inside the box.
Copperplate engraving,
around 1780

Le Joueur d'échecs
Marcelle Charles-Dullin,
Charles Dullin

59

feudal power has today given way to a catchy salute of welcome in the advertising world. While the clockwork automatons in the early modern era were modeled on the myths of the gods or the history of Christian salvation, and in the 18th century served to represent the power of the sovereign and at the same time the universal craftsmanship of the middle-class citizen, this technical skill becomes the real object of the man-machine constructions in the 19th and finally the 20th century: to reproduce the whole complex apparatus called man, albeit free of pain and defects, in a state of equilibrium. Engineers and artists, scientists and writers – significantly enough, mainly men – now work uninterruptedly on this project of the species, as if they somehow wanted to catch up with women's natural productivity and finally overtake it some day, with beings that are naturally more faultless than those to date, thereby eliminating the difference between the sexes.[28] However, these constructions initially differed from the "full-bodied automatons," which now tend to drift into the toy production sector: series productions of talking dolls or quick little fighting robots for under the Christmas tree. In the wake of the inventions of Reis, Bell, Edison, Marconi, and many others toward the end of the 19th century, the individual senses, their perceptions and forms of articulation, are reproduced, specialized or intensified in technical systems; speech and hearing, projection and vision are transformed, and the system of the technical media is further developed. Society is not just trying to maintain itself at a new level or to expand its productivity through these projections and extensions. It is moreover attempting to redefine itself, from the tiniest element to the largest system, from the individual to the state itself. By thus effectively transforming the individual senses into technical media, however, the two disintegrate, both individual and state. The technical reproduction, storage, and transport of voice and ear, eye, nose, and skin, divides the individual up into a field of sensory exchange processes. When national institutions are networked and coupled with global information processes, vital economic, political, and social decisions are transferred from the traditional legislative and executive "bodies" to dynamic, re-coupled media processes which are no longer localizable in space or time. In order to be somehow able to grasp this disintegration and reformation, which run counter to a traditional understanding of decision-making processes, and get an impression of the new bodies and their new communities, there are probably only two figures which in equal measure awaken both technical euphoria and culture-critical anxiety in the late 20th century: the android, robot, cyborg, or whatever the new individual is called, and his state supervisor, Big Brother, the intelligence service, the CIA, the Securitate, or the Internet, the greatest conspiracy medium of all time.

In the early 19th century, inspired by Freiherr von Kempelen's essay "Über den Mechanismus der menschlichen Stimme" (On the Mechanics of the Human Voice), Joseph Faber built his famous talking machine "Euphonia," which imitated human speech better than all prior attempts – even Kempelen himself had once built a talking machine. It could well be the model, utilized by the cultural critics, for the many artificial women that populate literature, at the latest since E.T.A. Hoffmann. Faber's talking woman did not bring him anything like the luck, fame, and money that, for example, Kempelen's "Chess Player" had brought its owner, Maelzel, who even had it challenge Napoleon to a game of chess.[29] Faber destroyed his machine and committed suicide, a fate prefigured in Hoffmann's story about the "Sandman" and repeated in Villiers de L'Isle Adam's "L'Eve future" (1886), and in 20th century science fiction literature, Lawrence Durrell's "Nunquam" from 1970, for example. Here literature is just continuing the work on that vexing "phantom" which holds societies and cultures together at their core: that material-immaterial system of signs, language's possibilities for combination. These stories, which have long since moved from the medium of the book to the theatre, cinema, and the latest media, there to be further processed, really have only one positively fixed idea: that it should be possible to talk to a self-steered machine, that the human Ego and the technical Id should be able to enter into communication with one another. Long before Turing's test – which tries to prove that when a technical medium is interposed, machine communication is indistinguishable from human communication on the basis of the data sent and received alone – writers, artists, and philosophers were working on this idea, doubtless in the interests of their own peculiar productivity. The idea that a wonderful machine – *the* machine – might one day be able to answer these lonely artists as they shape their texts, pictures, and sculptures, and might in fact be able to enter into an open dialogue with their creators, this displacement of the self, is surely their most irresistible temptation. The creators are not interested in passive partners, but want an active, interactive as we say today, counterpart that is unexpectedly independent, something whose movements, replies, actions are completely unpredictable.[30]

Virtual People

The substitution game outlined above has been continued in literature from Jules Verne's "Le Château des Carpathes" (The Chateau of the Carpathians) to Aldolfo Bioy Casares's "La invención di Morel" (The Invention of Morel) to Oswald Wiener's "Verbesserung von Mitteleuropa" (The Improvement of Central Europe) and finally William Gibson's "Neuromancer." More and more new Bellmer "dolls" are being put together in the fine arts, from Jean Tingueley to Jim Whiting's "unnatural bodies" to Cindy Sherman's photo works. From Fritz Lang's METROPOLIS to Rainer Werner Fassbinder's WELT AM DRAHT to ROBOCOP, BLADE RUNNER or Hollywood's TERMINATOR series, they trip fantastically in ever new variations through cinema and television – and are today stored on CD ROMs. Activated on the monitor of the multimedia PC, they wander from there in their hundreds and thousands through the Internet, unstoppable: a new odyssey with incomplete, incompletable circles. The latest transformations of the story of Dr. Frankenstein are available on three CD-ROMs. One presents the biography of Mary Wollstonecraft Shelley and her invention, complemented by sound and images. A second makes an interactive quick-time movie play out of THE ROCKY HORROR PICTURE SHOW, the cult film of the youth scene for many years.

The third version is certainly the most interesting in our context, a kind of surgical adventure game: the players put together their own monster out of a large arsenal of organs, and thus begin their story, the struggle for this new existence. In this world, imagination is definitely more advanced than its somewhat childish technical transformations.

Footnotes

1. Alex Sutter: Göttliche Maschinen. Die Automaten für Lebendiges bei Descartes, Leibniz, La Mettrie und Kant. Frankfurt am Main: Athenäum 1988, p. 144
2. Julien Offray de La Mettrie: Man a Machine. Ed. by Gertrude C. Bussey. Chicago: Open Court Press 1912, without pagination
3. Sutter, op. cit., p. 143
4. La Mettrie, op. cit.
5. Ibid.
6. Ibid.
7. Ibid.
8. Sutter, op. cit., p. 142
9. La Mettrie, op. cit.
10. Ibid.
11. Friedrich Schiller: Sämtliche Werke. Ed. by Gerhard Fricke, Herbert G(eorg) Göpfert, 5 vols., Munich: Hanser 1958/59, Vol. 5, p. 951
12. Dieter Mathhes: Goethes Reise nach Helmstedt und seine Begegnung mit Gottfried Christoph Beireis. In: Braunschweigisches Jahrbuch, Vol. 49, Wolfenbüttel 1968, pp. 121ff.
13. Cf. Hans H. Hiebel (ed.): Kleine Medienchronik. Von den ersten Schriftzeichen zum Mikrochip. Munich: Beck 1997. Hiebel also mentions the French mechanician P. Falcon, who used sets of small perforated wooden slats to guide looms; he refers to Vaucanson only as a builder of automatons. The imaginative interaction between work and play is closer in inventors, engineers, and artists.
14. On prosthesis see Marie-Anne Berr: Technik und Körper. Berlin: Reimer 1990
15. As with the corresponding metaphor in Heinrich von Kleist's famous Kant crisis, which refers to nothing more than a technical "support" instrument, i.e. spectacles.
16. Which has not yet been solved. Heinz von Foerster made an interesting if equally inadequate suggestion at a congress in Berlin early in 1997. With reference to Kant, for whom consciousness is that alertness, attentiveness or brightness that ought to accompany all our thoughts and emotions, he defines consciousness as a certain break in the inner neuronal routines. Consciousness, he argues, emerges the moment they are interrupted, when they do not simply run on, but run wrongly, when functions oppose one another, that is to say, have to be reorganized. If one wants to understand consciousness as light, as the Enlightenment did, then here in this context more as a will-o'-the-wisp in search of new exits. The difference between animals, men, and machines would in fact then be only a gradual one, measured according to the number and diversity of strategies available for mastering disruptions.
17. "Phantom-limb pain, sensation of pain in an amputated limb. The phantom-limb pain is caused by the fact that the nerve fibers responsible for the sensations in the amputated limb are still present in the main nerve. When the nerve stump is stimulated at the point of the amputation (where the amputated nerve strands are not insulated), sensations are triggered which the brain 'projects' onto the missing part of the extremities." (Translated from: Der große Brockhaus, 1992, Vol. 14, p. 141)
18. Hans Bellmer: Die Puppe. Frankfurt am Main, Berlin, Vienna: Ullstein 1976, p. 73
19. Sigmund Freud: Jenseits des Lustprinzips. In: Studienausgabe. Ed. by Alexander Mitscherlich, Angela Richards, James Strachey. Frankfurt am Main: Fischer 1975, vol. III, Psychologie des Unbewussten, p. 222. For a discussion of this model see Jacques Derrida: Freud and the Scene of Writing. In: Writing and Difference. London: Routledge 1978, pp. 196–231; Wolfgang Schivelbusch: Geschichte der Eisenbahnreise. Munich, Vienna: Ullstein 1977
20. Marshall McLuhan: Understanding Media: The Extensions of Man. New York: Signet Books 1964, p. 91
21. Ibid., p. 19
22. Ibid., p. 52. McLuhan too refers to the toothache, illustrating his theory with an apparatus that technically implements Bellmer's and Freud's theses: "Battle shock created by violent noise has been adapted for dental use in the device known as *audiac*. The patient puts on headphones and turns a dial raising the noise level to the point that he feels no pain from the drill." (p. 54)
23. Ibid., p. 53
24. This is to be understood literally. Freud illustrates his theory with the so-called "Fort-Da" (gone-back) game played by his grandchild, who used a wooden spool on a string to transform the disappearance/appearance of his mother into a game and thus make it more bearable. One can therefore read every "Once upon a time" in literature as an aestheticization or anesthetization of an injury or pain and its transformation into a game or story. Freud could have found one of the most amusing transformations in Kafka's story about Blumfeld, the "older bachelor" who fails to attach the little hopping balls to a string, unlike Freud's grandchild. Literature thus adopts psychoanalysis, while at the same time distancing itself from it.
25. Johann Heinrich Moritz von Poppe: Wunder der Mechanik oder Beschreibung und Erklärung der berühmten Tendlerschen Figuren, der Vaucansonschen und anderer merkwürdiger Automate. Tübingen: Osiander 1824, p. 53
26. Annette Beyer: Die faszinierende Welt der Automaten. Uhren, Puppen, Spielereien. Munich: Callwey 1983, p. 57
27. They can still be viewed today at the historical museum in Neuchâtel in Switzerland, and every Sunday morning they are in action.
28. Even the authors of the extensive literature on this project are mainly male, cf. Bernhard J. Dotzler, Peter Gendolla, Jörgen Schäfer (eds.): MaschinenMenschen. Eine Bibliographie, Frankfurt am Main: Lang 1992. Only when feminist cultural criticism became established was women's attention drawn to this attempt to elimi-

nate them, recently, for example, by Donna J. Haraway: Simians, Cyborgs, and Women: The Reinvention of Nature. New York: Routledge 1991

29 The "Chess Player" was so famous around the world that E.A. Poe felt called upon to prove, merely on the basis of the newspaper reports on its presentation, that an intelligent dwarf must have been hidden in the man-machine. Cf. Edgar Allan Poe: Maelzel's Chess Player. In: Southern Literary Journal. April 1836

30 On other aspects of this unpredictability see Peter Gendolla, Thomas Kamphusmann (eds.): Die Künste des Zufalls. Frankfurt am Main: Suhrkamp 1999

What is the Golem?

Legend, Literary and Cinematic Figure

Documents and Memoirs

1. The Golem saga has grown up out of two roots. One is the Talmudic and late Judaic legend of Adam, as it developed in various versions. Accordingly, the first man emerged from the hand of God as *golem*, i.e. unformed substance (Psalms 139, 16), was gigantic and bisexual. Later God breathed a soul into him and separated man from woman. The word Golem as a soulless, gigantic, artificially created human figure entered later belief and literature from this description.

2. Early on, the power to create artificial human beings was ascribed to individual rabbis. Clay was the material, *æmaeth* (אמת) was the word written on the forehead of the being, and *shem hamphorash* was the life-bringing formula. Under particular circumstances, such a Golem served its master as servant or maid, but certain safety measures had to be undertaken so that it would not become too powerful. In other words: the constant effort of the human mind to unravel the secret of life and take control of it found considerable nourishment and embellishment in this cabalistic-magical myth. It should born in mind, moreover, that sagas about living statues, human and animal automatons, and artificial human beings have been varied time and again since antiquity and have also found their way into the legends of the Middle Ages.

3. In the 17th century, when the Cabala exercised a strong influence on Jewish and Christian mystics and alchemy and magic renewed the longing to master nature by supernatural means, the Golem saga was awakened to new life and gradually developed and spread, orally at first, among Jewish circles in Eastern Europe. At the time the saga was closely attached to the figure of the once famous, later largely forgotten Rabbi Elijah of Chełm, who was said to have had such a Golem permanently in his service. And when human automatons became very fashionable in the 18th century and the Romantics enjoyed using them for poetic effect, the Golem saga seemed appropriate for literary adaptation. Jacob Grimm drew attention to it in 1808 (...), Achim von Arnim took it up as a rewarding motif in his novella "Isabella von Ägypten" (1811), and after that the Golem was released from its relative obscurity and placed in the bright light of the literature of the 19th century. The line leads from Auerbach ("Spinoza" 1837) and Annette von Droste-Hülshoff ("Der Golem", poem 1844) to Holitscher's drama "Der Golem" (1908) and finally Meyrink's gripping novel "Der Golem" (1916), to name only the better-known writers (...).

4. Hand in hand with this literary application came a transformation rooted in the 19th century. The creator and master of the Golem is now seen as the famous and wise Rabbi Loew of Prague, who in this way takes the place of the meanwhile forgotten Rabbi Elijah of Chełm. And it must also be noted that the mythical features of the old Jewish saga were set aside, and the subject matter was used independently to address universal problems of love and general belief.

Stammler: Golem. In: Handwörterbuch des deutschen Aberglaubens. (Handbook of German Superstition.) Ed. by Hanns Bächtold-Stäubli with the special participation of E. Hoffmann-Krayer and collaboration of numerous experts. Vol. III. Berlin and Leipzig: de Gruyter 1930/31, cols. 939, 940

What is the Golem? The Homunculus of the tragic people; not distilled from chemical elements, but formed of clay like that first God-nigh person whom a myth has made the most exalted of all beings, so that the angels who are subject to him envy him; not through the perhaps of science with the Devil's help: animated by the pure Spirit, the activating name of God, the Shem (Shenn, as the unwitting authors of a popular film put it) on the parchment under his tongue. But the Spirit, not flowing directly from its divine source, but rather diverted and subject to the conjuring Rabbi in a pale reflection, can only do a mere miracle; not to create a living creature after the kind and magic of natural beings, light-footed and possessing of a soul – but rather a soulless, only physically stalwart being stands there on his unsteady feet: the slave, the Golem; dull, obedient, without past, without future, without permanence, without memory, a hideous thing that possesses only actuality and strength of arm, whose world expires behind his eyes, alive without living, present without a soul, human-shaped and yet not human. He serves his master; on Friday afternoon, as the day of rest approaches, the master withdraws the life-giving name from his mouth, and the Golem falls into non-existence, that his existence may not disrupt the Sabbath. But one evening the Rabbi forgets this duty: and now the caged-in and abused power, incensed at the profanation, rages in the Golem; the helpful worker turns into a howling destroyer, a rampaging demon, until the Rabbi returns home and wrests from him the Shem with spellbinding word; the Golem falls to dust, and never was the likes again created. (...)

Basic error of the writer and actor: to humanize the Golem, to place him in a fate that goes against his own nature and is alien to him. For to shape the Golem with an aim to feelings, with a longing to be man, is to diminish, degrade and negate him. The Golem of the legend is a bound and lowly angel, a demon, an active, divine force locked in clay. The sorrow that surrounds him is the sorrow of the exiled, of the subjugated, of the sovereign as slave. Deep wisdom and grandiose stance of the legend: that this force remains conscious of its divine origin and breaks out in the frenzied rage of resistance when it is to violate the law of the Sabbath, which is of the same origin as itself; thus forcing arrogant man to break the chains forever and let it return home to its source, to unity, to God.

Arnold Zweig. Der Golem. In: Die Schaubühne, No. 10, March 11, 1915

DER GOLEM UND DIE TÄNZERIN
Rochus Gliese

What is the Golem?

Der Golem, 1914

Paul Wegener

Paul Wegener, Dore Paetzold

What is the Golem?

DER GOLEM, WIE ER IN DIE WELT KAM

Paul Wegener, Albert Steinrück

Ernst Deutsch, Paul Wegener

Loni Nest, Paul Wegener

Paul Wegener, Ernst Deutsch

Albert Steinrück (left), Paul Wegener (right)

Loni Nest, Paul Wegener

Paul Wegener

65

What is the Golem?

Der Golem, wie er in die Welt kam

They leaned him against the staircase along the wall that led from the middle of the laboratory up to the stone tower. The master put the strip of parchment with the word into the stone capsule and pressed the "shem" into the opening in the creature's chest.

They both stood breathlessly before the creation and stared into its clay countenance, in fervent anticipation. Suddenly, a shudder seemed to pass through the mighty body. It opened its eyes very slowly. They were set like pure glass in the earthen head, but the gaze was so terrible that the famulus sprang back into a niche in the room. He shook so hard that his teeth clattered.

The Rabbi had also stepped back. And it took a long time until he could pull himself together in order to address the creature. He ordered it to go ... and the Golem sauntered off with heavy, swaying footsteps in the direction the master had pointed. He ordered it to turn around and come back. ... The stone giant followed the commands it was given.

The famulus, full of curiosity, advanced and was so spellbound by the strange creature that he stood still as if paralyzed when the Golem came toward him. But it continued in the direction the master had ordered it, ignoring the fact that the little fellow was standing in the way. It strode on its way, grazing the youth's shoulder in passing so that he was hurtled to the floor as if blown over.

The master was pleased with this strength in the newly created being, although he could not overcome his shock. He motioned to the Golem to stop – and gazed in astonishment again at how it stood still and no longer moved. He took the "shem" out of its breast ... and at the same moment the creation fell against the wall as if it had never been alive at all.

The master wiped the sweat off his brow and took a deep breath. Then he called the famulus over, who still lay dazed on the floor, and both of them knelt down and thanked Jehovah for the miracle, and for having escaped unscathed the terror of the night.

Paul Wegener: Der Golem, wie er in die Welt kam. Eine Geschichte in fünf Kapiteln. (The Golem, How He Came into the World. A story in five chapters.) Berlin: Scherl 1921, pp. 34/35

Finally, I would like to describe the most unusual trick that has perhaps ever been made in the cinema – especially unusual because the viewer in the movie theater – every viewer – went along with it!!

Strange, isn't it?!

Subject of the scene: the awakening of matter to life!

Rabbi Loew has just forced the spirits through his conjuration to reveal the magic word by which the petrified figure can be awakened to life.

So he has the stone figure carried in from the courtyard by several strong men and set up in his laboratory. He has to take the little capsule out of the Golem's chest, write the magic word on a piece of parchment, put it in the capsule, and insert it back into the Golem's chest.

We had a reproduction of the stone figure molded – it had the features of Paul Wegener, of course, and was a perfect likeness. Well, we could have had the molded figure carried in, shot the scene in a number of takes and cut them all together, and then replaced the figure with the actor for the last phase when the Golem is supposed to open its eyes. For the few seconds it takes to insert the capsule and for the figure to come to life and open its eyes Wegener could have stood still without moving.

However, this technique of staging the scene would have destroyed the illusion from the very start. The viewer at the time was clever enough to know that to a certain degree he was being cheated in scenes like this through the editing. To be sure, everything that we were showing there was like a fairy tale and unreal. But at the moment when the scene is rolling, people believe these things. And an uncut, uninterrupted take would naturally have a documentary touch that would hold the audience spellbound. And it was only by filming it in such a way that it had the appearance of really happening, in other words that the photography would document the reality of the scene, so to speak, that we would be able to create the illusions that make the impossible seem possible!

So it became of prime necessity for the impact and success of the scene that it proceed without any cuts or inserts and not offer any possibility of committing an innocent swindle by replacing the Golem figure, and that it show the stone figure of the Golem without any interruption, no matter what happened.

So at first we tried to use Paul Wegener from the beginning without utilizing the molded figure of the Golem, in other words to carry him in and stand him up as if he were the stone figure itself.

And that is precisely what didn't work. He lacked the rigidity of an inanimate object, of course. Despite all the energy and effort he exerted to be rigid and stay rigid, his body was elastic and gave way here and there. It didn't look genuine when he was carried in; it wasn't like carrying stone, but rather like carrying a person who had fainted or was dead. You could sense too clearly that the body was made of flesh and blood ...

So we had to have the dead figure carried in. But how should we awaken it to life ...?

I will describe the solution the way the audience sees it in the film and the way it was able to show how dead matter came to life in a truly believable fashion:

Above all we had to stick to one thing: the take was shot without stopping, without cuts, and also without dissolves, in one uninterrupted go. The camera was on a dolly, which allowed everything to be seen very clearly from very close up. The viewer could not help recognizing that it was an inanimate figure.

During the entire rest of the scene the camera showed a close-up of the Rabbi – but it always kept the Golem (and this is very important!) visible in the background during the entire course of filming!

From nearby we see the Rabbi having the stone figure transported into the laboratory. When it is stood up, the camera moves back far enough to show clearly how this inanimate figure – owing to the unevenness of the floor – stands at an angle and almost topples over. It sways and tilts precariously: stiff, dead matter. This is particularly obvious in this scene. With the greatest difficulty it is prevented from falling over and is set straight again. Then the men leave the room.

The Rabbi looks at the figure. He takes the capsule with the Star of David out of the figure's chest. Again it sways in its stiffness. The Rabbi holds onto it, being very careful that it doesn't fall. Then he goes to his table upstage with the capsule: the camera moves back with him, always keeping the Golem in the background of the shot – even when the camera has to change its angle slightly to follow the Rabbi's actions.

The Rabbi picks up the strip of parchment with the magic word and demonstrates how he rolls it up and places it in the capsule. Then he returns to the Golem. The camera moves with him to the figure, keeping the Golem in the picture the whole time – so close up that we finally see the Golem in portrait format. The Rabbi is now only seen in part. In the lower half of the picture his hands can be seen placing the capsule into the Golem's chest.

At this very moment we see the Golem open his eyes up wide and stare at his surroundings. The dead figure is suddenly alive and begins to breathe…

So this is the scene, successfully shot in one take without stopping the camera – and yet at the end of the scene we have the actor Wegener in place of the molded, inanimate figure!

Time and again people have confirmed to me – and still do even today – the tremendous impact of the scene, its astounding credibility and authenticity. There was almost never anyone who spoke to me without asking how we actually did it.

At first we all kept the secret very strictly. Meanwhile, I have finally revealed to a close friend, once or twice, the device we used (it is almost too much to call it a trick). At the time I described it only to our boss, General Director Davidson. He didn't believe me at first.

And if I now explain here that at a certain moment, with the scene was running and the camera rolling and thus visible to every member of the audience, the inanimate, molded figure of the Golem was carried out of the picture by four men and Wegener put in its place – then nobody who has seen the film and this scene will believe me, just like Mr. Davidson!

And yet that is how it was done. I utilized a method to distract the eyes of the viewers from the process of replacing the figure with the actor so that nobody noticed the substitution, except for ourselves and Mr. Davidson, whom I finally got, after showing him the scene five or six times, to stop looking at the hands of the Rabbi, but rather at the Golem, by pinching his arm and screaming in his ear: "Look at the Golem now! The Golem!" Then Davidson, completely bewildered, said: "Yes, indeed! Now I saw it! I didn't believe it was possible!!"

The secret lies in the way it was filmed and especially in the moment chosen. I had told Steinrück, the Rabbi, to be a little bit clumsy with his hands when he put the strip of parchment into the capsule and to let the parchment and capsule fall, but just manage to catch them again, and then to finish putting the parchment in properly. And at the critical moment when every eye was spellbound by this happening in the foreground I had the substitution take place in the background!

To be sure, that was a very cheeky experiment – certainly the cheekiest one I ever dared to undertake in my career as a director. But the success, the effect achieved, have proven me right: thanks, incidentally, to every spectator in the movie theatre, who, as I said, "went along with it"…!

To be honest, I must admit that we made a reserve take just in case. This safety precaution was necessary for such an expensive film. So we shot the exact same scene, with the same dolly movements, and also without any interruption. But in the reserve scene we took care that the Golem was covered from view by the Rabbi in the foreground at the decisive moment when the actor was substituted for the figure. While manipulating the capsule, the actor had to lean forward between the camera and the figure of the Golem in an involuntary movement for three or four seconds.

However, it was not necessary to use this reserve take – fortunately: for the original, of course, was much more amazing and above all – much more beautiful!

Carl Boese: Erinnerungen an die Entstehung und an die Aufnahmen eines der berühmtesten Stummfilme: Der Golem. (Memories of the production and shooting of one of the most famous silent films: Der Golem). Unpublished typewritten manuscript (carbon copy), Filmmuseum Berlin – Deutsche Kinemathek, Collections, section: "Der Golem, wie er in die Welt kam"

I stand on the Golem's grave. It is on a hillock barely five meters high, sparse tufts of grass, sandstone crags, night is closing in, the factory sirens have already blared their message, the domes of the Wolschan and Straschnitz graveyard buildings have slackened their contours, a bright, frozen column of smoke hangs over the chimney of the Kapslovka like the swollen cloth of a banner.

A track-and-field athlete in training jogs around S.-C. Viktoria's soccer field; in the garden plots that crowd the land up to the hillsides with cottages as wretched as peasant outhouses, factory workers now begin to work for themselves.

A sentry stands stiff with boredom before the house of the firearms inspection commission.

Below are refuse pits; blue enamel pots, flowered metal washbasins, rusty cans, crushed griddles and casseroles, incurably crumpled pot-lids, rasps with hypertrophic holes, dented kettles lie in huge piles. The colors of these Zizkow dolomites blend to gamboge.

Soot-covered lovers seek out the narrowest hollows. Rachitic children, ten or twelve years old, creep up Indian-style to learn something about the love act.

A worker shovels sand; the spades have dug out many cavities under the hills overhanging them. A coffin with the Golem could be put down anywhere and covered by the collapsing overhang…

A small child has taken a tin chamber pot from the rubble and wants to bake a gugelhupf of sand in it; the mother, who sits somewhat apart with a soldier, notices it, kicks the vessel away with her foot and slaps the crying child; the soldier laughs.

Stooped workers, weary, broken, bloodless, leave the factories and head for Hrdlorez, Maleschitz or even further.

And standing over the grave of the Golem, I know why God wanted it so that the human automaton, unconditionally subjugated to a foreign will and working for the benefit of others, lies here irretrievably interred...

Egon Erwin Kisch. Dem Golem auf der Spur. (On the Trail of the Golem.) In: E.E.K.: Der rasende Reporter. Berlin: Reiss 1925. Quoted in excerpts from: Der rasende Reporter. Berlin, Weimar: Aufbau 1996 (2nd Edition), pp. 300/301

Granting Life

Blade Runner
Daryl Hannah

Granting Life
Impotence and Power of the Female Cyborg

by Elisabeth Bronfen

The notion that certain combinations of the 22 letters of the Hebrew alphabet can be used to create life originates in the "Sefer Yetzirah," or "Book of Creation," mentioned in the Talmud. There, it is said that man can partake of the divine power of creation by adopting formulae that regulate the exchange and combination of these letters. There are two premises of crucial importance in the Talmudic stories of the creation of a Golem: Jewish tradition not only assumes that language has the power to create life, but also envisages that an alteration of the combination of letters can take that artificial life away again. Man sees the mutual interdependence of creation and destruction confirmed in the figure of the Golem. The creation of a Golem is comparable to a mystic rite of initiation because it is an act that allows man to experience his oneness with the divine creator. At the same time, however, the figure of the Golem also provides him with a likeness of that lower form of life from which he wishes to set himself apart as a being in God's own image. For the Golem is a creature whose imperfection reminds man that he, too, was once no more than matter brought to life, a living creature with no soul, no sense of self, and no aim in life.

The Dream of the Subordinate Sex

As an unfinished human vessel, the Golem lends itself as a metaphor to describe persons who have not yet achieved their true spiritual potential, who possess intellect and moral virtue, but who are nevertheless in a state of mental confusion and disorder. In this sense, an unmarried woman used to be called a "golem." Only on conclusion of the marriage contract was her status raised to that of a useful member of the symbolic community by her husband. The question, embodied by the Golem, of man's proximity to God raises a double issue of gender difference: on the one hand in the sense of configuration of a sexual difference which involves allocating the female to the position of a creature dependent on and shaped by a male creator, and, on the other hand, in the sense of a configuration of tribal membership or family kinship that accords man the right to create non-human beings, to make use of their services, and to consolidate his rule over them by the fact that their existence depends solely on his will. In apodictic terms, the dream of the Golem fulfills the wish of the male subject to hold sway over the boundary between life and death and to regulate his needs in such a way that he seeks to secure his proximity to God by distinguishing himself from creatures he has declared to be a lower form of life.[1]

It is said that the poet and philosopher Solomon ibn Gabirol, who suffered from a skin disease and lived alone, created a female golem to be his servant. When the city fathers heard of this, they ordered him to deactivate the golem, suspecting that the artificial creature was his mistress. Loyal to the lawmakers of his community, he dismantled the woman of wood and nails. The fear that the male creator might lose control of the artificial creature he has created is not the sole preserve of tales involving female golems. While the male golem or vassal, generally made of clay, was esteemed for the enormous physical strength by which it could protect the Jews should a pogrom break out, this same potential also made it a risk. As in the anecdote about the golem wife, the golem vassal nurtures a reassuring fantasy only as long as the man creating him is certain that, if necessary, he can also destroy the figure he has created.

The legend of Rabbi Elijah of Chełm goes one step further, by telling how the Golem asks the rabbi to make him inanimate again. The artificial creature hems in the truth of God because it embodies the fluidity of the boundary between divinely animated life and artificially vitalized life. This is why the Golem asked his creator to erase the letter *alef* from the word *emet* (truth) written on his forehead so that only the word *met* (dead) remained. Although this anecdote does confirm the rule of the male subject, it also illustrates the ambivalence attached to the figure of the Golem. The Golem-maker is, on the one hand, a demiurge, yet at the same time, his act of creation invariably harbors within it a potential threat to his person and his community. The dream of creating a being for the purposes of self-defense or the satisfaction of erotic wishes constantly threatens to change into a nightmare in which either the woman subordinate to the male subject or the slave himself takes power.

Ridley Scott's film BLADE RUNNER (1992) offers what is, in visual terms, one of the most remarkable post-modern adaptations of the Golem myth. In it, the scientist Tyrell has genetically engineered a new race of humanoid replicants endowed with superhuman powers and intended to protect humans in much the same way as the Golem of Jewish lore. Banished from the company of humans, who are their physical inferiors, these artificial creatures are employed as fighting machines on the galactic front. Ridley Scott employs this traditional motif to deconstruct the notion of artificially created life as a God-like act. The hegemony of the male subject is radically called into question by the forbidden return of a small group of replicants to Earth, revealing the permeable boundary between the human being as a creature animated by God, whose death is unforeseeable, and the cyborg as a humanoid machine, whose life-span can be programmed by its creator.

BLADE RUNNER's portrayal of two different types of female cyborg sheds an interesting light on the niggling question of whether it is possible to distinguish with certainty between a human and what might be just a perfect android. The merciless female warriors Pris and Zhora, who shy no act of violence in pursuit of their aims, but who also display a distinctly human capacity for love and loyalty, are contrasted with Rachel, whom Tyrell has equipped with his daughter's memories. Rachel does not know she is a cyborg, though she suspects as much. Yet it is not only because she fully identifies herself as a human, denying her golem origins, that she confounds the clearly defined boundaries required by the male subject to maintain his rule over the beings under his command. Unlike the other replicants, she does not have a predetermined life-span of only a few years.[2] Rachel is above all a creature who wishes to serve the male subject – first her boss, the scientist Tyrell, and then his right-hand man Deckard. Yet it is precisely in this respect that her ambivalence is evident, for she, too, is prepared to destroy whatever might stand in the way of what she desires. In her case, that means the desire to rank unequivocally among the humans. There is a key scene in which she finds Deckard on a parking lot, where his life is threatened by Leon, an escaped replicant. In order to save Deckard's life, she shoots one of her own kind. Thus, in one and the same gesture, she signals both her willingness to subject herself completely to the male and at the same time her wish to be his superior. She grants him life so that he can save her.[3]

In Ridley Scott's film the dream of the female cyborg as a perfect artificial creature – stronger than the man and yet totally subordinated to him – acts as a bulwark against the nightmare of the omnipotent female warrior, the femme fatale who threatens the male power system with her powers of seduction. This figure is adopted in part from Fritz Lang's film METROPOLIS (1925/26), which, in terms of its visual aesthetics and its critique of technology, is a precursor of BLADE RUNNER. Maria, who is introduced at the beginning of the film as the friend and protector of proletarian children, and who gets Freder, the tycoon's son, to mediate between the unscrupulous intellect of the father and the mindless physical strength of the foreman, has a cyborg double in the figure of the "false Maria." While the good and merciful young woman preaches neighborly love to the workers, her golem counterpart incites them to revolt against the ruling machines. She, too, was designed by her creator, Rotwang, as a female cyborg to defend the male ruler. The tycoon hopes to use this figure to subjugate the insurgent workers. When she triggers the destruction of the workers' city on grounds of a revolt against the machines (which condemn the workers to their golem-like existence), the figure of the "false Maria" acts as a vehicle for the message that the violence used against the political hegemony is in fact inherent to the system. One might even go so far as to speculate that the "false Maria," at a latent level of meaning, also unveils the "true Maria" as a cyborg herself. Her boundless willingness to sacrifice herself, and the message she represents – that sentimentality can erase the differences between ruler and vassal – can only come from a machine being. Though she does not reflect the primordial lower form of life for Freder and his father, she does represent the kind of total self-deference of which the human subject – once self-awareness and a concomitant individualistic self-assertion have been attained – is not capable.

The Dream of Cyborg Life beyond the Pale of the Gender Difference

The traditional Talmudic notion that the generation of artificial life is to be understood as a fulfillment of human creative potential has also been adopted by women writers, primarily as a gesture of intervention against the notion of a male subject whose omnipotent fantasies of creation violate the laws of maternity. An example is the young Mary Wollstonecraft Shelley, who wrote her 1816 novel "Frankenstein, or The Modern Prometheus" primarily in order to expose the dangers of male creation fantasies. She has her Dr. Frankenstein frequent slaughterhouses and cemeteries in search of body parts. From these, he plans to create a life that, unlike the Golem, will be superior to humans, since it is not born of woman, but animated artificially – in imitation of God – by a male power, and does not bear the flaw of mortality. As we know, Dr. Frankenstein's dream of creating a new species freed of all traces of physical weakness turns into a nightmare. The perfect, immortal creature turns out to be a death-bringing monster.

What is particularly remarkable about Mary Shelley's moralistic diatribe against the generation of artificial life is the fact that she discovers the female monster at the traumatic core of male creation fantasies. The trail of destruction wreaked by Frankenstein's monster, in the tradition of the Jewish Golem myth, is triggered by the fact that the scientist refuses to create a female helpmate for his melancholy monster. It is only at this point, on seeing all his hopes of companionship crushed, that this late Romantic forerunner of the cyborgs decides to kill the family and friends of his creator. Having had to watch Frankenstein dismantle the half-finished female monster and sink her remains in the lake by his laboratory, he now drives his own father into the open countryside, pursuing him to the North Pole, far from all civilization, so that he, too, can feel the deadly consequences of solitude. In this text, which sanctions only life flawed by mortality, the figure of the mother as the symbol of natural birth, too, must remain unscathed. The menacing aspect of the female monster is the coupling of artificial and natural life – the act of giving birth naturally to a species of monster whose origin is artificial. Thus, if the female monster – as the epitome of the twofold minority of her sex – were to prove capable of generating life, this female golem figure, declared as the lesser form of life, would have successfully appropriated the position of power of the ruling male subject, namely by attaining the capacity to hold sway over the boundary between life and death.

The same notion that represents a vision of horror for Mary Shelley, with her criticism of the male creator and her propagation of the conservation of traditional kinship bonds and natural motherhood, is turned into a tongue-in-cheek utopian fantasy of political change by Donna Haraway, who sees herself as a postmodern theoretician of feminist socialism. In her 1984 "Cyborg Manifesto," she presents her own version of the Jewish myth. She assumes that the inhabitants of the highly technologized world of the late twentieth century are in a sense comparable with the cyborgs, and for this reason she calls for recognition and acceptance of the pleasure that comes with blurring the boundary between machine and human organism. For the cyborg is the fruit of a symbolic, post-gender community that has transcended the laws of sexual difference: a world without genesis and therefore also a world that is no longer teleologically destined to meet an inevitable end. It is not so much because its hybrid nature blurs the difference between natural or self-empowered and artificial or externally developed organism that the figure of the cyborg fascinates Haraway, but because it is a figure that does not originate in the dyadic unit of mother-and-child. This means that a notion of symbolic community can be developed in relation to the cyborg that transcends all questions of belonging to a natural family or biologically prescribed species and goes beyond the question of acceptance or rejection strategies determined by such cultural attributions.

On the one hand, a world inhabited by cyborgs could unleash the horror scenario of the ultimate imposition of external control; after all, in the world of the late twentieth century, the machines that serve us are already disturbingly lively, while we ourselves seem frighteningly inert. On the other hand, however, according to Haraway's ironic speculation, a blurring of the boundaries between the world inhabited by people and that inhabited by cyborgs could also mean the creation of social and physical realities in which people no longer fear kinship with so-called lower forms of life, such as animals and machines, and in which communal relationships exist that are not regulated by kinship but by a mutual sense of affinity. The cyborg represents a creature that can be disassembled and reassembled and which, by dint of this endless re-figuration, circumvents sexual reproduction. In order to counter this with the game of regeneration, according to Haraway, the female subjects of the postmodern world in particular are faced with the challenge of coding this changing being according to their needs and interests. In this respect, she departs considerably from the Talmudic notion of the female as the passive creature under the control of the ruling male. Instead, she calls upon women to appropriate the act of deconstructing and constructing for themselves. For feminists, according to her utopian fantasy, both political power and social responsibility are situated at the leaky boundary between animal-human (organism) and machine, for the blurring of gender and species difference can also reveal the weaknesses in the cultural matrix of paternal rule based on the notion of male identity.[4]

Although Donna Haraway underpins her "Cyborg Manifesto" with references to contemporary texts by women writers of science fiction, the male dominated science fiction film also provides some particularly lucid examples of how her project of new kinship relationships is treated as a circumscription of conventional views of gender difference. James Cameron's film THE TERMINATOR (1984) adopts the nightmare scenario inherent in the myth of the Golem. In his post-apocalyptic world, the survivors of a nuclear holocaust not only struggle against the victorious machines, but also seek to re-code the future by intervening in the events of the past. They send a destroyer cyborg, the Terminator, into the world prior to the catastrophe, with the mission of killing Sarah Connor before she can give birth to her son, John Connor, who will become the leader of the revolt. The cyborg played by Arnold Schwarzenegger fails in his mission, and Sarah Connor, who is both the mother of the savior of the human race and the only person not to succumb to the golem-like indifference of her fellow humans in respect of the dangerous experiments being conducted in the field of Artificial Intelligence, has a vision – in TERMINATOR 2: JUDGMENT DAY (1991) she sets herself the task of executing computer engineer Myles Dyson, because he is the one who will be responsible for new cyborgs being generated from the individual parts of the Terminator she has destroyed and which will one day unleash the genocide against the human race.

TERMINATOR 2: JUDGMENT DAY aims to make a radical distinction between the human capacity to act on the basis of moral principles and a machine existence in the world – no matter whether this refers to the scientists blinded by their own research and creation mania, or the warrior machines they construct. At the same time, it is interesting to note that the blurred boundary between cyborg and human is visualized by means of a gender crossover.[5] Whereas the heroine, played by Linda Hamilton, increasingly takes on the traits of a merciless warrior machine in her fanatical conviction that she has to kill Dyson, seeking to achieve her aim at any price, the good cyborg sent back in time from the freedom fighters of the future to protect her and her son turns out to be a motherly father. The postmodern Golem, also played by Arnold Schwarzenegger, is benign and patient in caring for the freedom fighter's son (one is reminded of the "true Maria" in Metropolis) and blindly follows his orders. As in BLADE RUNNER, subordination is also a sign of strength: his boundless obedience is the precondition for the equally boundless mercy with which he is prepared to sacrifice himself to save human life. What is explosive is the fact that James Cameron ascribes to this figure all the traits that are otherwise culturally associated with femininity. In a scene that is of key importance to the question of newly negotiated family relations, Sarah observes a game between the Terminator and her son, who is trying to teach the heavily armed figure a more socially acceptable way of communicating. We hear her voice-over explaining that the Terminator will never stop, that he will always be there, and that he would sacrifice his life to defend that of her son. She deduces that he would be the best possible father for him. In the exchange between human and machine, the cyborg has taken on the attributes of the mother: trust in the survival capacity of human sympathy. Although in TERMINATOR 2: JUDGMENT DAY the golem is both the better person and the more reliable parent, James Cameron nevertheless implicitly ascribes the crucial position of power to his heroine. When she succeeds in preventing the research that will generate that species of Artificial Intelligence, it is not her son John Connor, but Sarah herself who is the savior of humankind. It is no longer necessary for the son to lead the resistance.

In the film THE MATRIX (1999) by the brothers Andy and Larry Wachowski, the fear of the Talmudic Golem has become reality. The war of humankind against the machines they themselves have made is lost and time can no longer be turned back. The nightmare scenario based on ancient Jewish legend is intended as a warning that in the age of Artificial Intelligence and cyber-reality, the challenge faced by the creator of the Golem is not one of producing bigger and better machines. Instead, our humanistic task is to protect people from becoming golems themselves, with the machines they have created completely regulating and controlling their lives. In this world in which human dependence on the machines under their control has been reversed in a tragically ironic way, the animate but soulless human beings are wired up to a complex machine. Thousands of them lie in a nutrient solution in glass cocoons, their body warmth providing the machines with the necessary energy. Mere batteries, these people live an illusory life that is entirely in the spirit of the incomplete Golem of Jewish lore. Instead of the life-giving word on their forehead, they have a power point in their necks linking them to a coding and decoding program entitled Matrix, which allows them to experience cyber-reality as though it were actual reality. In keeping with ancient Talmudic tradition, this scenario also addresses the idea that man is capable of imitating God, which enables him to make an Adam-man from an Adam-golem. Those who master the rules of combining the letters can animate the still incomplete human beings so that they live out their individuality and freedom of action to the full.

Although THE MATRIX plays out the rather terrifying side of Donna Haraway's design for a world in which the boundary between man and machine has become totally fluid, the Wachowskis do adopt one aspect of her "Cyborg Manifesto." The humanistic project of maintaining a world in which man is capable of determining his own actions is borne by a movement that transcends gender difference. Morpheus, the leader of the resistance, a figure echoing God the Father, releases his chosen son Neo from his golem-like existence and instills in him the belief that he is the one who can free humankind from their slavery. Yet it is his helper Trinity, with her elements of the Holy Mother Mary, whose words in the film's key scene give new life to the young man when he has already been shot dead. Like the addition of the letter *alef*, which turns the Hebrew term for death into the word for true life, Trinity's claim that Neo cannot be dead because her love for him is true resurrects the young hero, whose body has indeed died in the realm of reality because his spirit has gone through a death experience in the Matrix. It is only through her words that he can at last take on his role as savior and irrevocably damage the cyber system of the machines.

It is interesting to note that Trinity is also presented as the perfect amalgamation of machine and human. In the first scene, she appears as a cyborg endowed with supernatural powers. The policeman who is supposed to arrest her tells his superior, special agent Smith, that he does not need his help because his men will be able to handle "a little girl." But the agent knows better. His men, he retorts, are already dead. Then we see how Trinity, with the merciless precision of the female warrior machines in BLADE RUNNER, effortlessly exterminates the policemen, and can even escape from the agent (the true cyborg who has been played into the Matrix system by the machines) thanks to her superhuman ability to run and jump. She is also comparable to the cyborgs proper in that, like Pris and Zhora in BLADE RUNNER, she is driven by a consummate will to fight. Totally focused on her mission, which she is carrying out for her master, the leader Morpheus, like a classic female golem, she asserts herself like a machine. Yet as the name Trinity suggests, her body unites the attributes strength of will, physical power, and kindheartedness, which Fritz Lang distributed among three figures. She grants new life, but she does it more along the lines of the female monster in FRANKENSTEIN (1931). Although she strives for Neo to be liberated from his golem-like existence in order to assert the possibility of natural birth against the birthing fields controlled by the machines, where humans are artificially produced, the family that she helps to found – by first convincing Neo to follow Morpheus' instructions unconditionally like she does and then bringing him back to life through her faith in her love – is artificial. The life that she grants Neo is not one of natural reproduction, but of artificial regeneration. Maternity and the artificial generation of life coincide. In the figure of Trinity, the boundary between machine and human is fluid, as is the boundary between transcending the limitations of gender-specific identity and re-establishing precisely that gender difference.

THE MATRIX
Keanu Reeves, Carrie-Ann Moss

Footnotes
1 These remarks on the Talmudic and rabbinical tradition of the Golem are based primarily on the outstanding study by Byron L. Sherwin: The Golem Legend. Lanham: University Press of America 1985, pp. 1–49. See also the foreword by Isaac Bashevis Singer in the exhibition catalogue of Emily Bilski: Golem! Danger, Deliverance and Art. New York: The Jewish Museum 1988, and the two-volume anthology edited by Klaus Völker: Künstliche Menschen. Dichtungen und Dokumente über Golems, Homunculi, lebende Statuen und Androiden, Munich: Hanser 1971

2 The limited life span is the postmodern variation of the reversibility of the combination of letters from which *emet* can be rendered as *met*. The ancient fear that the human warrior machines cannot be brought under control again also prompted the Tyrell Corporation to train replicant hunters such as Deckard to trace escaped cyborgs, hunt them down, and "retire" them, using their own weapons.

3 For a survey of the visual repertoire in which the artificially created female is repeatedly designed as a fantasy of the boundlessly servile creature in the service of the male subject, see Joachim Paech: Cyborgs! Sind Roboter weiblich? Oder was sonst? In: Journal Film, No. 29, Summer 1995, pp. 52–59. For a detailed analysis of the film, see also Scott Bukatman's monographic study of BLADE RUNNER (London: British Film Institute 1997).

4 See A Cyborg Manifesto. Science, Technology, and Socialist-Feminism in the Late Twentieth Century. In: Donna J. Haraway: Simians, Cyborgs and Women. The Reinvention of Nature. New York: Routledge, London: Free Association 1991

5 See also Forest Pyle: Making Cyborgs, Making Humans. Of Terminators and Blade Runners. In: Jim Collins, Hilary Radner, Ava Preacher Collins (eds.): Film Theory Goes to the Movies. New York, London: Routledge 1993, pp. 227–241

Granting Life

BLADE RUNNER
Sean Young

Daryl Hannah

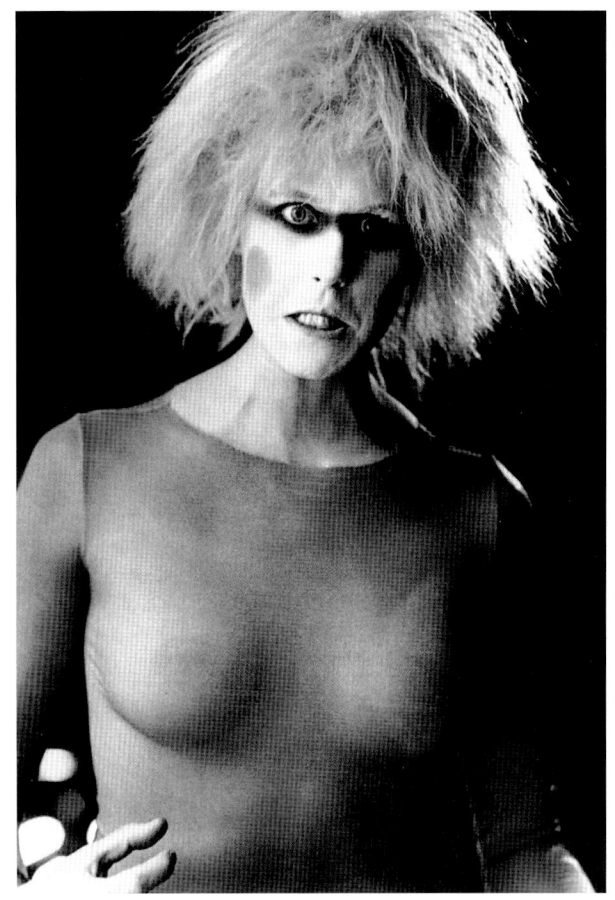

Daryl Hannah, William Sanderson

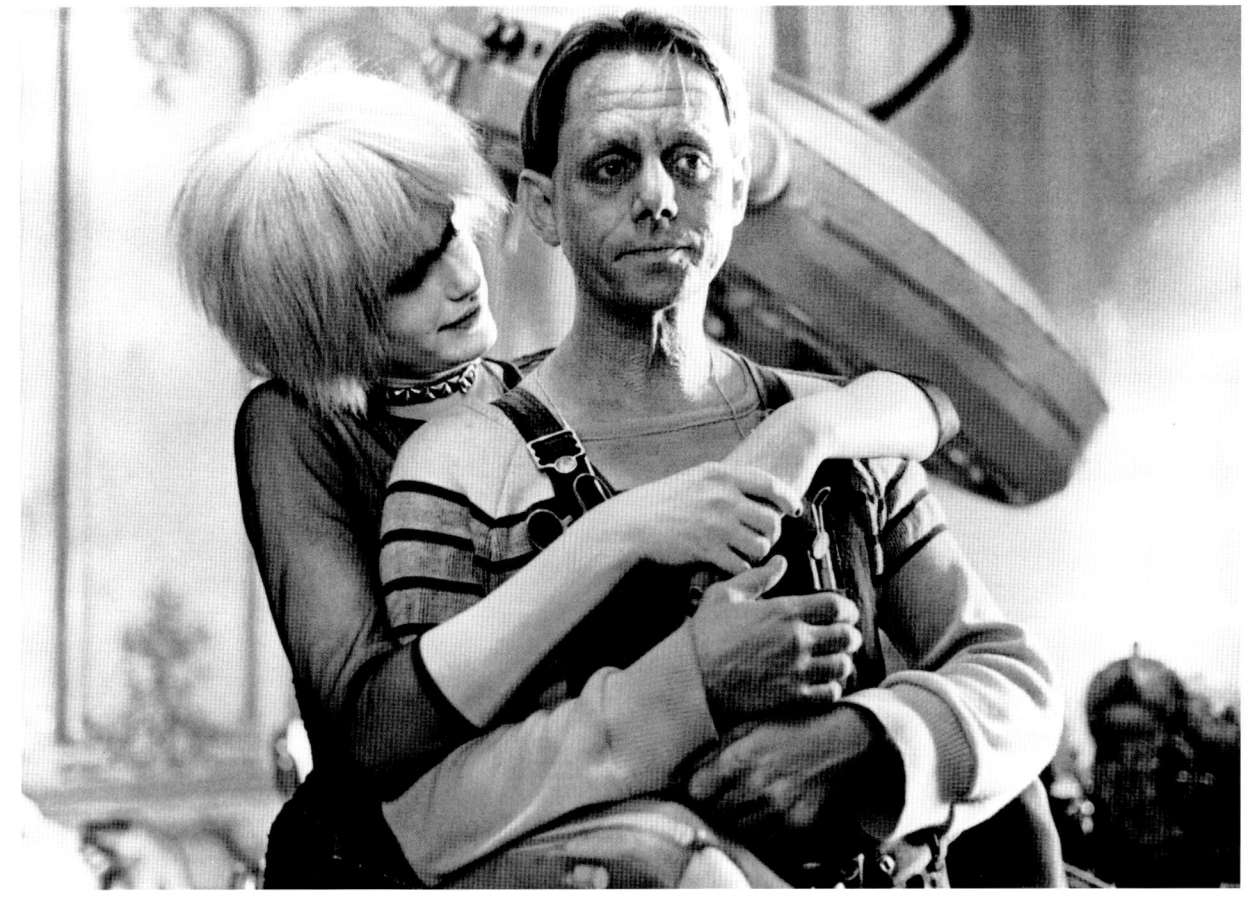

75

ALRAUNE, 1927
Brigitte Helm

From Vampire to Vamp
On the Background of a Cinematic Myth

by Klaus Kreimeier

A comparison of the world with a laboratory had now rekindled an old notion in him. He had often thought of life in terms of a large laboratory where the best ways of being human had to be tried out and discovered anew, if it were to please him. (Robert Musil, "The Man Without Qualities")

The idea of the world as laboratory has been a driving force in the history of technology, setting in motion the very development of civilization itself. There has never been any dearth of attempts to determine the best way to be human. Such experiments have brought forth a huge variety of cultures and spawned diverse forms of barbarity in equal measure. In short, the history of the world is a series of experiments, successful and failed, conducted by mankind upon himself. "Artificial man" – whether in utopian and mythical terms or as a particularly appealing subject in literature and art – was and remains the fantasy of a civilization incessantly striving to harness nature and change humankind, little knowing what the outcome might be.

A New Theater of Marionettes

In broaching the subject of artificial human beings in the history of film, it would undoubtedly be appropriate to describe cinematography as a machine, as part of a great laboratory in which people can observe themselves and the shadows they cast into the depths of history, studying the human condition as a historical process. Cinematography is nothing but the puppet theater of the modern age, moved by machine operators whose finger movements are "something quite precise" in relation to the movements of the puppets attached to them, "like the relation of numbers to their logarithms or asymptotes to the hyperbola." The dancer that Kleist has contemplate the puppets thinks in terms of the mathematical relations from which the computer will emerge 150 years later – and he even anticipates cinema when he speculates that the dance of the puppets "could be entirely transferred to the realm of mechanical forces and could (...) be controlled by a crank."[1] The stage machinery of Romantic drama forges the link between this vision of the mechanical operators' work and the projectionists of early cinema. The grace of the puppets, according to Kleist, owes much to a total absence of affectation – that egotistical intrusion of reason by which "the soul (*vis motrix*) is somewhere other than in the center of gravity of the movement. The puppeteer, with the wires or strings, controls no other point than this center, so that all other limbs are lifeless, simple pendulums (...)."[2] In short, they are mere matter that has nothing to do with (self-)reflection.

Victor Hugo placed more trust in the inanimate puppet than in organic life when, seeking a model for the figure of Déruchette in his novel "Les Travailleurs de la Mer" (1886), he arranged for a dummy dressed in the traditional garb of a woman from the island of Guernsey to be placed in his study.[3] Organic life fell from grace when it ate of the Tree of Knowledge and took on human form. Yet, "grace will return when our consciousness has (...) journeyed through the infinite, and appear most pure in that human form which either has no consciousness at all or possesses infinite consciousness – that is, either in a marionette or in a god."[4]

The notion of man as a hybrid between matter and God that grasps infinity only in yearning was to become the martyrdom of Romantic thinking. Artificiality and death became the focus of speculation. Art, it appeared, harbored a potential that enabled consciousness to "journey through infinity" and encounter God. The nullity of life, of the living hybrid that is man, was the price to be paid for such theories. What appears alive, according to the apocryphal "Nachtwachen des Bonaventura" (The Night-Watches of Bonaventura, 1804), is "the art of nature," and with that all things organic are the product of artifice, of a technique that we call "Nature."[5] Nature grasped as *tekhnikos* – as a technical deity – unleashes mankind upon the world as technical apparatus, as machines that, in turn, produce other machines in order to be nearer to God. According to this notion, beings emerge who are "more natural" than man himself, because they embody his lost grace, while at the same time machines are also created that are "more artificial" (that is to say, technically more perfect) than their human makers – and who may well end up gaining the upper hand.

If a theory of digital cinema existed, it could hardly ignore the texts of early Romanticism. The computer is, for the time being, the ultimate approach to the notion of the perfect technicity of nature and the perfect naturalness of the technical. It is also the culmination of Kleist's vision of the marionette theater, in that the actor (Kleist's dancer) first had to become a shadow and give up his life to the "realm of mechanical forces" in order to rise again as a digital human: bodiless, beyond the organic, "lifeless, simple pendulums," and even less than that.

Admittedly, the computer marks the end of film history. Making films meant watching death at work. In digital production, on the other hand, death has already done its work, for knowledge is on its infinite path to God. The result is sobering. A cursory glance at the monitors and interfaces among which we have set up camp shows us a world, as far as artificial beings go, that is positively riddled with metastases. It would seem to us that there is nothing but artificial beings anymore – from TV announcer to Lara Croft. The history of cinematography is coming to a close because our entire daily life – from cell-phone display to computer-aided organ transplants – has become cinematographic. In digital film, there is nothing sensational about artificial beings. They are run of the technical mill. They are not an attempt to upstage God, just a means of doing what is good for business. Not even the films of George Lucas bear comparison with the Paradise of, say Hieronymus Bosch, peopled as it is by organic automatons, anthropomorphic plants, machine-like embryos, winged apparatuses, and biological monsters of every kind.

From Vampire to Vamp

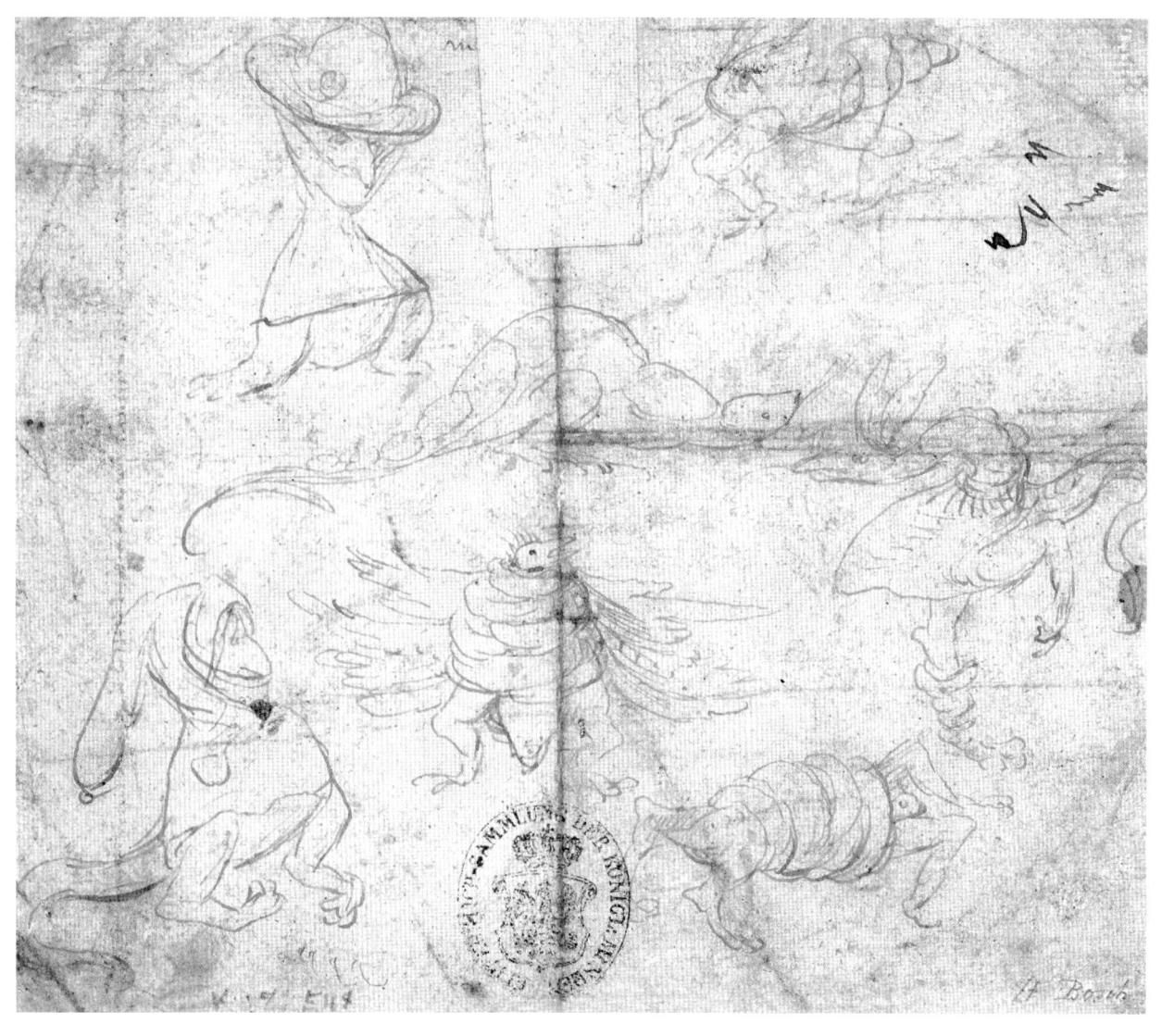

Hieronymus Bosch
Sketch. Seven fabulous creatures.
Staatliche Museen zu Berlin –
Preussischer Kulturbesitz,
Kupferstichkabinett

Hieronymus Bosch
Human head striding to the right
on animal legs, on the left a toad-
like creature on two long legs.
Staatliche Museen zu Berlin –
Preussischer Kulturbesitz,
Kupferstichkabinett

STAR WARS – EPISODE I:
THE PHANTOM MENACE
Yoda and other fantasy beings

The difference is not George Lucas's fault, nor that of computer technology. Bosch was a heretic, a priest of the night. Post-modernism turned night into day. The *electronic day* of telecommunications is no longer identical with the astronomical day, as Paul Virilio points out: "The indirect lighting of the electronic images now follows on from electrical lighting just as the latter once took the place of the sunrise."[6] In this garishly illuminated world, heresy has become obsolete – it no longer exists.

It must have evaporated somehow in the course of the 19th century; at the latest by its end, by the heyday of Décadence, it had become little more than a rumor, a pose, mere aesthetic trappings. At the threshold of modernism, cinematography emerged – evoking memories of heresy and cult, and at the same time foreshadowing what was to come as the technical prelude to a new and transhistorical universe of images in which we move today like uncertain Argonauts, seeking to discover whether there is any future for us.

This interface between the literary hothouses of the 19th century and the glasshouses of the early film industry is the subject of the following discourse: the nightmares, vampires, and artificial humans constructed by an enlightened era already tired of its enlightenment, in images and books, and handed on to cinema.

Excursus on a Virtual Man

"If there is a sense of reality, there must also be a sense of possibility," says Robert Musil in his novel "The Man Without Qualities," the most important literary construction of a virtual human ever created in our century.[7] A sense of possibility, according to the protagonist Ulrich, implies having a "mind" (and the desire) to be another than the person one is; of having other qualities than those one possesses. A sense of possibility also means not only wishing, but actively endeavoring to be another, that is to say, seeking to discard the qualities with which one has been born or which one has acquired, in order to gain qualities that move within the realms of the possible and thereby remain unknown. Ulrich, the man without qualities, is a man in transition, a man seeking to discard his "old" qualities, but who is not yet certain of his "new" qualities. He is a man who undertakes to create a construct: himself.

God, too, had a sense of possibility when he created the world. Ulrich considers the alternatives between which the Creator had to decide; the world could be the way it is, but it could well be different. God, too, thinks Ulrich while he is still at school (for which he was almost expelled), "probably preferred to speak of his world in the subjunctive of possibility."[8] Moreover, given that he is the projection of man, God can also be described as the first artificial being, and also as the first being to create a being in his own image, that is to say a construct: mankind. All myths of creation contain, in outline, the myth of the artificial being.

"Pourquoi donc ne suis-je pas Dieu, – puisque je ne puis être homme?" (Why am I not God if I cannot be a man?), asked Théophile Gautier.[9] In his words, we can trace an echo of Romantic yearning and inner turmoil, a reflex of desperation at an existence vegetating as a hybrid between matter and divinity – a sense of desperation that is a source of inspiration and the basis for all visions of artificial humans. In Musil's novel, the *homo technicus* of the developed industrial age (Ulrich is a mathematician) appears as a counter-design to the *homo faber* of the 19th century and the machine operators of the Romantic era. He is interested in the "architectural blueprint" of man, which may well be more simple than generally assumed. "If you analyze a thousand people, you will find two dozen qualities, emotions, forms of development, types of structure and so on, which are what they all consist of."[10]

Presumably the visions of artificial man such as the Golem or the Homunculus are based on the assumption that these "types of structure" and "forms of development" merely have to be schematically recreated – in order for the qualities and sensibilities with their calculable number of variants to result automatically.

The opposite of this architectural blueprint, its "deconstruction," was applied by the Marquis de Sade in "Juliette": "And what is murder but a little disorganized matter, a few compositional changes, a few molecules ruptured and thrown back into nature's crucible to be returned to the soil in a different form in a few days, and where's the harm in that?"[11] Often in literature and film, as in the Frankenstein complex, murder is regarded as the dismemberment of matter, as the prerequisite of the construction of an artificial being.

Musil's Ulrich is far from losing himself in the dreams of de Sade. His interest in the architectural blueprint results from his distinctly scientific curiosity about the disillusion of the modern persona that increasingly delegates its component parts and their unity to the implied suggestions of society. "B had always followed A whether in battle or in love. Therefore he had to suppose that the personal qualities he had achieved in this way had more to do with one another than with him; that every one of them, in fact, looked at closely, was no more intimately bound up with him than with anyone else who happened to possess them."[12]

It is difficult to imagine the man without qualities going to the cinema – yet Ulrich would surely have at least taken pleasure in cinematography as a laboratory of the artificial and as a place of production of artificial people. In the conversations he has with his sister Agatha about love, he reflects on the genre of the still life or *nature morte* in painting: "(I)n real still life – objects, animals, plants, landscapes and human bodies conjured up within the sphere of art – something other than what they depict comes out: namely the mysterious, demoniacal quality of painted life."[13] Although a marginal feature in the still life, the human body is expressly mentioned. Gradually, the discussion about love develops into a discussion about death: "The world speaks of the consecration and dignity of death; the poetic theme of the beloved on his bier has existed for hundreds, if not thousands of years; there is a whole body of related, especially lyric, poetry of death. This obviously has something adolescent about it. Who imagines that death bestows upon him the noblest of beloveds for his very own? The person who lacks the courage or the possibility of having a living one!"[14]

If Ulrich had been a cinema spectator, one of the educated and intellectually inspired aficionados of the new medium in the years before the First World War, he would have found that "mysterious, demoniacal quality of painted life," the necrophiliac enchantment of the *nature morte,* in the vamps of the silver screen. He would have found in Lyda Borelli and Theda Bara, Asta Nielsen and Pina Minechelli the faded, ghostly, rekindled frenzies of the 19th century and, at the same time, the coldness of the new era, but above all: he would have found in them the configuration of a completely artificial creature.

Medusa and Satan

When Percy Bysshe Shelley saw the head of the Medusa by an unknown Flemish artist (erroneously attributed by him to Leonardo da Vinci, however) in the Uffizi galleries in Florence in 1819, he praised the "metallic sheen" of its snakelike hair and described its unity of beauty and cruelty, a key concern of the Romantic era, as the "tempestuous loveliness of terror."[15] In this connection, Mario Praz[16] recalls Mephisto's warning to Faust when he thinks he has seen Gretchen's image: "It is an enchanted phantom / a lifeless idol; with its numbing look / it freezes up the blood of man and they / who meet its ghastly stare are turned to stone, like those who see Medusa." Faust deliriously cries, "What joy! What suffering!" (Welche Wonne! Welch' ein Leiden!).[17] In his "Psychologische Fragmente," Novalis ponders, "It is strange that the true source of cruelty should be desire."[18]

The synthesis of superficially incompatible elements – grace and terror, joy and suffering, desire and cruelty – was already part of the inventory of the mannerists of the Renaissance period; in the 19th century they became the program of the European Romantics and the movement of Décadence, and several decades later were adopted by the Surrealist avant-garde. These obsessions invariably aimed not only at considering beauty and cruelty as a single unit, but also at grasping horror in beauty and enjoyment of beauty in horror. The cruel beauty of the Medusa is the epitome of this synthesis – and her petrifying gaze is revenge on man for overstepping a boundary of the possible. To the extent in which she unites enchantment and death, the Medusa is also the epitome of the artificial being: the perfection of the possible in the image and at the same time the punishment for the presumption of regarding the image of man as perfection. In his "Journaux intimes," Charles Baudelaire drew from this the conclusion that he could barely conceive of any type of beauty where "there was not unhappiness" as well and saw in Milton's Satan the "most perfect type of male beauty".[19]

The image of the vamp that conquered the silver screen in the early years of cinema was the fruit of centuries of labor. The notion of the bloodsucking vampire was the father of this concept, yet the original image of the exotically made up, dangerously shimmering, and often stonily distanced face of the star can be found in the design of the "cruel beauty" that through the ages had been accorded to the ancient Medusa. The heroines of Italian, French and American historical and costume films between 1905 and 1914 were Lucrecia Borgia, Salome, the Queen of Sheba, Agrippina, the biblical figure of Judith, and Cleopatra – merciless rulers of monadic bearing and unfettered drive, martial nymphomaniacs who took pleasure in imprisoning their lovers, torturing them, decapitating them, or dismembering them. In the aura of these figures, we find a blend of legend, historic tradition, and artistic stylization (through literature and painting) that fitted so well into the "decadent" mood of the fin de siècle and the years prior to 1914, and this was the climate in which such cinema vamps as Theda Bara were to thrive in the studios of William Fox.

Their predecessors paved the way for this career, though they were still shaped by the stylistic concepts of their respective studios, or else they were rooted in a precinematic culture in the manner of Gabrielle Robinne, originally from the Comédie Française, who dominated the image of the heroine for the first decade at Pathé, and tended to be found in the more intellectual *films d'art*, most notably in the *films bibliques* of Henri Andréani (as late as 1913, Andréani was to film LA REINE DE SABA with her).[20]

Florence Lawrence, an early American SALOME (1908), became the first star of film history as the Biograph Girl, because the company needed a counter figure to Florence Turner in their competition with Vitagraph. But even Lyda Borelli, the diva of the Turin-based film company Gloria Film, fits the mold of the femme fatale: "Her outward appearance, underlined by makeup and costume, suited her perfectly to the roles she played: flowing locks of hair, dark, shadowy eyes, supple limbs and a pale skin. Her preferred pose was to drape her body fluidly on a soft ground. Sensual desire and doom were the message of her film titles."[21] Her role in MA L'AMOR MIO NON MUORE! (1913) as an actress who misuses the love of an aristocrat and becomes a spy revolves around that interdependent relationship between Eros and crime, desire and cruelty, that structurally defines the role of the vamp and its aura.

The type of vamp to be found in the first two decades of cinema differs from that of the later, already domesticated vamp of the tamer, more bourgeois "society film," in that "in this figure, the struggle for domination still appears unreconciled with the subject," as Enno Patalas points out. The early vamps, according to Patalas, are themselves "victims of their senses, who ruin themselves just as they ruin the men." As Salome and Salammbô, Judith and Cleopatra, they are the "mythical embodiments of sexual emancipation" in a far more radical sense than their famous successors Greta Garbo, Marlene Dietrich, Mae West, and Jean Harlow. They live "apart from social reality both in terms of space and time."[22] In a no-man's land of sumptuous, bloodthirsty, archaic and atavistic rituals associated with Eros and Thanatos.

"The Beauty of the Medusa, beloved by the Romantics," writes Praz, is "Beauty tainted with pain, corruption and death."[23] The women that Baudelaire adores in his poems are configurations of beauty and cruelty, subjects of desperate desire with "a hint of melancholy, lassitude, even satiation" ("qui comporte une idée de mélancolie, de lassitude, même de satiété").[24]

According to the fevered constructs of the Romantic era, a yearning for death and sexual desire converge in a desire for experience beyond sacrosanct boundaries. In an era in which capitalism was already expanding, and industry already ousting artisanal craftsmanship, an era in which the economic rationality of the bourgeoisie was triumphing over the heroically romantic world views of feudalism, the specter of the Medusa once more haunted European culture before it was passed on to the film industry:

Head of the Medusa, Dutch, around 1620/30 (previously ascribed to Leonardo da Vinci). Florence, Galleria degli Uffizi

From Vampire to Vamp

Lyda Borelli

Florence Lawrence

81

an artificial creature and a product of the radically lyrical imagination.

Like the serpent-haired Medusa of mythology, the vamp of cinematic history has no male counterpart. Yet Baudelaire's respect for John Milton points not only towards the "black" obsessions of the European Romantics and their artificial, and often untempered, intellectual game with the fires of Hell, but also points to Satan as a hybrid figure, tantamount to a superstar of cultural history. Undoubtedly, the Devil of illustrated books and puppet theaters, is an artificial figure – no less than the Satan that stalks the world wanders through literature: in Torquato Tasso, for example, in which "Satan keeps his terrifying medieval mask like that of a Japanese warrior."[25] Incidentally, Tasso's monumental crusade epic, "Gerusalemme Liberata," from 1581, was filmed three times by Enrico Guazzoni, the first time in 1911, then in 1918, and finally in a talking version in 1934. From Tasso to Giambattista Marino, the figure of Satan gains the melancholy of the fallen angel who shares with Prometheus the rebellious attitude and the spirit of revolt against the powers of Heaven. The Devil as "prince of angels": with him, in Milton, "the evil one definitely assumes an aspect of fallen beauty, of splendour shadowed by sadness and death."[26]

The Satan of "Paradise Lost" (1667) was followed towards the end of the 18th century by rebels in grand style, including Schiller's robbers and their ilk, who made their mark on the English Gothic novel. They can still be found in the French novels of the 19th century where they take on such forms as the fallen aristocrat in Eugène Sue – and only a few decades later they were adopted by the film industry. When Louis Feuillade made Judex in 1916, he created a figure struggling for justice and right, and, as such, a positive counterpoint to his great criminal Fantômas (1913) and to Les Vampires (1915), following complaints by the French Minister of the Interior. However, looking at Judex and Fantômas, both of whom employed the masquerades and ingenious techniques of disappearance, as marks of a *single* personage, the contours of a magical figure emerge: that of the fallen angel and melancholy rebel, a hyper-construction in which construction and deconstruction coincide.

Chateaubriand and Lord Byron spring to mind here. Chateaubriand describes Milton's Satan as "one of the most sublime and pathos-laden designs ever to have sprung from the mind of a poet."[27] The term "design," or "conception" in the original, refers here to the artificiality of construction in much the same way as the term *concetto* is used in the Italian Renaissance, and later in European Baroque, to describe the cleverly exaggerated, abstract mind play operating with extreme images as an eloquent and lyrical form. Baudelaire hails the creation of such a design as a stroke of genius, and calls the *concetto* a masterpiece.[28] Satan is a *concetto* by which man re-designs himself and reflects on his affinity to God and his own imperfect construction. Praz writes of Byron that, "given the vanity of his own nature, what is more probable than that he should have deliberately modeled himself upon the accursed angel."[29] The identification of the subject with the hybrid ego, that is to say, the artificial and artificially enlarged version of the self, is very probably an integral component of the mythology of the artificial being.

In the popular literature of the late 19th century and in the film industry, the Devil, hardly surprisingly, finally loses his horns. "The Byronic heroes of the *romans-feuilleton* of such writers as Eugène Sue and Paul Féval are in reality, under their Satanic exterior, apostles of Good."[30] The satanic element remains an external attribute – the inner nature is transformed into the philanthropic, beyond the tragedy of the fallen angel. The new figures, Praz continues, "loom gigantic in the midst of a net of intrigues which have for their object the salvation of the State – a curious popular reflection of the end of Byron's career, as the champion of Greek independence." Satan as benefactor and *homo politicus*. Often, the artificial figure succeeds in saving a state and possibly even the whole world. This is the mission of the global detective and agent that is to dominate the century of cinema. In the managed world, even James Bond is an employee, and with Arnold Schwarzenegger's Terminator, the Devil is extraterrestrial – and at the same time the high-tech icon of prevalent sports megalomania.

Even early cinema, admittedly, had a satanic repertoire broad enough to accommodate innumerable variations on the "bad guy," from the burglar to the male vampire, in multiple and genre-specific forms, so that the satanic archetype can occasionally be sensed, though it does not come anywhere close to the importance accorded to the she-devil, the vamp, and its variation, the femme fatale. The construction of the vamp as an artificial figure and a code of demonic eroticism forms one of the most outstanding achievements of cinematography in terms of cultural history. Its "architectural blueprint," however, originates in the 19th century; the European Romantics and the fin de siècle paved the way for her aura, her cosmetic details, her attributes, and her "enigmatic demonism."

Construction of an Allegory

If we accept Walter Benjamin's theoretical reflections on the essence of the allegory as outlined in his "Trauerspiel" book to the effect that the "core of allegorical observation" is to be found in the "exposition of history as the story of the world's suffering,"[31] the images of the artificial being can be ranked as allegories. The strategy of enigma that determines its aesthetics is preceded by gloomy brooding, aporetic thinking that remains captive in the mourning of the breach in the world and the imperfection of man. "Classicism was unable to retain the unfree, imperfect and broken aspects of the sensual and beautiful body. Yet this is what the allegory of the Baroque presents with unexpected emphasis, concealed beneath its sumptuous opulence."[32] He adds, "Allegories are to the realms of thought what ruins are to the realms of things."[33] Allegories are "the only diversion, albeit a potent one, in which the melancholic indulges."[34]

In addition to the depressive groundswell from which the figure of the allegory emerges, the European Romantic movement has a tendency towards demonism and the glorification of vice. The Medusas of the 19th century exude an air of eroticism which is closely related to madness and desperation, and which immerses the Classicist notion of ideal man and the body beautiful as well as the ideal of erotic success, quite literally, in murder and blood. They are

Eugène Delacroix: Liberty Leading the People, 1830. Paris, Musée du Louvre

synthetic allegories of the equally inhuman and superhuman crime and formulate, programmatically, not only the nullity of moral conventions, but also the overwhelming power of terror over civilization.

As goddesses of the night, they also lend "positive" ideas a satanic spark. With a view to the pandemonium presented by Delacroix's œuvre, Mario Praz notes that even his famous painting of Liberty, though it is meant to inspire hope, shows a figure trampling over bodies, inciting to murder, and looking as much like a goddess as the courtesan Phryne or a fishwife, as Heine remarked.[35] While the fishwife ("poissarde," as she is called by Heine)[36] points towards the social symbolism that Delacroix's painting offers of a close but superficial political exegesis right up to the present day, Phryne and the murdering goddess are rooted in other sources of inspiration: archaic predecessors on the one hand and on the other the repertoire – in other words the "divertissement" – of a contemporary, "black" romanticism that is fixated on the allegories of destructive Eros.

One of the precursors of the cinema vamp is the figure of the "grande voluptueuse" Cleopatra created by Théophile Gautier ("Une Nuit de Cléopatre," 1845) with her "sublime cruauté" (sublime cruelty), who massacred in the morning the lovers who had passed the night with her.[37] Another such precursor is the lyrical prototype created by John Keats in his "La Belle Dame sans Merci": "I met a lady in the meads, / Full beautiful – a faery's child, / Her hair was long, her foot was light, / And her eyes were wild." The fairytale floating image takes on a gloomy tone towards the end when the reader dramatically realizes what this figure has done to the men: "I saw pale kings and princes too, / Pale warriors, death-pale were they all; / They cried – 'La Belle Dame sans Merci / Hath thee in thrall!'"[38] In 1921, Keats's poem was to inspire Germaine Dulac to film La Belle Dame sans Merci.

The genealogy of the romantic vamp, as proposed by Praz – from the figure of Matilda in Matthew G. Lewis's novel "The Monk" to Chateaubriand's Velléda and Flaubert's Salammbô, Mérimée's Carmen, and Eugène Sue's Cécily – is, according to the author, itself "an arbitrary arrangement, certainly, but it enables one to make some general remarks which are not without significance in the history of taste and manners."[39] This history of taste and manners comes into focus when we determine the metamorphosis of the romantic vamp figure in the fin de siècle, in the trivial literature of the turn of the century, and finally, in early cinematography.

Matthew G. Lewis's novel "The Monk," the prototypical Gothic novel, was not hailed only as a literary sensation when it was published in 1795, but was also seen as an attack on the philosophy of reason and moral conventions of society. Lewis, who was familiar with the German literature of his day, also influenced E.T.A. Hoffmann and Franz Grillparzer, and an excerpt from his novel was published by Schiller in his "Musenalmanach." The story tells of the passionate love felt by Matilda for the monk Ambrosio, in whose monastery Matilda has become a novice. In the course of the novel she undergoes a transformation from loving woman to enchantress who collaborates with Satan in order to draw Ambrosio away from the influence of celestial powers. Her physical appearance lends this transformation an expression of literal "ecstasy" in the sense that the vamp steps beyond the cocoon of human form: "(H)er neck and arms were uncovered; in her hand she bore a golden wand; her hair was loose, and flowed wildly upon her shoulders; her eyes sparkled with terrific expression; and her whole demeanour was calculated to inspire the beholder with awe and admiration."[40] Goddess of love, witch, and angel of death in one, she already has all the attributes of the Romantic femme fatale.

François René Vicomte de Chateaubriand adds, in the figure of his witch Velléda in "The Martyrs," the glow of the militant patriot, also attired with the black habit, the tousled hair, and the dagger of Matilda. In Gustave Flaubert's novel "Salammbô" (1862) the figure finally becomes "frigid, unfeeling, idol-like."[41] Flaubert's detailed description reads almost like a script for the costume designers and makeup artists of the monumental films that were to be created shortly after the turn of the century in the French and Italian film studios: "From her ankles to her hips she was enmeshed in a close-knit net like the scales of a fish that shimmered like mother-of-pearl. Around her waist was a swathe of blue with two crescent-shaped cut-outs revealing her breasts with their bejeweled nipples. Her headdress was of jewel-encrusted peacock feathers. A mantle white as snow flowed behind her and, with her elbows by her side, her knees together, and diamond bangles adorning her upper arms, she struck the aloof pose of a priestess."[42]

The extent to which Lewis's Matilda caught the imagination of writers throughout the 19th century is evident not only in Prosper Mérimée's figures – such as Mariquita in the comedy "Une Femme est un diable" (1825) and his "she-devil" Carmen – but also through the motif of the Inquisition, which Mérimée adopted from Lewis. It is remarkable, admittedly, that the vamps of the Romantic era, when they are pursued by the Inquisition, as Matilda is, are able to escape its clutches by their devilish arts. The system of the Inquisition itself (whose diabolical machinery is also the subject of innumerable novels) also stands less for the defense of true faith than for the dark tribunal that conspiratorially seeks to rule the world under the device of rooting out carnal desire as the work of the devil.

As a synthesis of all attributes of the Romantic vamp, the Creole Cécily electrified a mass audience around the middle of the 19th century when she appeared in Eugène Sue's "Les Mystères de Paris." As a whole, the novel, which was originally published in installments between 1842–1843 in a Paris daily newspaper, meets every criterion of the emergent cultural and media industry of the day in terms of its means of production, its mode of narration, and its figures. In a foreword that he wrote for a German edition published in the 1920s, Victor Klemperer clearly describes the pressure of production to which Sue was subjected in order to adapt his mixed material – based on facts, reports, and pathos-laden social comment – to the demands of serial publication. "He wrote breathlessly and hastily for the day; he wrote his novels as reviews, intended to create tension, he had to break off at climactic points, had to finely tune the threads of the story, and then he had to carry on, picking up somewhere, weaving in intrigues and still using the greatest possible clarity for the simplest of minds."[43] On this basis, the vamp cannot but emerge as a cliché. Yet it is the literary cliché, in particular, that foreshadows and clearly outlines the images that are to appear on the cinema screen decades later. Sue describes Cécily: "That big Creole, svelte and full-bodied, strong and supple as a panther," as a "personification of the burning sensuality that can only ignite in the heat of the tropics. Everyone has heard of these colored women, positively fatal to Europeans, these enchanting vampires! (...) Instead of pouncing on her prey and, like her ilk, dreaming of nothing but to destroy another life and happiness, Cécily aimed her magnetic gaze at her victims and began to draw them gradually into the fiery maelstrom that seemed to emanate from her."[44]

"Les Mystères de Paris" was first filmed in 1911 by Albert Capellani (at 1500 meters, the film exceeded all feature film lengths previously known in France[45]). That same year, Arturo Ambrosio helped to revive Flaubert's "Salammbô" on the cinema screen in Italy. With the "panther cat" Cécily and her many vampish sisters of the 19th century, with their "burning sensuality" and their hypnotic gaze, the "glow of the tropics" and the exoticism it implied became a firmly established part of the vamp program. The smoldering-eyed exotic Medusas of the early cinema years had their roots in literature, most notably in the figure of Sue's Cécily, thanks to the phenomenon of mass marketing throughout Europe: the man-eating woman, impassioned to the point of self-destruction, the "mysterious" seductress as erotic idol.

The film stars had to be constructed, and the nascent media industry rose to the task and set about constructing their backgrounds and their private lives. For Pola Negri, the "exotic beauty" of German film around 1920, who starred in Ernst Lubitsch's Carmen (1918), they invented the story that she was of gypsy blood, and indeed she aroused the impression, when she arrived in the USA with Lubitsch in 1923, of actually being the very kind of woman that Gloria Swanson, the girl from Chicago with the distinctly Anglo-Saxon name, could only play: "(W)ith her challenging and at the same time tragically florid gaze, her deep black hair, and her cat-like movements, Pola Negri appeared to her fans as the embodiment of Slavic unfathomability."[46] It is interesting in this context to note Patalas's remark that Pola Negri had "made human" the type of vamp created by Theda Bara. With her, and many other female stars of film history after the First World War, the Medusa once again takes on "human" traits, and the artful feminine machine of the vamp is returned to its origins.

Excursus on Arabian Death

In 1909, at the age of eighteen, Theodosia Goodman, the daughter of a Jewish tailor in Cincinnati, left her parents' home to make her career on Broadway. She failed. Five years of hardship and deprivation followed in which she spent much of her time keeping the white-slavers of Hollywood's film factories at bay. Theodosia abhorred cinema. It was only at the age of twenty-three, when her room and all its contents were devoured by flames, that she decided to call Frank Powell, who was filming The Stain (1914) for William Fox. Powell took one look at Theodosia, saw the dark, deeply melancholy eyes set in a pale and malnourished face, and decided that she had an erotic aura. Fox agreed with him and commissioned his two best advertising agents, Johnny Goldfarp and Al Selig, to come up with something good.

First of all they found a name for Miss Goodman: Theda Bara – an anagram of "Arab death." Then they created an interesting biography for the new creature. Theda Bara, as the newspapers were soon to report, had been born in the Sahara Desert, in the shadow of a sphinx, the daughter of an Arabian princess and a French artist, who had lost his soul and his mind in the arms of his beloved, and perhaps even his life. Finally, she was given a mystically romantic ambience. Skulls and other gruesome relics with which she was photographed stylized Theda Bara as the priestess of the "Black Mass." When Fox moved its studios from New York to California, she was given a mock-Tudor palace in the desert, full of tiger skins, crystal balls, pearl-studded skulls, mummy cases, and all the accoutrements of Gothic novels from a past but still virulent culture. The first female vampire of film history had thus been created and had entered the limelight of the modern, dynamically expanding media industry.[47]

The star became the program – and literature provided her with the desired aura. The first film of the new genre, A Fool There Was (1915), took Rudyard Kipling's poem "The Vampire" as its motto: "A fool there was and he made his prayer / (Even as you and I!) / To a rag and a bone and a hank of hair / (We called her the woman who did not care). / But the fool he called her his lady fair / (Even as you and I!)."[48]

In this film Theda Bara drives a respectable citizen to ruin (Edward José as the government employee John Schuyler). She accompanies him on a cruise to Europe, betrays his wife, and engineers his physical and mental downfall. In England and then on the bohemian Italian Riviera, Schuyler is gradually transformed into a shadow of his former self. Rapidly aging, with illness and weakness encroaching, disowned by his friends, he turns to drink – until, in the end, he breaks his neck falling down stairs. Theda Bara, in mourning, scatters roses over his corpse. Here, a man is brought low by the merciless "bloodsucking" gaze of a vampire. Indeed, he is robbed of his life's juices. (In the artificial figure of the vamp, around the turn of the century, an underlying metaphorical sexual aspect was still prevalent: the notion that it was not the loss of blood, but the "frivolous" spending of sperm that weakened the man and led to his physical and mental decline.)

Theda Bara worked for William Fox for five years. She made almost forty films, all of them variations on the vamp – until the vampire itself was wrung dry, reduced to a mere image, and no longer able to drive men to madness and women to hysteria on stage. Before that, however, she went through the entire "classical" vamp program imported from the Romantic era. She is the only actress who can claim to have played the entire repertoire of Romantic archaic heroines and fin-de-siècle Medusas – women who have driven their men to destruction and are then dragged down with them.[49]

In 1915, with Raoul Walsh as director, she played the title role in the film Carmen, and told reporters that she herself was Ar Minz, the original image of Carmen, and that she must have met Mérimée as a vampire in a previous life. By way of proof, she interrupted the press conference to have raw meat served to her.

CLEOPATRA, 1917
Theda Bara

Theda Bara played Alexandre Dumas's "Dame aux Camélias" in CAMILLE (1917) and told the fan magazines that an admirer had once taken his life with her poison snake bracelet. She played MADAME DU BARRY (1917), starred in CLEOPATRA (1917), danced the role of SALOME (1918) – and thus fulfilled the repertoire of "frenetic" sex figures that had dominated literature and fine arts only a few decades before. Phantoms situated on the thin line between "black" Romanticism and Modernism: "The vampire that Bara played was really a 19th century character that thrived on the silver screen for a brief period before the Modern Age took hold in the 1920s and the nation conceded that gender roles were not entirely separate and unequal."[50]

Among the myths that Fox and his advertising agents constructed around Theda Bara is the legend of her own inability to love: "Every woman must choose whether she will love or be loved. She cannot hope for both."[51] The "Woman Vampire" drives men mad with a yearning for fulfillment that remains beyond reach. The contract that Theda Bara signed in 1917 was modeled to give legal form to an artificial figure that had nothing to do with daily life (let alone "life" itself). She undertook never to marry, never to appear in public without a heavy veil, never to use any means of public transportation, and, on no account, to enter a Turkish Bath. Yet Theda Bara herself lends the nun-like image of a celibate Medusa a touch of radical feminist rebellion: "For every Woman Vampire, there are ten men of the same type, men who take everything from women – love, devotion, beauty, youth – and give nothing in return! V stands for Vampire, and it stands for Vengeance. The vampire that I play is the vengeance of my sex upon its exploiters. You see, I have the face of the vampire, perhaps, but the heart of a feministe."[52]

In the years following the First World War, America was split into two camps – torn between two icons, both artificial figures created in Hollywood's factories. The disciples of "European" decadence, "Romanesque" sensuality, and "Romantic" seediness of all kinds stare with fascination at the "Franco-Arabic" Theda Bara, and every second dark-haired starlet practices the poses of this gloomy goddess in front of the mirror. Meanwhile, on the other hand, prudish America mobilizes its women's clubs against the premiere of CLEOPATRA, in which Theda Bara's ample flesh can be seen naked, draped in garlands of precious jewelry. And those who still uphold decency and traditional American virtues, turn towards the good girls – above all the flaxen-haired virgin Mary Pickford, that antithesis of the vampire par excellence – emanating from the light and boredom of the endless cornfields of Iowa. The artificial figures of the American cinema now represent – not unlike Asta Nielsen and Henny Porten in Germany, two "role models" of a society seeking to decode its inner contradictions in complementary and contrasting images.

When Theda Bara wears the dress of a peasant in KATHLEEN MAVOURNEEN (1919) and appears on the screen in corkscrew curls, her time is already over. William Fox shows her the door without further ado when her contract runs out. She is succeeded by true exotics from faraway, "decadent" Europe: the Russian Alla Nazimova, the Italian Nita Naldi, and Appolonia Chalupek alias Pola Negri from Warsaw. Pola Negri in BELLA DONNA (1923) – that is the epitome of Kipling's "Vampire," according to the "New York Times." With her, however, we also lose the synthetic myths woven around the early vamps, enveloping them to the point of unrecognizability in the small-talk of the gossip columns, which still continue to determine what is news, when it comes to marketing idols, artificial people, irrespective of their origins, in the interests of successful product placement.

While Theda Bara was bringing to the screen her pale echo of Romantic frenzy and evoking Medusa and Satan in American cinema, William Randolph Hearst was running after baby-faced chorus girls and launching their careers.[53] It was media mogul Hearst, of all people, who was soon to mobilize virtuous America against all manner of real and imaginary vice, against dissidence and minorities, against deviations from the American way of life. Truly good girls and didactically constructed bad girls gradually pushed out the vamp, and with that blotted out the shadow the 19th century had still been casting upon the cinema screens of the early 20th century.

Media History, Universe of Images

What began as literary history in the first half of the 19th century was soon to continue as media history. The motifs of the Romantics became popular and conquered the boulevard, the theater, so-called trivial literature – and finally the technical media of the daguerrotype and photography, the illustrated press, and the fantasy worlds of advertising.

"Allegorical, tragic, sentimental and coquette female figures"[54] are predominant in the representational photography of the turn of the century and the Belle Epoque. Historicism and a tendency to prefer "living images" fostered inter-media strategies – in the German speaking world as well, where, for example, the actress Charlotte Wolter stood model for all Hans Makart's Cleopatra paintings, performing in 1878 at the Burgtheater in Vienna not only in a Cleopatra tragedy in the Markart style, but also having her photograph taken in the pose of the dying heroine. "With transfigured gaze, she looks towards Death, that has already come upon the slave lying on her death bed."[55] In France, theatrically staged photographs featuring allegorical female figures had been in fashion since the mid-19th century, though the allegory tended to be little more than an excuse for indulging in a sinister form of eroticism in a sumptuous and pathos-laden setting, such as the "Veiled Nude" with a coat of armor in the background on an 1854 albumin print by Braquehais.[56]

Dancers and actresses from the boulevard theaters of Paris – and the aura that veiled them in the gaze of the Décadents – mediate between the last phases of Romanticism and the romantic inclinations of early cinematography. Théophile Gautier writes of the dancer Fanny Essler: "The outline of her arms has something both soft and nervy which recalls the shape of an extraordinarily handsome and slightly effeminate youth, like Bacchus and Antinous."[57] Paul Verlaine's youthful poem on the actress Marco doubly stylizes the vamp as an artificial being: "Quand Marco passait, tous les jeunes / Se penchaient pour voir ses yeux, des Sodomes / Où les feux d'Amour brûlaient sans pitié." (When Marco passed by, all the young men / strained to see her eyes, those Sodoms / in which the fires of love burned without pity).[58] Texts such as these hail an actress (or dancer) in terms of an artificial figure, and the stylization transposed to the text places her artificiality on another aesthetic level that adds a literary element (tragic, mythical, demonic).

"Now they have returned to the cemetery of the Past, these ghouls, vampires and incubi," writes Praz in 1930, "but the Danse Macabre was prolonged till after the dawn of the present century."[59] It was to survive, thanks, above all, to film.

In the early years of cinematography, at least, the Danse Macabre so popular in the Gothic novel continued to flicker across the screen – a number of titles from the opulent œuvre of Georges Méliès spring to mind in this regard, among them LE MIROIR DE CAGLIOSTRO (1899); COPPÉLIA OU LA POUPÉE ANIMÉE (1900); LA DAMNATION DE FAUST (1903); UN MIRACLE SOUS L'INQUISITION (1904); LE JUIF ERRANT (1904); LES QUATRE CENTS FARCES DU DIABLE (1906). More important still, however, both in terms of cultural history and technology, is the "romantic" atmosphere of the pre-filmic "fog pictures" or images of clouds of smoke and gauze curtains in the work of the Belgian Etienne Gaspar Robertson (1763–1837), that represents the link in media history between popular aspects of the Romantic era in the light novel and painting on the one hand, and cinematography on the other. The place and the atmosphere projected in Robertson's scenes of horror with their artificial beings constitute a Gothic novel situation par excellence: "Soon the citizens of Paris, filled with eager curiosity, began to gather in the gloomy chapel of the old Capuchin monastery at the Place Vendôme. By the dim light it was just possible to see the strange ornamentation, the mysterious images, gravestones, bones and skulls. (...) In the deathly silence, few dared even to whisper. All awaited with trepidation the appearance of the spirits that were to rise from the tombs. The lamp goes out. Suddenly the oppressive silence is broken by the howling of a stormy wind and the patter of rain, followed by thunder and lightning. The death knell tolls, invoking the spirits: in the distance a faint light appears and a ghostly figure can be seen."[60] With the introduction of the stereoscopic process of photography around the middle of the century, ghosts and other ghoulish subjects became popular; the portrayal of the black mass in such images as the stereographic photograph "Le Sort Satannique" (1865) can even be found on calling cards of the period.[61]

Camera obscura and laterna magica, machines from the long prehistory of cinematography, are part and parcel of the inventory of European romanticism. E.T.A. Hoffmann's "engineers" were already constructing imaginary scenarios and peopling them with artificial beings, forerunners of those pale figures that were to haunt the silent movies of German Caligarism until the early 1920s as harbingers of the uncanny. Until the First World War, and to a degree long beyond that time, cinematographic images appeared to be merely the longed-for realization of a dream, which – removed from modernity, enlightenment, and technical civilization – clung to magical notions and, in the 19th century at least, had sought its escape in Romantic "divertissement," artificiality, and illusion.

The vamps of early film history not only mark the end of a long development that, for reasons of erotic obsession, sexual fatalism, and destructive fantasy, has driven the image of woman as subject and object of love into a situation of extreme artificiality, but also mark the culmination of a sub-history of arbitrary and highly subjective interpretations of a celebrated art-historical heritage that had long since found its way into museums. Shelley with his "Ode to the Medusa in the Uffizi" is not alone. Charles Swinburne's description of women's heads from the school of Michelangelo in a text written in 1868, for example, is not so much an art-historical study as an enthusiastic celebration of his own idiosyncrasies and his obsession with woman as Medusa: "In one drawing she wears a head dress of Eastern fashion rather than Western, but in effect made of the artist's mind only; plated in the likeness of closely welded scales as of a chrysalid serpent, raised and waved around it the likeness of a sea shell, in some inexplicable way all her ornaments seem to partake of her fatal nature, to bear upon them her brand of beauty fresh from Hell; and this through no vulgar machinery of symbolism, no serpentine or otherwise vestal emblem: the bracelets and rings are innocent in shape and workmanship; but in touching her flesh they have become infected with deadly and malignant meaning. Broad bracelets divide the shapely slender of her arms; over the nakedness of her firm and luminous breasts, just below the neck, there is passed a band as of metal. Her eyes are full of proud and passionate lust after gold and blood; her hair, close and curled, seems to shudder in sunder and divide into snakes. (...) She is the deadlier Venus incarnate."[62]

Praz notes soberly: "It is hardly necessary to point out how little Swinburne's imagination sticks to the drawings he is discussing: Michelangelo is translated into terms of Gautier."[63] Yet only a few decades later, Swinburne could well have described the hairstyles, snakelike bracelets and rings, metallic nakedness and cruel facial expressions of innumerable vamps from the early silent movies in much the same way.

The artificiality of classical and late Hellenistic figures can be traced back to the Italian Renaissance. The "black" Romantics and the Décadents of the turn of the century transformed the figures of female beauty and enigma, on which painters and sculptors had worked for centuries, into embodiments of their own crises of emotion and consciousness. The unfettered synchretism of the period pictures before 1914 with their elaborate settings and costumes nonchalantly draws upon traditional and constantly reworked material, adopting attributes for their cruel beauties wherever they can find them. The saturnalia and bacchanalia of the early monumental films, in Italy at least, are positively teeming with artificial figures of motley Oriental, Ancient Egyptian and Greek provenance, kitted out with the morbid fantasies of the fin de siècle and placed in a setting of fashionable, "modern" stylization. As the sinister master of ceremonies of European Décadence, we find the poet Gabriele d'Annunzio, who put his signature to Giovanni Pastrone's script for CABIRIA (1914), and probably contributed no more than that, although Mario Praz believes that he imbued it with his "contagio della frenesia funebre" (contagion of funereal frenzy).[64]

The production of artificial figures has invariably involved different "notional worlds", both traditional and modern; these involve synthesis and artifact, configura-

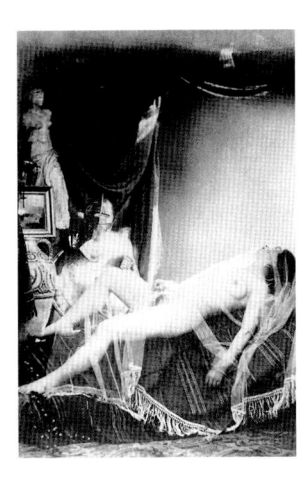

Braquehais: Veiled Nude with Knight's Armor, 1854

tions of traditional and virtual material. The British writer Walter Pater described Leonardo's "Mona Lisa" as follows in 1873: "All the thoughts and experience of the world have etched and molded there, in that which they have of power to refine and make expressively outward form, the animalism of Greece, the lust of Rome, the mysticism of the Middle Age with its spiritual ambition and imaginative loves, the return of the pagan world, the sins of the Borgias. She is older than the rocks among which she sits; like the vampire she has been dead many times, and learned the secrets of the grave (...)."[65]

At the same time, the Gioconda is, in the history of painting, the most distinctive example of an artificial construct which, in every era, has been interpreted imaginatively and speculatively: the face of a star long before the stars of the cinema were constructed. As Pater further describes it, "certainly Lady Lisa might stand as the embodiment of the old fancy, the symbol of the modern idea." It is a distinctive quality of media history that it allows the images and their reception, the idols and the fashions that they trigger, to be brought together in complex systems – and that, at the same time, the expectations of the intellectuals and the desires of everyday life, the institutions of representative culture and the sphere of consumerism are all included. Among the courtesans of Paris in the 1880s, it was fashionable to wear the enigmatic smile of the Gioconda. And in 1915, in THE DEVIL'S DAUGHTER (based on a novel by Gabriele d'Annunzio), it would be Theda Bara who added yet another vamp to the world of contemporary cinema with her role as La Gioconda. The promiscuous liaison between art/literature and cinema/mass culture was fed at the turn of the century by operettas and boulevard life, photography and fashion salons, by the boudoir and the brothel.

"The year 1900 no more marked the date of a cataclysm than did the year 1000. The philosophy of Schopenhauer, the music of 'Götterdämmerung,' the Russian novel, the plays of Maeterlinck – all these were absorbed and digested, after doing no more than create an impression of a delicious death-agony."[66] Yet the year 1900 was anticipated with a particularly lustful anxiety *(Lustangst)* as a year of catastrophe because the 19th century had changed the world more enduringly and had caused upheaval in European society to a far greater extent than any century before.

Visions of catastrophe and the euphoria of a new beginning are indiscriminately mixed in the media of the turn of the century. Countless popular novels around 1900 are dedicated to the fall of Byzantine culture thirteen centuries before as the backdrop for a giddy panorama of decadent contemporary Western culture. Literature precedes cinema, supplying the material: "Great choreographic movements seek to disguise under a false sparkle of picturesqueness the absence of any real thinking."[67]

Choreography and splendor find their opulent revival in the historicizing monumental films of the first two decades of cinema. Cinematography, the most technically advanced medium of the era, is regressive in its early beginnings, looking towards the 19th century, from whose nightmares it cannot liberate itself. Its artificial figures present themselves as copies of the decadent literature that recycled their "Black Masses" in the darkness of the cinema. At the center of all saturnalia, slaughter, and twilight of the idols stands the vamp.

Androgynous Alternation

Is the vamp(ire) male or female? In Goethe's ballad "Die Braut von Korinth" (The Bride of Corinth), the figure is unequivocally female: "Wie der Schnee so weiss, / Aber kalt wie Eis / Ist das Liebchen, das du dir erwählt" (Like snow so white / But cold as ice / Is the beloved that you have chosen).[68] According to Praz, vampirism came into fashion in the 19th century mainly through Byron. "In the 'Giaour' (1813) Byron mentions vampires; three years later in Geneva, in company with Shelley, Dr. Polidori, and M.G. Lewis, he read some German ghost stories and invited his friends each to write one. Thus Mrs. Shelley conceived Frankenstein (...)."[69]

In Polidori's ghost novel "The Vampire" (1819), the bloodsucker is male. Yet the sexual fantasies and phobias change. "We shall see how in the second half of the 19th century the vampire becomes a woman as in Goethe's ballad; but in the first part of the century the fatal, cruel lover is invariably a man (...)," writes Praz. More clearly still, he explains that "the function of the flame which attracts and burns is exercised, in the first half of the century, by the Fatal Man (the Byronic hero), in the second half by the Fatal Woman; the moth destined for sacrifice is in the first case the woman, in the second the man. It is not simply the case of convention and literary fashion; literature, even in its most artificial forms, reflects to some extent the aspects of contemporary life."[70]

The French Revolution and the Reign of Terror were a male tragedy that spawned a towering, internationally active political vampire in the figure of Bonaparte. Yet by the July Revolution of 1830, the working-class women of the *faubourgs*, the market women of *les halles*, and Heine's *poissardes* could no longer be overlooked. In his painting of "Liberty" Delacroix had even created a buxom and voluptuous monument to them, to the horror of many male spectators. Clearly, the entire 19th century was straining to create a complex androgynous construct that alternately allocated priority to the male and the female principle.

The respectively dominant (artificial) figure is also split between "all-devouring" love and an unfettered desire to destroy the object of that love. The female stars of early film history – from Italia Almirante Manzini to Pina Menichelli, from Theda Bara to Gloria Swanson, from Fern Andra to Mae Murray – continue this history of ambivalence and dichotomy. Admittedly, as the film industry (and its subject matter) became increasingly commercialized and bourgeois, they began to transpose the great Romantic motifs to the everyday themes and social mores of a contemporary world regarded as "modern," with elegant interiors where the female vamp lived on as a "woman of the world." Among the later Hollywood stars, only Elizabeth Taylor can still claim to have risen to the stature of a Medusa and ancient love goddess for the new era (albeit for fundamentally altered audience expectations) in her role as CLEOPATRA (1963). Costing 40 million dollars, it was, at the time, the "most expensive film ever made."

Leonardo da Vinci: Mona Lisa, around 1503. Paris, Musée du Louvre

From Vampire to Vamp

CLEOPATRA, 1917
Fritz Leiber, Theda Bara

CLEOPATRA, 1962
Elizabeth Taylor

89

Not only the screen vamps, but indeed the entire history of cinema, until today, has drawn countless variations from a cultural history of sexual ambivalence and the enigma of our sexual desires. In German cinema around 1920, Richard Oswald highlighted the ambiguity of gender roles with his artificial figures (Anita Berber, Conrad Veidt, and Werner Krauss among them) – and with that the aporia inherent within them. Dietrich Kuhlbrodt has described the "undisguised pleasure" with which Werner Krauss and Maria Forescu celebrate a sado-masochistic game with remarkable nonchalance in the alternation and interaction of their roles in Dida Ibsens Geschichte (1918).[71]

Countless Hollywood films have taken the subject of sexual ambivalence and used it to create hilarious and tragic figures and situations. Tony Curtis and Jack Lemmon in Billy Wilder's Some Like It Hot (1959) are artificial figures who (re)discover their "first" and perhaps "authentic" nature in the artificial guise they are forced to adopt in the interests of their own survival. Tony Curtis undergoes a double process of transformation that is akin to a second shedding of the skin. This mediocre woman-chaser has to dress as a woman in a humiliating experience that makes women inaccessible to him, at the very moment when, to make matters worse, he is constantly in the company of the ultimate symbol of sexual desire, Marilyn Monroe. Only his second masking as a sexually inhibited millionaire helps him to enjoy this proximity – if only he could enjoy it instead of having to play impotent. It may be a role that enables him to be seduced, but at the same time it forces him to abandon the role of permanent seducer. Here we have a role play that breaks down all role clichés, banning Curtis to a purgatory from which he will emerge a different, more gentle, and more sensitive man.

The androgynous joke of this famous scene had already been worked out in detail in the 19th century: in the novel "A cœur perdu" by the otherwise artistically uninspired writer Joséphin Péladan (1888). Here, an act of seduction is described as follows: "Resisting his desire for the women instead of fueling it, Nebo reversed roles and foresaw that the young girl, androgynous as she was, would dare to act like a man, for he was being evasive like a woman. This was further emphasized by Nebo's feminine behavior, lending the princess' desires masculine traits. (...) He allowed himself to be wooed and desired like a coquette, in order to delay the process of sex."[72]

In the photography of the late 19th century, sexual ambiguity characterizes the artistically staged figures of young boys that Baron Wilhelm von Gloeden had pose for his camera as hermaphrodite ephebes – like the nude studies of prostitutes photographed by E.J. Bellocq around 1912 in New Orleans.[73] The bizarre side of androgyny, however, that is carried on in the bearing, gestures, and swaggering ostentation of many a cinema vamp, was captured by Aubrey Beardsley in his drawings. Here we see artificial people that are peeled out of plants, vegetables or organic ornamentations or converge with them: man as an aesthetic construct and an arrangement of forms stylized to the extreme. As late as 1922, the Russian actress Alla Nazimova made her mark as Salome wearing costumes based on Beardsley's drawings in an already outmoded Art Nouveau style.

In 1926, the "Chicago Tribune" launched its "Real America" campaign, railing against the social consequences of an androgynous Hollywood icon: "When will we be rid of all these effeminate youths, pomaded, powdered, bejeweled and bedizened, in the image of Rudy – that painted pansy?" In Chicago, the newspaper reported, a dance hall had opened that was "a boudoir for men, frequented by boys of dubious mien," and where there was even "all manner of cosmetics, pomades, ingredients, lipstick and eyeshadow, even an automatic powder dispenser. So this is 1926! We undoubtedly owe all these refinements to such 'men' as Valentino, that pink powder puff."[74]

Calls for a "long overdue reappraisal" of Rudolph Valentino – against "photos explicitly typing him," "wild rumors," and the suspicion of homosexuality[75] – were to be voiced time and again by film historians, and they would be perfectly entitled to do so and probably even have the facts on their side. Yet even "serious" film historiography will not get around the fact that artificial luminaries of the film industry are made up not only of their undoubtedly existing human substance and their equally unquestionable artistic capabilities. The love and hate of the consumer, rumor and gossip, staged photographs and infamous slander, the publicity campaigns of major companies and the tirades of the press all contribute decisively to creating their nimbus. These form the machinery and the climate of vitality in which only the star can blossom, fueling the illuminating glow that typifies and reflects the superficialities of 20th century media culture and makes them indistinguishable from its very being. Rudolph Valentino – the "women's hero who never had a woman,"[76] the seducer of youth at whose funeral even men cried – will continue to remain identical with the icon of the feminine, soft, refined, sensitive, melancholy, perfumed man: an artificial product whose myth will survive its reduction to the *pars pro toto* of the "pink powder puff" for quite some time to come.

Madonna and Whore

How are artificial beings created? Probably much in the same way as allegories are created, if, according to Musil, "this is understood as an intellectual device to make everything mean more than it has any honest claim to mean."[77] The myth of the "Woman Vampire" and the iconography of the vamp are characterized by overcharged sensuality, emotional overdrive, and hypertrophy. In the developmental history of the romantic metamorphosis of the Medusa to a cinema icon, an ancient dialectical relationship between the image of the saint and the whore is rehabilitated and transformed into a sensually bewildering and intoxicating identity. The media civilization, our modern culture of the superficial, the "tailors, fashion fads and coincidences" (Musil), and, finally, the publicity departments, have undoubtedly speeded up this development – but here, too, the authors and artists of the 19th century paved the way.

The figure of the Medusa in Flaubert, according to Praz, is to be regarded "as the profanation of the image of the Madonna."[78] Medusa and the femme fatale are inconceivable without the image of the Virgin Mary: the thrill of the gruesomely beautiful replaces the thrill of the saintly. Profanation is not the same as the secularization of a *sanctum*,

Aubrey Beardsley: John and Salome, 1893. Illustration not used for Oscar Wilde's "Salome," 1894

Rudolph Valentino

but rather the reversal (literally: per-version) of the artificial image of the woman close to God and its no less artificial allocation to the circle of Satan. It is the femme fatale of the cinema after 1918 that first links the original pious image and its Medusa-like satanic antithesis to the social conditions of the modern world and dresses it in the costume of the grande dame with the face of an angel and the lifestyle of a worldly prostitute.

In Flaubert's "La Tentation de Saint-Antoine," which he rewrote three times between 1849 and 1872 (filmed by Méliès in 1898), he says of the whore Ennoia that she is innocent, like Christ, who died for man, whereas she devoted herself to women ("Innocente comme le Christ, qui est mort pour les hommes, elle s'est dévouée pour les femmes...").[79] Ennoia figures as a mythical whore, as a union of the classical Helen, the patrician Lucretia, the biblical Delilah, and the daughter of Israel "who gave herself to the beasts, taking pleasure in adultery, idolatry, lies and foolishness, prostituting herself to all and singing at every crossroads" ("qui s'abandonnait aux boucs. Elle a aimé l'adultère, l'idolâtrie, le mensonge et la sottise. Elle s'est prostituée à tous les peuples. Elle a chanté dans tous les carrefours.")

Perhaps it is here that we can find the key to a deeper understanding of all the mythical whores and the man-eating vamps of cultural history: Ennoia, as the destructive principle and embodiment of sin, hypertrophically heightened to an artificial female figure of "diabolical" lust and insatiable desire for destruction, is the counterpart to the artificial figure of the Christian redeemer, because it is her calling to sacrifice herself for the purity of women, just as Christ sacrificed himself for the redemption of mankind. (Theda Bara, the first Hollywood vamp, was to remodel this image in a feminist way: the "Woman Vampire" as an angel of vengeance – and as a chaste Medusa sacrificing herself on behalf of her exploited and humiliated sisters who had been subjugated to male sexism.)

This would mean that the daughters of Medusa and Satan should not be regarded simply as a reversal of the Christian theory of redemption or an antipode to the Divine principle, nor as mere objects of some "forbidden" reverence, heightened by the consciousness of sacrilege, but rather as representing the notion of redemption itself. In the works of the "divine Marquis" de Sade, and in Baudelaire, we can glimpse this notion, but in the Gothic romanticism and literature of the fin de siècle, it gets lost in the trimmings and the staging of the effect. In the age of cinematography, the saint as sinner returns to a world from which all secrets have disappeared, and from now on rules as the diva of show-business – with the task of bridging the endless discrepancy between the way the world is and our dreams. "What 'temptation' was among the ruins of a world still inhabited by phantoms, has become 'education' in the prose of the modern world," writes Michel Foucault in his afterword to the German edition of "La Tentation de Saint-Antoine" in reference to that other great work by Flaubert, "L'Éducation sentimentale."[80]

The stars of the film industry, especially the female stars, were equipped by the publicity departments of the production companies with equivocal, exotic, and at the very least mysterious biographies that gave their radiant nimbus an "unfathomable" shadow, and added a "satanic" sparkle to their divinity. Theodosia Goodman alias Theda Bara set an example that was to be followed by many. It was said of Fern Andra that she spent much of her life languishing in a nunnery to escape the sinful excesses of her existence as a diva and her private life. Mae Murray was reputedly sent to a convent as a young girl, where she was whipped for her immoral actions. Seen from a distance, these biographical constructions are as much subjects of Gothic romance as the figure of Matilda in Lewis's novel "The Monk." Even the serialized novels and pulp literature of the turn of the century took her as their model. With the advent of cinema, she became a legend in the literal sense – a guide to the fantasies of the modern media industry, revived by the marketing strategies of the major companies.

With regard to the 19th century, Michel Foucault notes a "library phenomenon": the fantasies, according to Foucault, "no longer have their place in the night, in the sleep of reason, in the uncertain void that opens up before yearning, but in a waking state, in indefatigable attention, in scholarly industry, in alertness"[81] – in other words, in the world of books. In the 20th century, the audiovisual has become heir to the night and the books; the fantasies live on in the media industry, they determine hairstyles and decor, coloring and lighting, standards and conventional formats of a culture that has raised distracted viewing to the norm. Even the construction of the artificial being follows this law: in the balance sheets of the majors it is an item of the advertising budget rather than the production budget.

Femme Fatale

Sainte-Beuves's description of the beauty of the femme fatale foreshadows the screen figures who seem to be made of malleable steel – to be admired but not desired – and who promise any lover who approaches them deadly torment or, in the mundane bourgeois version of the social film, deadly embarrassment: "The beauty that is painted neither in the ideal expression of the face nor in the mirror of the eyes nor in the delicacy of a smile nor yet in the subtle veil of the eyelids; the human face is nothing, almost nothing, in this beauty; eye and voice, gently coupled, are so close to the soul, so much a par of what is desired. (...) Oh, I have understood this beauty. I have also grasped that this beauty is not true beauty, that it is contrary to the spirit itself, that it kills, that it crushes, but that it does not bond."[82]

In the closing decades of the 19th century, European literature begins to depart from the myths, from the oriental exoticism and excesses of an imaginatively staged antiquity; turning instead towards the real vamps who populate contemporary salons and theaters, who frequent the roulette tables, and are to be found in the arcades, on the boulevards, and at the Grand Hotels. "The type which eventually crystallized around Salome's grizzly passion, and still continues to find favour with novelists, (...) the historical woman of exasperated desire, in whose hands man becomes a submissive instrument."[83] Again, we find the literature of the late 19th century forging a link to the cinema and to the "secularized" vamps of the movies after 1918 – to

Lya de Putti, for example, who, in F.W. Murnau's film Der brennende Acker (1921/22) and in E.A. Dupont's Varieté (1925), appears to belong partly to the here and now, and partly to some "unfathomable" otherness or some mythical era.

For at least three decades, however, the biblical Salome remained the true femme fatale of the era – not only in the lasciviously Romantic culture of the bourgeoisie, in the world of Aubrey Beardsley's drawings, or on the opera stage of Hugo von Hofmannsthal and Richard Strauss, but also on the cinema screen. Oscar Wilde's "Salome" (1893) was followed in 1905 by the Strauss opera of the same name, and in 1908 by the first American Salome, filmed by J. Stuart Blackton (with Florence Lawrence). In 1909 came the first German Salome film, by Oskar Messter, and in 1918 the version with Theda Bara, until, in 1922, we find Alla Nazimova, as we already noted, appearing against that Beardsley backdrop.

The decadent Huysmans wrote of Gustave Moreau's painting "Salome": "She had become, as it were, the symbolic incarnation of undying Lust, the Goddess of immortal Hysteria, the accursed Beauty exalted above all other beauties by the catalepsy that hardens her flesh and steels her muscles, the monstrous Beast, indifferent, irresponsible, insensible, poisoning, like the Helen of ancient myth, everything that approaches her, everything that sees her, everything that she touches. (...) Moreover, the painter seemed to have wished to assert his intention of remaining outside the bounds of time, of giving no precise indication of race or country or period, setting as he did his Salome inside this extraordinary palace with its grandiose, heterogeneous architecture, clothing her in sumptuous, fanciful robes, crowning her with a nondescript diadem like Salammbô's, in the shape of a Phoenician tower, and finally putting in her hand the sceptre of Isis, the sacred flower of both Egypt and India, the great lotus-blossom."[84]

Hysteria and rigidity, a body language in which all the emotions seem to have turned to stone or are about to explode: once again, as in Shelley's visit to the Uffizi galleries, in Swinburne's view of Michelangelo's female heads, and in the countless interpretations of Leonardo's "Mona Lisa," we find that the performers themselves (and their own highly subjective obsessions with a view to works of fine art) contribute enormously to shaping the artificial figure of the vamp. In the world of fine art, the Belgian painter Félicien Rops, who was a celebrated artist at the turn of the century, did more than any other to drive the identification of the feminine with cold evil to the point of allegory, and was encouraged in his endeavors by the critics of the day: "Rops is truly eloquent in painting the cruelty of contemporary woman: her steely gaze and her ill-will towards man is neither concealed nor hidden but clearly expressed in her entire being,"[85] wrote the Goncourt brothers in their "Journal" of 1868.

In German cinema of the 1920s Brigitte Helm is featured with a hypnotic radiance as the robot Maria in Metropolis (1925/26), as an "artificial" being in Alraune (she played this role in 1928 under the direction of Henrik Galeen and in a talkie by Richard Oswald in 1930), as Antinea in G.W. Pabst's Herrin von Atlantis (1932), and once again in Karl Hartl's Gold (1934), in which she plays the role of the demonic vamp "beyond the centuries": small breasted, yet dangerous with her bony shoulders bent forward, her cat-like movements and her coldly sparkling eyes. In Pabst's Abwege (1928), by contrast, she plays the (semi-)emancipated housewife who slips into the role of the pleasure-seeking, diabolical woman of the inflation years, with a talent for evil and intrigue: half yearning lover, half femme fatale with steely gaze.

The Parody of the Lurid Corpse

"The detailing of female beauty so popular in the poetry and literature of the Baroque era, in which each is highlighted by means of comparison, secretly adheres to the image of the corpse," writes Walter Benjamin in his notes for the "Passagen-Werk."[86] Thus, centuries ago, literature was already taking recourse to the same method as film montage, whereby both use the deconstructive process of "detailing" and, in doing so, shift the organic body closer to the anorganic. This "fragmentation of female beauty into its most fabulous components," as Benjamin puts it, "is like a dissection, and the popular comparisons of body parts with alabaster, snow, jewels or other generally inorganic entities does the rest."

Benjamin's "Passagen-Werk" presents a fragmentary theory of fashion and sexual mores, at the center of which we find death, for all fashion stands "in contradiction to the organic" and "couples the living body with the anorganic world."[87] Moreover, according to Benjamin, "fashion was never anything but a parody of the lurid corpse, a provocation of death through the female and a dialogue with decay whispered bitterly among the pools of memory."[88] The stylization of the film star to an artificial being is foreshadowed by the eccentric fashion of the Belle Epoque and the torture of the human body in the literature of the Romantic era. Perfect beauty is the aim: a perfection that is celebrated in literature in the gruesome death of the victim, in fashion by the hindering of the female body through the crinoline, and in cinematography by the pale, corpse-like rigidity of the beautiful face. The truth of the refined "artificial" being has the death of nature as its pre-condition; the living is eliminated and has to make way for a "second nature" that has nothing but the "architectural blueprint" or structure in common with the first.

The star thus embodies a truth of life after the end of nature. The operations to which the star's body is subjected are akin to the torturing of the body in the Romantic era in order to celebrate the corpse as the ultimate and highest state of beauty. In order to describe the eroticism of a "male corpse half veiled, half disclosed by the moonlight as it lay," Charles Robert Maturin evokes the aura of martyrs in his "Melmoth the Wanderer" (1820), such as that of "Saint Bartholomew flayed, with his skin hanging about him in graceful drapery" or of Saint Laurence, "on a grid iron, and exhibiting his finely formed anatomy on its bars, while naked slaves are blowing the coals beneath it."[89] In "L'Âne mort et la Femme guillotinée" by Jules Janin (1829) the operation of an injured courtesan is described as a work of art: "When he had finished with the iron, he used fire, pitilessly branding, occasionally admiring his work with the contentment of a young painter creating a landscape."[90]

Varieté
Lya de Putti

Gustave Moreau: Salome

In Thomas de Quincey's "Murder Considered as one of the Fine Arts" (1827) such necrophilia turns to humor, yet when murder is raised here to the status of a legitimate "work of art" of dismemberment, the murderer hailed as an "artist" and his criminal calculation as a "design,"[91] the balance is maintained, as throughout his writings, between a tongue-in-cheek critique of culture and "black" Romanticism.

In the work of the artists of the Decadent Movement, and in the trade of the couturiers, the costume designers and the makeup artists of the film industry, there is a certain amount of fetishism involved. "In fetishism," according to Benjamin, "sex removes the barrier between the organic and the anorganic world. Clothing and jewelry are involved. It is at home in death as it is in flesh." In passion, the fetishist explores "the landscapes of the body." These landscapes are "criss-crossed by paths that bring sex into the world of the anorganic. Fashion itself is merely another medium that draws it still deeper into the material world."[92]

Not just in the film industry, but in the fashions of every era, the attempt to transform the human body into an artificial figure has always started and finished with alterations to the skin. Even in everyday language, the skin is used to refer to something we might otherwise describe as our identity. We tend to inhabit our "identity" to the extent that we even describe resolving a difficult or threatening situation as "saving one's skin."

Tattooing may be regarded as an attempt to transform the skin – which cannot be stripped off – into a surface for the illustration of someone else, a possible other, a screen for projection. In everyday life, makeup is fashion's declaration of war on nature, of the inorganic on the organic – applied to the human face. When the fashion of the living "takes account of the rights of the corpse,"[93] as Benjamin writes, then this applies expressly to the garishly whitened faces of the silent movie stars. "The fetishism that underlies the sex appeal of the anorganic" paints its tableau here.

Baudelaire, writing in praise of cosmetics, says: "I ask you to review and scrutinize whatever is natural (...), and you will find nothing but frightfulness. Everything beautiful and noble is the result of reason and calculation."[94] Makeup is nothing but the shroud that a sense of beauty, by way of reason and calculation, spreads over the nature of the female face. It is a sense of beauty that is aware of perfection in death and, by making the skin disappear under artificial layers, undertakes a reversed shedding of skin.

"She penciled her eyebrows with a painter's loving care and enameled her forehead and cheeks for a heightened effect that reached beyond naturalism and mere reality into a style of religious art," writes Robert Musil, describing Ulrich's lover Bonadea, a Cleopatra-like figure of 1913.[95] It is also worth considering Musil's further observations on fashion: "Clothes, when abstracted from the flow of present time and their transmogrifying function on the human body, and seen as forms in themselves, are strange tubes and excrescences worthy of being classed with such facial decorations as the ring through the nose or the lip-stretching disk. But how enchanting they become when seen together with the qualities they bestow on their wearer! What happens then is no less than the infusion, into some tangled lines on a piece of paper, of the meaning of a great word. Imagine a man's invisible kindness and moral excellence suddenly looming as a halo the size of the full moon and golden as an egg yolk right over his head, the way it does in old religious paintings, as he happens to be strolling down the avenue or heaping little tea sandwiches on his plate – what an overwhelming, shattering sensation it would be! And just such a power to make the invisible, or even the non-existent, visible is what a well made outfit demonstrates every day of the week."[96]

Fashion as the medium in which the virtual achieves visibility. The aesthetic of the early vamp added that very "halo the size of the full moon and golden as an egg yolk" to the choice figure in the form of fantastic costumes – and occasionally took it quite literally, by creating towering hairstyles and glittering headwear. The face beneath it rarely has the "ideal expression" or "soulful mirror of the eyes" described by Sainte-Beuve. Instead, it is Prosper Merimée's "Venus d'Ille" (1837) that foreshadows the strange grimaces of the painted silent movie stars: the slight distortions in the white face, the slanting, deeply shadowed eyes – the entire face appearing not as the mirror, but as the mask of a life burnt out by its own passions: "Disdain, irony, cruelty, can be read on this face, though it is nevertheless of incredible beauty. In truth, the more one considered this admirable statue, the more one had the disconcerting feeling that a beauty so marvelous could go hand in hand with a complete absence of all sensibility."[97]

"The typical Fatal Woman is always pale, just as the Byronic hero was pale," writes Praz.[98] With color, nature too has left this face; the pallor is the pallor of near death, of evil, and the predominance of the anorganic over the traces that write "life" onto a face. The tools of beauty were regarded by the "effeminate" Romantics and Decadents not as the necessary accessories to fashion and everyday life, but as the tools of an exacting aesthetic which, together with the sensitivity of the poet, the colors of the painter, and the palate of the gourmet, formed part of the instrumentarium of an Epicurean lifestyle: "Poetry is connected to the arts of painting, cuisine and cosmetics," wrote Baudelaire.[99]

Cosmetics, then, the subtle work on the skin of the artificial being, is linked with poetry and painting by the demand for the highest possible artificiality: the result, here as there, is an artificial product in the sense of the definitive, deliberately undertaken detachment from nature. It is not by coincidence that the memoirs of film stars so frequently describe the patience they applied to their makeup, or the time they spent with the cameraman, often many hours before shooting began, for the lighting of their facial landscapes.

Branding Women

The rest is burnt skin. Between 1915 and 1931, Hollywood told the same tale of evil no less than three times: a socialite loses $10,000 gambling and borrows it from a playboy. When she wants to pay the money back, he refuses it, attacks her and presses a branding iron onto her naked skin. The name of the film is THE CHEAT. Directed by Cecil B. De Mille in 1915, with Fanny Ward as the victim, it was remade in 1923 by George Fitzmaurice with Pola Negri, and again in 1931 by George Abbott with Tallulah Bankhead.

Félicien Rops: Naturalia, around 1875. Brussels, Galerie Patrick Derom

METROPOLIS
Brigitte Helm

Sessue Haykawa, cast as the playboy in the 1915 version, reappears in the same role in the French version of 1937, *Forfaiture* by Marcel L'Herbier. Haykawa is said to have recalled that it was a pleasure to torture Fanny Ward with the branding iron. By 1959 this material had been filmed sixteen times.

"Branding women was a popular theme in movies of this era," write Lottie Da and Jan Alexander,[100] referring to the period when cinema was making the transition to bourgeois subject matter, perfumed social film, and the commercial standards of an entertainment industry running at full tilt. It almost looks as though cinema was wreaking revenge on its own beginnings, on its own wild, untamed and barely controllable creature, the vamp – that dark shadow of the 19th century that had become the demonically shimmering artificial figure of a young and not yet saturated film industry, still unstable by bourgeois moral standards. But what had Medusa done to the people of that era to deserve such terrible torment, quite literally before the eyes of the world, and to be branded with a hot iron? How great were the sins of Theda Bara and Lyda Borelli, Geraldine Farrar and Pola Negri, that they should appear to justify the branding iron as a suitable punishment?

A hidden explanation may perhaps be found in a statement by Pola Negri, who, recalling her role in *The Cheat*, admitted that she had felt very unhappy in this film – except in the scene in which she was branded by her enemy. The actress perceives with pleasure what is done to the figure she portrays. In this, she becomes one with the audience that wishes to suppress neither its sympathy with its victim nor its pleasure in watching the torture.

The "tempestuous loveliness of terror" that Shelley perceived in seeing the Medusa in the Uffizi galleries was potent still – and it continued to have an effect well into a century that wished to rid itself once and for all of the ghosts of times past, and to cast out the vampires, the nightmares, and the artificial creatures brewed in the witches's cauldrons of the Romantic era, in order to achieve the triumph of Rationality in its own way. The vamp was a reminder that the promise of Enlightenment had not yet been redeemed. It is this grim undertone that the vamp continues to hold for us today.

Footnotes

1 Heinrich von Kleist: On a Theatre of Marionettes. (Tr. by Gerti Wildorf.) London: Acorn Press 1989, p. 4
2 ibid., p. 5
3 Walter Benjamin: Das Passagen-Werk. In: Gesammelte Schriften. Vol. 2. Ed. by Rolf Tiedemann. Frankfurt am Main: Suhrkamp 1982, p. 849
4 Kleist, op. cit., p. 11
5 Die Nachtwachen des Bonaventura. Afterword by Adolf von Grolman. Heidelberg: Schneider 1955, p. 66
6 Paul Virilio: Ereignislandschaft. (Paysages Evenements.) Munich: Hanser 1998, p. 116
7 Robert Musil: The Man Without Qualities. (Tr. by Sophie Wilkins and Burton Pike.) London: Picador 1995, p. 10
8 ibid., p. 14
9 Quoted in: Mario Praz: The Romantic Agony. (Tr. by Angus Davidson). New York: Meridan 1956, p. 157
10 Musil, op. cit., p. 64
11 Praz, op. cit, p. 105. Praz quotes in French: "Et voilà donc ce que c'est que le meurtre: un peu de matière désorganisée, quelques changements dans les combinaisons, quelques molécules rompues et replongées dans le creuset de la nature qui les rendra dans quelques jours sous une autre forme à la terre; et où donc est le mal à cela?"
12 Musil, op. cit., p. 157
13 ibid., p. 1324
14 ibid., pp. 1325 f.
15 Percy Bysshe Shelley. The Poetical Works. London, New York: Frederick Warne and Co., undated, p. 493
16 This groundbreaking study of the darker side of the Romantic era has proved an invaluable source of inspiration and information for this essay. First published in Florence in 1930 under the title "La carne, la morte e il diavolo nella letteratura romantica," it was reprinted in 1948 by Sansoni Editore. An English translation by Angus Davidson was published by Meridian, New York, in 1933 and reprinted in 1956. (See note 9.) The German translation used in the original version of this essay appeared in paperback at dtv in 1970.
17 Johann Wolfgang Goethe: Faust. Der Tragödie erster Teil. The present quotation is taken from Percy Bysshe Shelley's translation of Goethe's Faust, Part I, excerpted in Praz, op. cit., pp. 26 f.
18 Quoted in Praz, op. cit., p. 28
19 ibid., p. 30. Praz quotes Baudelaire in French: "(…) je ne conçois guère (…) un type de Beauté où il n'y ait du *Malheur*" and, on Milton's Satan "le plus parfait type de beauté virile."
20 Georges Sadoul: Histoire du Cinéma Mondial des Origines à Nos Jours. Paris: Flammarion 1966, p. 74
21 Enno Patalas: Stars – Geschichte der Filmidole. Frankfurt am Main and Hamburg: Fischer 1967, pp. 30 f.
22 ibid., p. 79
23 Praz, op. cit., p. 45
24 Charles Baudelaire: Journaux intimes. Cited by Praz, op. cit., p. 29
25 Praz, op. cit., p. 53
26 ibid., p. 56
27 ibid., p. 69. Praz quotes in French: "une des conceptions les plus sublimes et les plus pathétiques qui soient jamais sorties du cerveau d'un poète."
28 Wolfgang Kraus (ed.): Symbole und Signale. Frühe Dokumente der literarischen Avantgarde. Bremen: Schünemann 1961, p. 43
29 Praz, op. cit., p. 70
30 ibid., p. 78
31 Walter Benjamin. Ursprung des deutschen Trauerspiels. In: Schriften. Vol. I. Frankfurt am Main: Suhrkamp 1955, p. 290
32 ibid., p. 300
33 ibid., p. 301
34 ibid., p. 310
35 Praz, op. cit., p. 144
36 Heinrich Heine points out the allegorical character of the portrayal. He describes Delacroix's painting in his review of the Salon of 1831: "It represents a group of the people during the Revolution of July, from the centre of which – almost like an allegorical figure – there rises boldly a young woman with a red Phrygian cap on her

head, a gun in her hand, and in the other a tricolour flag. She strides over corpses calling men to fight – naked to the hips, a beautiful impetuous body, the face a bold profile, an air of insolent suffering in the feature – altogether a strange blending of Phryne, *poissarde*, and goddess of liberty." Originally published in German in the periodical "Morgenblatt" in Augsburg in Sept./Oct. 1831, this present extract is excerpted in the 1893 translation by Charles Godfrey Leland, in: Charles Harrison and Paul Wood (eds.). Art in Theory 1815–1900. An Anthology of Changing Ideas. Oxford: Blackwell 1998, p. 82

37 Praz, op. cit., p. 204
38 The Oxford Book of English Verse 1250–1918. New Edition. Ed. by Sir Arthur Quiller-Couch. Oxford: Oxford University Press, undated, pp. 757 f.
39 Praz, op. cit., pp. 191 f.
40 Matthew Gregory Lewis: The Monk. Cited by Praz, p. 192
41 Praz, op. cit., p. 195
42 Gustave Flaubert: Salammbô. Paris: Gallimard 1970, pp. 102 f. "Des chevilles aux hanches, elle était prises dans un réseau de mailles étroites imitant les écailles d'un poisson et qui luisait comme de la nacre: une zone toute bleue serrant sa taille laissait voir ses deux seins, par deux échancrures en forme de croissant. Des pendeloques d'escarboucles en cachaient les pointes. Elle avait une coiffure faite avec les plumes de paon étoilées de pierreries; un large manteau, blanc comme de la neige, retombait derrière elle, et les coudes au corps, les genoux serrés, avec des cercles de diamants au haut des bras, elle restait toute droite, dans une attitude hiératique."
43 Victor Klemperer. Preface to the German edition of Eugène Sue's "Mystères de Paris." In: Eugène Sue: Die Geheimnisse von Paris. Berlin: Karl Voegels, undated, p. 8
44 Praz, op. cit., p. 197. Praz quotes in French: "Cette grande créole à la fois svelte et charnue, vigoureuse et souple comme une panthère, était le type incarné de la sensualité brûlante qui ne s'allume qu'aux feux des tropiques. Tout le monde a entendue parler de ces filles de couleur pour ainsi dire mortelles (...), de ces vampires enchanteurs (...). Au lieu de se jeter violemment sur sa proie, et de ne songer, comme ses pareilles, qu'a anéantir au plus tôt une vie et fortune de plus, Cécily, attachant sur ses victimes son regard magnétique, commençait par les attirer peu à peu dans le tourbillon embrasé qui semblait émaner d'elle (...)."
45 Sadoul, op. cit. (see 20), p. 73
46 Patalas, op. cit. (see 21), pp. 50 f.
47 Based on the outline provided by Lottie Da and Jan Alexander, in: Bad Girls of the Silver Screen. London, Sydney, Wellington: Pandora 1990, pp. 17 ff.
48 ibid., p. 17
49 See Patalas, op. cit., p. 33
50 Da, Alexander, op. cit., p. 20
51 ibid., p. 23
52 ibid., p. 23
53 ibid., p. 32
54 Ursula Peters: Stilgeschichte der Fotografie in Deutschland 1839–1900. Cologne: DuMont 1979, p. 248
55 ibid., p. 249
56 Bruce Bernard: Foto-Entdeckungen 1840–1940. Cologne: DuMont 1981, plate 26
57 Praz, op. cit., p. 464n
58 Cited by Praz, op. cit., p. 378
59 Praz, op. cit., p. 143
60 Friedrich v. Zglinicki: Der Weg des Films – Die Geschichte der Kinematographie und ihrer Vorläufer. Berlin: Rembrandt 1956, p. 70
61 Gus Macdonald: Camera: Victorian Eyewitness. A History of Photography: 1826–1913. New York: Viking Press 1980, p. 51
62 Cited by Praz, op. cit., pp. 239 f.
63 ibid., p. 241
64 ibid., p. 258
65 Walter Pater: Studies in the History of the Renaissance. London: Macmillan 1873. Cited by Praz, op. cit., pp. 243 f.
66 Praz, op. cit., p. 382
67 ibid., p. 385
68 Johann Wolfgang Goethe: Sämtliche Gedichte. Erster Teil. dtv-Gesamtausgabe. Vol. 1. Munich 1961, p. 136. Goethe wrote this ballad in 1797.
69 Praz, op. cit., p. 76
70 ibid., pp. 77 and 206
71 Dietrich Kuhlbrodt: Dida Ibsens Geschichte. In: Richard Oswald – Regisseur und Produzent. Ed. by Hans-Michael Bock, Wolfgang Jacobsen, Jörg Schöning. Munich: edition text + kritik 1990, pp. 19 f.
72 Cited by Praz, op. cit., pp. 323 f., in the original French: "Résistant au désir de la femme au lieu de le provoquer, Nebo inversait les rôles et prévoyait que la jeune fille, en sa qualité d'androgyne, oserait comme un homme, puisqu'il se dérobait comme une femme. Ce phénomène fut aidé par la mise de Nebo, mise féminine qui dotait de mâleté le désir de la princesse. (...) Il se faisait faire la cour et désirer comme une coquette et son but, cependant, était de retarder la sexualisation."
73 Kunstforum International, Vol. 22, 4/77. 150 Jahre Fotografie III. Mainz 1977, pp. 78–86
74 Cited by Patalas, op. cit. (see 21), p. 61. Quoted in part by Ephraim Katz: The Film Encyclopedia. New York: Harper Perennial, 2nd Edition, 1994, p. 1401
75 Liz-Anne Bawden (ed.): rororo Filmlexikon. Vol. 6. Reinbek bei Hamburg 1986, p. 1427
76 Patalas, op. cit., p. 60
77 Musil, op. cit. (see 7), p. 442
78 Praz, op. cit., p. 155
79 Cited by Praz, op. cit., pp. 212 f.
80 Michel Foucault: Nachwort. In: Gustave Flaubert, Die Versuchung des heiligen Antonius. Frankfurt am Main: Insel 1966, p. 217
81 Foucault, op. cit., p. 221
82 Sainte-Beuve's novel "Volupté," published in 1834, is cited in French by Praz, op. cit., p. 191: "(...) celle qui ne se peint ni dans l'expression idéale du visage, ni dans le miroir des yeux, ni dans les délicatesses du souris, ni dans le voile nuancé des paupières; le visage humain n'est rien, presque rien, dans cette beauté; l'oeil et la voix, qui, en se mariant avec douceur, sont si voisines de l'âme, ne font point parti de ce qu'on désire (...) oh! J'ai compris cette beauté là. J'appris aussi comme cette beauté n'est pas la vraie; qu'elle est contraire à l'esprit même; qu'elle tue, qu'elle écrase, mais qu'elle n'attache pas."

83 Praz, op. cit., p. 267
84 Joris-Karl Huysmans: Against Nature. (Tr. by Robert Baldrick). Harmondsworth: Penguin 1959, p. 65. The French original, "A Rebours," published in 1884, is cited by Praz, op. cit., p. 293: "Elle devenait, en quelque sorte, la déité symbolique de l'indestructible Luxure, déesse de l'immortelle Hystérie, la Beauté maudite, élue entre toutes par la catalepsie qui lui raidit les chairs et lui durcit les muscles; la Bête monstrueuse, indifférente, irresponsable, insensible, empoisonnant, de même que l'Hélène antique, tout ce qui l'approche, tout ce qui la voit, tout ce qu'elle touche (...). Le peintre semblait d'ailleurs avoir voulu affirmer sa volonté de rester hors des siècles, de ne point préciser d'origine, de pays, d'époque, en mettant sa Salomé au milieu de cet extraordinaire palais, d'un style confus et grandiose, en la vêtant de somptueuse et chimériques robes, en la mitrant d'un incertain diadème en forme de tour phénicienne tel qu'en porte la Salammbô, en lui plaçant enfin dans la main le sceptre d'Isis, la fleur sacrée de l'Égypte et de l'Inde, le grand lotus."
85 Cited by Praz, op. cit., p. 369, in the original French: "Rops est vraiment éloquent, en peignant la cruauté d'aspect de la femme contemporaine, son regard d'acier, et son mauvais vouloir contre l'homme, non caché, non dissimulé, mais montré ostensiblement sur toute sa personne."
86 Benjamin: Das Passagen-Werk, op. cit. (see 3), p. 130
87 ibid., p. 130
88 ibid., p. 111
89 Cited by Praz, op. cit., p. 120
90 Cited by Praz, op. cit., p. 124. Praz quotes in French: "Quand l'opérateur en eut fini avec le fer il employa le feu; il brûla impitoyablement, regardant par intervalle son ouvrage avec le complaisance d'un jeune peintre qui achève un paysage."
91 Thomas De Quincey: On Murder Considered as one of the Fine Arts. First published in 1827 in the February issue of "Blackwood's Magazine." Excerpted in: The Faber Book of Murder. Ed. by Simon Rae. London: Faber and Faber 1994, p. 379
92 Benjamin, op. cit., p. 118
93 ibid., p. 130
94 Charles Baudelaire: The Painter of Modern Life. Excerpted in Harrison & Wood, op. cit. (see 36), p. 502. The original text of 1859, first published in 1863 under the title "Le Peintre de la vie moderne," is cited in French by Praz, op. cit., p. 146: "Passez en revue, analysez tout ce qui est naturel, vous ne trouverez rien que d'affreux. Tout ce qui est beau et noble est le résultat de la raison et du calcul."
95 Musil, op. cit., p. 573
96 ibid., pp. 573 f.
97 Praz, op. cit., p. 208. Praz quotes in French: "Dédain, ironie, cruauté, se lisaient sur ce visage, d'une incroyable beauté cependant. En vérité, plus on regardait cette admirable statue et plus on éprouvait le sentiment pénible qu'une si merveilleuse beauté pût s'allier à l'absence de toute sensibilité."
98 ibid., p. 221
99 Cited by Praz, op. cit., p. 310
100 Da, Alexander, op. cit., p. 34

The Index is the Umbilical Cord
On Photo Doubles and Digital Chimeras

by Katharina Sykora

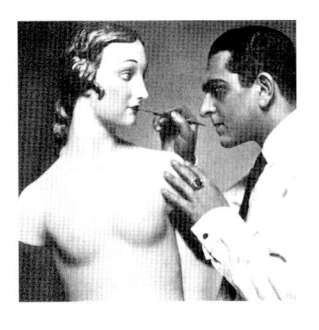

Karl Schenker: Schenker bei der Arbeit (Schenker at Work), 1925

The enduring fascination of artificial humans throughout the centuries, in all their manifestations in every field of life and art, is fuelled by two diametrically opposed factors. On the one hand, such figures demonstrate man's own power and ability to transcend mortality by creating a being "in his own image." On the other hand, even in this day and age, it still entails associations of magic, and a sense of trepidation at the possibility of life being breathed into the artificial figures, granting them independence. Oscillating between inanimate object and human being, the anthropomorphic creature bears within it the potential of emancipation from its creators. What we see with our own eyes is the terrifying prospect of a revolt of inanimate things in human form: a natural perception of the unnatural. These artificial creatures in human guise are ever capable of deceiving us; inhabiting the zone between nature and artifact, they constantly thwart our attempts to remain objective.

The medium of photography, too, possesses some of the qualities of the *doppelgänger*. These are the qualities that inform its relationship to pre-photographic reality and its potential for infinite technical reproducibility. The direct physical relationship between light-reflecting objects and their "take" in the chemical surface of the film makes photography analogous to the world of material objects beyond the picture. The index is the umbilical cord that binds the photograph to a spatially and temporally determinate reality. This binding link is forged at the very moment of "taking" a photograph. Yet in that same instant, it is severed again, and remains a mere trace on the photograph. Wrenched out of the ceaseless flow of time and developing reality, the photograph transforms itself from the Siamese twin of reality-and-image into a double separated from its counterpart by dint of its posteriority, thereby inaugurating its own history of perception. Nevertheless, it is photography's capacity as index that has dogged our notion of reality for more than 150 years.

The belief that the photographic image is "no longer a sign, but the thing itself"[1] has been used time and time again to gloss over the fundamental dichotomy between reality and photographic image. This initially took the form of asserting the mimetic correlation between the photographic (im)print and its referents. Although the similarity between reality and the photographic image proved untenable, it nevertheless became ensconced, in an act of symbolic enhancement, as a fundamental characteristic of photography. Ever since, index and mimesis have remained in the service of a discourse that hails photographic seeing as the blueprint for a realistic world view. For the past 150 years, it has informed the optical unconscious of our perception of reality in terms of photography. Not only is the photograph regarded as the double of the reality that goes before it, but it also generates doubles of its own. The negative, that shadow of reality that seems to cling to it like a specter, can produce an endless number of the same positives. Yet rather than canceling out the uniqueness of the recorded moment, they confirm it instead with each new print. If the negative projects reality as the original, then it is the photographic reproductions that make the negative the secondary original. The merry-go-round of original and duplicate begins here, and with it emerges the niggling doubt about which came first. Ever since, there has been no end to the debate as to whether it was photography that created the conditions for perceiving reality in the sense of an authentic model in the first place.

Certain shared structural aspects situate the photograph and the android within a highly complex relationship to one another. After all, the drive to create artificial man has a historical genesis comparable to that of photography. Initially, it involved the creation of an (im)print (effigy) and a three-dimensional reproduction of the human body, but the more perfect it became – for example, as an anthropomorphic automaton – the further it distanced itself from the human body, so that it was no longer a representation or effigy but a bewilderingly independent counterpart. Photographed androids are, theoretically, capable of overlapping both these systems without blurring the edges. The capacity of the photograph to "quicken," in the sense of constantly reviving a past moment, together with its capacity to "deaden," in the sense of suspending a segment of time-in-motion, is perplexingly mirrored in the *trompe l'œil* figure of the apparently undead androids. Photographs of artificial beings thus multiply the respective "doubling" qualities of medium and subject, while reflecting them reciprocally.

There are many photographs that play with the question of "puppet or person?" in the avant-garde and journalistic photography of the first half of the 20th century, bearing witness to a keen early interest in this topic. Karl Schenker's series of photographs "Models or wax figures"[2] initially leaves us in some doubt as to the character of the figure portrayed. The nondescript spatial setting and the handling of light leave us uncertain as to whether this is a doll or a living model. Here, photography becomes a virtuoso "life-giving" machine that brings the doll alive by lending its eyes a brilliant sheen and its skin a semblance of vitality. Given that the demiurgic gesture of creative power is absorbed by the transparent medium in a way that cancels out the authorial gesture of the photographer, narrative reaffirmation of the creator is required at the end of the story. This involves drawing the female figure out of the intended misunderstanding of a real-life figure of reference and leading it back into the realms of the artificial figure produced by the hand of the artist and photographer. This redeeming resolution goes hand in hand with the destruction of the previous, self-generated, illusionist presence of the female protagonist. As such, it follows the conventional pattern of "romantic agony" that represents man and artist as producer and destroyer of his ideal female creature.

The destruction of photographic illusion, however, still retains a trace of the uncanny when the artist and his creature face one another in the same medium, for it is then that the equivocal status of the photographed female double begins to rub off on its male counterpart. This is caused by the shared space of the photograph and its double capacity to "quicken" and to "deaden" everything "taken" by it. Erwin Blumenfeld used this photographic capacity to create a complex, self-referential, pictorial configuration in his self-portrait of 1937, in which he is seen demonstratively placing his hand on the shoulder of his partner, as though drawing her towards him. He is leaning his head towards her as though he were about to kiss her. The spectator's attention is drawn completely towards the tension of the "moment" that binds the couple. The almost hypnotic merging of their gaze, however, is interrupted by a fine "cut," or rift, between the lovers. Blumenfeld stages this fine separation with a hint of irony, running it right between the tips of their noses. The tiny gap between them defines the brief lull in which profound emotions are suspended for a moment and frozen in a formula of pathos. Passion seems arrested in a gesture of self-awareness. In this respect, what we find here is a referential indicator of photography itself, for Blumenfeld clearly addressed the cut as a media interruption that sabotages the notion of the ideal couple and tips the image into the realms of the uncanny. At the point where the man tenderly places his hand on the shoulder of his lover, the spectator is immediately confronted with abyss and insight at one and the same time. A hard edge marks the sectional cut through the female body and opens up a cavernous black void instead of compact corporeality. The lover turns out to be one of those old-fashioned wax figures whose sophisticated facial expression has enchanted so many artists. Yet Blumenfeld is not content with this simple gesture of revelation that leaves us, after the brief shock of temporary illusion, with the certain knowledge that the natural male creator and his artificial female model dwell in different worlds. He also applies the photographic cut to himself. He has the hand of the creator jut into the picture as though it did not belong to him. Moreover, he separates his face sharply from his body on the right hand edge of the photograph so that his face becomes the mask, and the photographic detail its cosmetic transformation.

This "cut" that severs the perfect android body and the mimetically illusionist photograph including its creator was eventually to become a key theme of the classical avant-garde in photographic studies of the artificial body. These are optimistically projected as hybrid beings that increasingly break away from their anthropomorphic form to become arsenals of new physical compositions. Hans Bellmer's first "Doll" photographs of 1933 bear witness to this fascination with breaking down the structures of the female body limb by limb and its arbitrary recomposition. In both cases, he creates an uncanny vitality through the authenticating authority of the photograph. The second "Doll," which was to become the sole model of his photographic cosmos from 1935 onwards, introduces a horizontal dimension of physical metamorphosis which can be described in arithmetic terms as the doubling, multiplication, and permutation of individual body parts, but which also plays with the organic appearances of distorted protrusions and self-generating body parts. This was linked by Bellmer himself, as it was by many others, to the linguistic forms of the anagram and the palindrome.[3] A central ball-bearing joint was used to permit kaleidoscopic attachment of various body parts. By duplicating doll components that stand in for each other erotically in a structure of inversion and substitution, Bellmer pursued a semantic emancipation, dislocation, and recoding of certain body parts, with the aim of creating a pan-erotic cosmos in which not only female genital forms and their phallic substitutes of leg, arm, and shoe play a role. Instead, all body forms, but also objects such as spheres, tires, fabrics, and even photography itself were to become triggers of erotic fantasy. The fact that the ambivalent effect of his "Doll" was further heightened by the medium of photography is something that Bellmer himself addressed. He links the oscillation between a promise of empowerment and denial, already inherent in the figure of the doll itself, with the magic potential of photography: "Its possession meant available pleasure and danger," he wrote. "It was not far from the pleasures of imaging to be found in books of magic, but also in the camera."[4]

Unlike Bellmer, Pierre Molinier does not take the artificial female body as the point of departure for rolling back media boundaries in a way addressed primarily at a spectator who is assumed to be male. The artist includes himself as part of a mix of dolls' limbs and "real" body parts, thus canceling out not only the binarity of real and false, live and dead, but also that of male and female. In his photographs, Molinier uses a dense layering technique in pursuit of his complex blend of "real" body and its artificial double. Even in the pre-photographic phase of staging the photo, Molinier furnishes his body with numerous addenda. After removing his body hair, he applies makeup and covers his body with a second skin of tricot and stockings, and his face with close fitting leather masks, or full masks of paper to which he applies makeup, as well. He also practices striking poses that make his male member disappear, enhances his breasts by using corsets, or attaches a dildo to his heel. What happens here is an exploration of erotically cathected signs comparable to those in Bellmer's second "Doll." The gender signs leave us in the dark as to their physical or objective character, playing out their charades on the body of the artist himself, like figures on a chessboard. Once this masked body enters the photographic system, a further layering ad infinitum begins. Here, in the tradition of photomontage, Molinier includes photographed doll parts and his photographed body parts to create anthropomorphic figurations. He then photographs the montaged bodies and retouches the points of overlap where the physical and artificial body parts meet. "La Poupée" leaves us wondering whether the head with the facial traits of Molinier is a retouched photograph of a mask with makeup, or a montaged doll's head with the join between neck and upper body disguised by the chain drawn on it. The photographic surface placed yet like another skin over the first skin, constituted by the masked performance, and the second skin, constituted by the sketched-over montage, brings the chimerical figure together on a third media foil. Depending on the density of overlap between the photographed layers, certain body parts seem to protrude sculpturally in the final print, while

Erwin Blumenfeld: Selbstportrait mit Mannequin (Self-portrait with Mannequin), 1937

Hans Bellmer: La Poupée, 1938

Hans Bellmer: La Poupée, 1935

Hans Bellmer: La Poupée, 1938

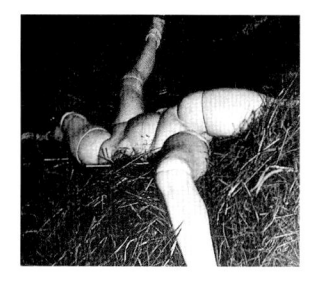

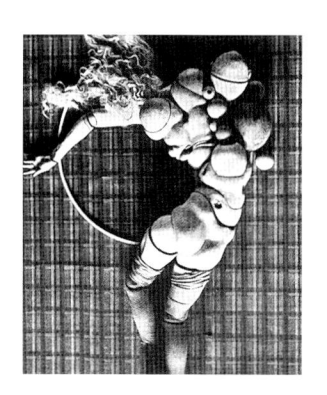

The Index is the Umbilical Cord

Pierre Molinier: Moignons, 1968

Pierre Molinier: La Poupée, 1965

Pierre Molinier: L'Œuvre,
le paintre et son fétiche, 1963

99

Karl Schenker: Mannequins oder Wachspuppen? (Mannequins or Wax Dolls?), 1925

others fade into the soft background in varying degrees of blur. Molinier also placed great importance on the use of soft prints and warm-toned paper. The photograph is thus not only optically the outermost skin constituted by the artificial figure, but actually becomes immediately tangible as its distinctly palpable realization.

Molinier, too, has applied forms of reversal, doubling, and multiplication to this layering of chimerical bodies, which is both deep and eruptive, albeit without revealing any inherent natural, biological, or gendered character beyond the ultimate shell of the medium in which it is presented. In the multi-part photograph "Moignons," artificial leg stumps are juxtaposed with artificial buttocks, rising in a phallic echo of the horns on the doll's head. Molinier's spread legs embrace the face of the doll standing on its head as though this were the birth of a female android. The whole thing finally develops like a blossom from a chalice formed by a pair of arms and two thighs. The aureole of light fixes the complex configuration like a medallion. It appears to place it in a potential rotation that continues the kaleidoscope of the limbs. The body of Molinier as a primary reference is lost among these multiple body ornaments and in the deep layering of the photos. Amid the plethora of dolls' limbs and human limbs, it becomes just one component among many others.

In his photographs, Pierre Molinier anticipates something that digital photography has made a central theme of its body configurations *mutatis mutandis*. Though he takes as his starting point the modularly constructed body, he increasingly breaks away from the "enlightened" claim of modernism that so demonstratively made the composite body its icon, in order to protest against the normative aesthetic of the "whole" body beautiful. Molinier's retouched montages negate both the ideal body of classical antiquity and the composite body of the classical avantgarde. By increasingly wearing away at the body's breaking points, the montages lead us into a surreal chimerical logic of the body.

Vilém Flusser has outlined the difference between photographed and digital bodies as follows: "'Chimaera' is an ancient word meaning composite fabulous beast: a goat with a lion's head and a tail of serpents. One might thus be led to believe that the mythical Ancients knew how to calculate and compute, but one would be mistaken. The mythical chimaera was a collage, a patchwork. If Bellerophon, who fought the Chimaera heroically, had kicked it instead of fighting it, its head would have rolled to one side and its tail to another. This is quite different from the newly emerging 'true' chimaeras. (...) The new 'true' chimaeras are consistent, autonomous phenomena. That is the way with myths; as soon as they become real, they look different from what was expected of them."[5]

And so the composite photographic bodies in Cindy Sherman's "Sex Pictures" are entirely in the tradition of Bellmer's "Doll" photos in the sense that they are put together. On the other hand, their demonstratively presented breaks between the various components neither prompt us to find out whether they are "real" or "unreal," nor do they trigger obsessive fantasies. Their artificiality is perfectly obvious. What is confusing is merely that they appear to be saturated with references to a pre-photographic and pictorial reality that cannot be unequivocally fixed. For example, the sexual prostheses of "Untitled No 263" from 1992 vaguely suggest the artificial body arsenals of a porn shop or Bellmer's anagrammatic "Doll" photographs. On the one hand, they show the fragmentary character of the brightly lit leg stumps, while at the same time concealing the join between male and female lower body with an oversized bow. Here, Sherman presents that ancient chimera – the hermaphrodite ideal of undivided gender – as a grotesque gift-wrapped package of wishful thinking that barely conceals what a motley jumble it is. Sherman uses the medium of photography in a similar way. She allows pre-photographic reality to appear only in the form of a quotation and shows it as a reality that has always been shaped by the medium itself. Photography's gesture of authentication – the claim that what the photograph shows is what was really there – no longer certifies the bodies as authentic and natural originals, but as inhabitants of an artificial world shaped by the world of material objects and photography in equal measure. Analogous thinking and seeing appear to have become obsolete where reality and image derive from the same artificial space and there is no gap left to bridge. In this respect, Sherman has already visualized fundamental elements of digital pictorial worlds in the photographic medium.

Finally, digitalized images are also technically beyond the pale of binary coordinates of reality. The body images they create are thus no longer indexically linked to anthropomorphic models. Nevertheless, they are oriented towards them, as is clear in the innumerable digitalizations of photographed bodies. Their computer-aided manipulation can only be seen where they take "old" models of the body and the media as the point of departure for their transformations. The photographic element, with its symbolic content of direct reference to reality, also plays an important role in digital worlds, albeit as a mere quotation that cannot be recognized as such on the digital surface. We tend to read a digital anthropomorphic body image as a photographically "real" image that has existed in a certain place at a certain time. When the heads of shop dummies are coupled with female nudes and the bodies attired in a naturalistic epidermis, as they are in Inez van Lambsweerde's "Thank you Thighmaster" series from 1993, their amalgamation on one and the same digital surface no longer reveals them as *composita mixta*. Lambsweerde, however, succumbs to the seductive capacity of digital images to create "invisible chimeras" in the sense of ideal artificial bodies that deny their character as artifacts. By lending the female body the epidermis of the doll at the "wrong places" and sealing the genitals or adding "unnaturally" hyper-realistic veins and redness to hands and feet, she confuses our pre-photographic visual experience while appealing to it at the same time. The contorsions in the body of "Sasja 90-60-90" (1992), her smooth and cemented skin, as it were, are immediately recognizable as artificial to any eye practiced in the observation of human anatomy. Yet the picture itself offers no indication of any seam that might make the body recognizable as composite. Ironically enough, the artificial digital bodies thus re-establish the power of a "real" body – as opposed to their own artificiality – as their empirically founded corrective. The fact that this pre-photographic or photographic body is by no means "entirely other" or even "natural" cannot be circumvented.

The newly emergent difference between the photographic image and the digital image, however, sets it up as a critical instance that allows us to doubt the digital image.[6] After all, the greatest challenge is posed by images that show no visible trace of unauthorized intervention, are apparently free of inner contradiction, and yet contradict our previous knowledge and experience.[7]

Because they embody this prior knowledge, the photo doubles, those artificial bodies of the photographic age, become specters of the children they have spawned: the digital chimeras. They have now taken on the role of the "digital unconscious" and safeguard the computed body from becoming entirely free of contradiction.

Footnotes

1 Roland Barthes: Camera Lucida. (Tr. by Richard Howard). London: Vintage Books 1993, p. 45
2 Fotogeschichte von Karl Schenker, Texte von "M.O." und "Johanna Thal". In: Die Dame, No. 23, 1925, pp. 6–9
3 See Hans Bellmer: L'Anatomie de l'Image. Paris: Le Terrain Vague 1957, and Anagramme. In: Unica Zürn: Hexentexte. Berlin (publisher unknown) 1954
4 Hans Bellmer: Die Puppe. Berlin: Gerhardt 1962, p. 19
5 Vilém Flusser: Chimaera. In: European Photography 1988, cited in: Hubertus von Amelunxen, Anthony Aziz (eds.). Photography after Photography. Memory and Representation in the Digital Age. Munich: G+B Arts 1996, pp. 151–152
6 Florian Rötzer looks at the demise of the photographic from a different angle when he claims that "photography ends where interaction and real time begin, where the body and as many senses as possible are drawn into an artificial virtual environment (...) with the complete elimination of the distance between it and the observer." Cited in F.R.: Re: Photography. In: Photography after Photography, op. cit., p. 18. In my view, Rötzer fails to recognize the opportunity and the practice of many artists in taking the end of the photographic as a relaxation of the symbolic connection between image and model in the sense of regaining territory that can be regarded as fertile soil for a critical empirical view of media reality.
7 William J. Mitchell: The Reconfigured Eye. Visual Truth in the Post-Photographic Era. Cambridge/Mass.: MIT Press 1992, p. 87

Ideal Idols

New Stars in Global Networks

by Ulrich Gutmair

Don't look at the idoru's face. She is not flesh; she is information. She is the tip of an iceberg, no, an Antarctica, of information. (William Gibson in "Idoru," 1996)

At the threshold of the new millennium, virtual personalities are redefining stardom. In place of figures with whom the masses identify, we find iconographies of individual consumption. In 1996, science fiction writer William Gibson published his novel "Idoru,"[1] in which the phenomenon of the pop star is addressed within the context of a computer-generated economy. With the precision so typical of his approach, Gibson designs Idoru's world as the logical extension of a society in which the Internet has become the accepted means of communication and an important economic factor.

In "Idoru," the global digital network serves as marketplace, mass medium, and instrument of personal communication. The personality of his protagonist Rei Toei consists of a patchwork of artificial memories that draw on the wishes and needs of her fans, mined from the Internet. Whereas Rei Toei's existence as artificial intelligence is based on a constantly growing databank, her visual representation as a marketing icon can be found on the Internet or in videos. In the form of a holograph, her media presence extends into real space.

The story revolves around the love affair between the "real" pop star Rez and the "virtual" singer Rei Toei. As Gibson tells it, the fact that Rez falls in love with Rei Toei does not suggest a near future in which virtual personalities will have a human side, but points instead towards the inherent virtuality of human stars. In this respect, Gibson follows an interpretation of the star system that "Situationist" Guy Debord posited as fundamental to the "Society of the Spectacle": "The agent of the spectacle placed on stage as a star is the opposite of the individual, the enemy of the individual in himself as well as in others. Passing into the spectacle as a model for identification, the agent renounces all autonomous qualities in order to identify himself with the general law of obedience to the course of things."[2] Debord cites by way of example the great rhetorician John F. Kennedy, whose persona to all intents and purposes survived him when his speechwriter Theodore Sorensen continued to work for his successor.

If stars have to be artificial and supra-individual personalities by definition, the question arises as to what distinguishes a "traditional" star from a "virtual" star. One explanation might be that the new stars are post-Fordian stars. They are no longer dependent on the traditional mechanisms of the culture industry that once provided the means of identification for a culture based on the industrial mass production of goods. The existence of stars, as we have known them until recently, was based on the distribution channels of the film and music industries – to wit, film, video, records, CDs, and audiovisual channels. The new stars, on the other hand, are children of the new media who are no longer dependent on hierarchical structures of broadcasting and receiving that function from top to bottom, but rather organize themselves like networks from the bottom up.

Thus, Rei Toei can be regarded first of all as a metaphor for the already virtual character of the star, and secondly as an "embodiment" of digital information, as an anthropomorphic figure made up of interactively obtained data. As such, she becomes a sign of herself, a symbol of the new digital information and communications technologies. Thirdly, Rei Toei is situated at the interface between the highly personal individual needs and wishes of her fans and an industry that seeks to satisfy these needs equally individually. In short, Rei Toei is the model of a new and interactive form of "personalized" marketing.

These functions also appear to be fulfilled by those "virtual stars" that have come to populate the media in recent years. Alongside new digital formats, new forms of stars and virtual celebrities are emerging which, like Rei Toei in the novel, no longer need human beings as "carriers." They are designed as protagonists in films, television shows, and video games, and as pop stars, and can be visited "at home" – at their own home pages. The Elite model agency recently announced that in the future, apart from Cindy Crawford and Linda Evangelista, it would also be able to provide virtual models.[3]

Kyoko Date: the "Ideal Idol"

While Gibson was writing his novel, the Japanese agency Hori Productions was already working on a completely new product that was launched with a young audience of fans in mind just a few months after the publication of "Idoru." Kyoko Date's persona corresponds to that of an average Japanese teenage girl. Kyoko is evidently the result of intensive empirical studies of the relevant target groups, and her biography the perfect blend of the wishes, expectations, and life-forms of her fans. She is what Debord called the "consumption celebrity": "The consumption celebrity superficially represents different types of personality and shows each of these types having equal access to the totality of consumption and finding similar happiness there."[4]

In fact, Kyoko's personality is almost entirely defined by her consumer behavior. Thus, she mirrors a world in which "lifestyle" is a question of choosing the "right" product. As her biography[5] indicates, Kyoko is slightly myopic. She likes eating sweets, playing computer games on her Mac, and surfs the Internet with Microsoft Windows. Her favorite actors are Christian Slater and Kyozo Nagazuka. She loves comics, likes drawing, and has a middle-class father who tinkers with his Harley Davidson when he gets home from work.

No fewer than ten animation specialists spent six months teaching Kyoko Date to smile. In her video clips she moves the 40,000 polygons of her body in Madonna-style

Kyoko Date

dance-steps through New York and Tokyo, and in Japan her single "Love Communication" has sold 50,000 copies. She is the virtual and thus most efficient variation on an *aidoru kashu* – a singer idol, as the many young female pop stars are known in Japan. Behind the digital interface of the star there is a dancer whose movements can be converted into data by motion capture process, a singer who records Kyoko's singles, a speaker who moderates Kyoko's radio show, a number of people who run Kyoko's chats on her own home page, and, above all, the specialists at her talent agency, Hori Productions.

Her traits and the way she works thus indicate first and foremost that the traditional stars of the entertainment industry are already virtual, confirming once again Marshall McLuhan's dictum that a new medium invariably incorporates an old medium. Kyoko Date has achieved enormous popularity as the first totally digital personality. She has given a face to the discourse of revolutionary new possibilities of digital production in old media.

The Star as Interactive Application

Whereas Kyoko Date embodies the idea of the star in its current "idealized" form of a star whose role model character is defined in consumer terms, Lara Croft possesses an entirely new characteristic generated by her function. She is the heroine of the internationally hugely successful computer game "Tomb Raider" – and is thus interactive. In Lara Croft, a figure from a game was promoted like a pop star for the first time: to promote the introduction of the adventure game, the building site billboards of European inner cities were adorned with her image.

There is more to it than this, however. There is an entirely new dimension involved in this cross between adventure game, shootout, and animated cartoon that has undoubtedly fueled the Lara Croft mania. The player is cast in the role of the young archeologist and can move the figure remarkably freely through more or less three-dimensional settings. Lara Croft is equipped with a sophisticated repertoire of movements between Kung Fu kick, diving and free-climbing, calling for considerable joystick skill on the part of the player.

Such predominantly asexual representations (for fear of censorship) of "ideal" women, however, have awakened quite different desires among her adolescent male fans. Kids with access to the appropriate software have been putting their own Lara Croft images on the net, enhancing screen shots from the game by adding natural-looking breasts and even, on occasion, bright pink genital labia. In keeping with the doctrine of integrated media, copy-and-paste techniques have permitted a marriage of genres: lavatory graffiti meets the pin-up.

In such figures as Lara Croft, the inaccessibility of the old-style stars, an inevitable result of traditional media, has been replaced by an interactive intimacy with the new-style stars. In place of mere identification a form of interactivity has emerged that actually grants users an active role. To be one with Lara Croft means to achieve a mastery of her functions with the help of a mouse or joystick.

Lara Croft

Avatars: Moderators of Consumer Desire

The virtual entity E-CYAS[6] owes its existence to the fact that marketing has become difficult in a society whose consumer habits are constantly diversifying and whose entertainment worlds are becoming increasingly blurred. E-CYAS is a product of the German I-D group of companies, one of Europe's most successful multimedia agencies, which has made a name for itself through, among other things, the Internet presence of major companies. E-CYAS recently released their first CD, with a title that addresses the question of virtuality: "Are you real?"

E-CYAS's image is actually very "real." It looks as though someone had digitalized an average twenty-something. In fact, it is precisely this impression that the "Endo-Cybernetic Artificial Star" is meant to convey. The E-CYAS has been equipped with a "biography" that compresses the notion of the target group's identification with the star into a single image: "23 students were selected according to their various talents and attitudes. Collectively, they represent the knowledge, the culture, the lifestyles and the diversity of an entire generation (…). Their brains and the experience and emotions stored in them were read by a neuronal scanner and logged into a super-computer in order to unite the various talents in a kind of mega-personality. (…) Then one day the unthinkable happened: the figure on the screen started to communicate."[7]

Thus the myth of the Golem merges with the fiction of artificial intelligence. Unlike Kyoko Date, however, E-CYAS's potential status as a hypermodern pop star is merely a means to an end. It is not a question of selling records with E-CYAS, but of bringing a whole new generation of newcomers to the Internet. E-CYAS is first and foremost the advertising flagship and symbol of Cycosmos,[8] a "world of experience" on the Internet that has been provided free of charge by the I-D group.

There, visitors can put together their own so-called avatar out of various figures, items of clothing, hairstyles, and accessoires. This digital anchorman can be used to contact other users: with the aid of a databank, Cycosmos selects potentially interesting contact persons who gather in "virtual communities" according to their preferences. As I-D manager Bernd Kolb explained in an interview for the Internet magazine "telepolis,"[9] it is a question of targeting no less than the bulk of consumers. Anyone who can ensure that Internet newcomers land on their own home page first is able to accumulate virtual capital that can rapidly generate more value, and does so not only through advertising revenue. Above and beyond this function as anchorman, E-CYAS is set to take on a further role as a "human interface."

Magic tools

Even today, intelligent programs persuade users to take up certain offers based on their membership in a certain social group. The more data available on a user's behavior and his preferences, the more precisely that user can be allocated to a specific social group. A software agent can deduce from the behavior of the respective groups which information or offers he should put forward. "I can imagine that people

Ideal Idols

106

Ideal Idols

find their identity in this system like a twin asking his brother, when faced with some unknown food: 'Hey, do we like that?' It is a kind of help that we can get in forming our identity by way of smart information systems which are not search engines but companions. They give us a more coherent view of who we really are."[10]

When Guy Debord formulated his social critique of the "spectacular society," he defined another class of stars apart from the "consumption celebrities": "The decision celebrity must possess a complete stock of accepted human qualities."[11] The new stars, as agents of information, not only represent the role of the decision-maker. They actually make the decisions themselves. The question that keeps cropping up in this decision-making process is the question of our identity.

The star as mediator between the world of commodities and the consumer finally comes into his own in the form of such avatars. As reflectors of potential wishes, avatars know more about the identity shaped by consumerism than the individuals themselves. Avatars are thus "technologies of the self" that have gelled as technical instruments.[12] They are magic tools of direct communication between their own desires and the world of material objects.

It is well known that it is a short step from animism to animation. Avatars, as digital ghosts, fill the gap that arises between the user/consumer and the information jungle of new technologies that cannot be fully grasped even by the elite caste of programmers. The user faces the Internet the way pre-modern man faced the dark forest. Lightning, thunder, and deluge are replaced by system failures and stock market crashes, triggered by hyper-rapid transactions on the net, which thus becomes the quasi-natural object of a real post-modern animism. It is no coincidence that, in Sanskrit, "avatar" actually refers to a divine being that takes on human form. In this sense, the digital avatars of today are the benevolent spirits of tomorrow – interfaces to an autonomous parallel world in which new technologies and consumerism are inextricably woven into the fabric of a self-regulating system.

Footnotes

1 William Gibson: Idoru. New York: Putnam's Sons 1996. See also William Gibson on Idoru. Interview. In: Salon1999 (http://www.salon1999.com/weekly/gibson3961014.html)
2 Guy Debord: La Société du Spectacle. Paris: Buchet/Chastel 1967. (Complete text, published in Paris by éditions champ libre, 1971, cited on: http://www.multimania.com/laplage/d_spec/index.html). All quotes here are taken from the English translation by Donald Nicholson-Smith, published in Detroit by Black & Red 1970, and cited on http://www.nothingness.org/SI/debord/SOTS/sots3.html
3 See Florian Rötzer: Agentur für virtuelle Topmodels. (Agency for Top Models.) In: telepolis. Das Magazin der Netzkultur (http://www.heise.de/tp/deutsch/inhalt/te/5085/1.html); a web address for cyber models is http://www.illusion2k.com; see also Jana Galinowski: Konkurrenz für Claudia Schiffer. In: Der Tagesspiegel, Berlin, 1 August 1999
4 Debord, ibid.
5 http://www.dhw.co.jp/horipro/talent/DK96/index_e.html
6 www.e-cyas.com
7 ibid.
8 www.cycosmos.de
9 Artur P. Schmidt: E-CYAS, E_ndo-CY_bernetic A_rtificial S_tar im Internet. (On avatars and a conversation with Bernd Kolb, managing director of the I-D group.) In: telepolis. Das Magazin der Netzkultur (http://www.heise.de/tp/deutsch/inhalt/te/2367/1.html)
10 Intime Technologien. Gary Wolf im Gespräch mit Ulrich Gutmair. (Intimate Technologies. Gary Wolf in conversation with Ulrich Gutmair.) In: telepolis. Das Magazin der Netzkultur (http://www.heise.de/tp)
11 Debord, ibid.
12 Michel Foucault: Technologies of the Self. In: Luther H. Martin, Huck Gutman, Patrick H. Hutton (eds.): Technologies of the Self. A Seminar with Michel Foucault. Amherst: University of Massachusetts Press 1988, pp. 16–49

Annotated Bibliography
A Selection

by Holger Schnell

Do robots read books? The question itself is rather anachronistic, since robots, needless to say, do not read. At most, they might log in to some electronic databank to quench their thirst for information. As for us lesser mortals, the only way to knowledge is by more classic means. Libraries are full of analytical texts and literary criticism on the subject of artificial human beings, and new publications are appearing all the time. The following is intended as a selection of some of the more important books on this subject, with the emphasis on film-related publications. They are organized by subject matter, and listed in chronological order within each field.

Bibliographies and reference books

1. Bernhard J. Dotzler, Peter Gendolla, Jörgen Schäfer: MaschinenMenschen: Eine Bibliographie. Frankfurt am Main, Bern, New York, Paris: Lang 1992. (Bibliographien zur Literatur- und Mediengeschichte 1.)

This bibliography provides a chronological list of 1,778 publications in the field of literature and literary criticism. The period covered is remarkable, starting with a work dated 1420. What is more, this publication is unusual in that it includes magazine articles as well as books. However, there is not much on film-related works.

2. Thomas P. Dunn, Richard D. Erlich, Clockworks: A Multimedia Bibliography of Works Useful for the Study of Human/Machine Interface in Science Fiction. Westport, Connecticut; London: Greenwood Press 1993.

"Clockworks" is an extended and updated book version of a bibliography already published in the anthology "The Mechanical God" (see 5). It includes works of reference, anthologies, literature and literary criticism, writings on theater, film and television, as well as music. Most entries are commentated, making this publication easy to use.

3. Jeff Rovin: Aliens, Robots, and Spaceships. New York: Facts on File 1995.

Structured like a lexicon, this book provides a survey of materials, topics and fictional characters in the field of science fiction in comics, literature, radio, theater, film, television, and mythology. There is a particularly useful section listing STAR WARS and STAR TREK figures and a comprehensive index of film titles, book titles, and persons. However, since it is restricted to the field of science fiction, there is no reference to such figures as the Golem or Frankenstein.

Anthologies and monographic studies

4. Klaus Völker (ed.): Künstliche Menschen. Dichtungen und Dokumente über Golems, Homunculi, lebende Statuen und Androiden. Munich: Hanser 1971. (Paperback edition: Frankfurt am Main: Suhrkamp 1994.)

Klaus Völker provides a comprehensive anthology of fiction and non-fiction from classical antiquity to the present day. The detailed afterword gives an authoritative survey of the subject matter with a wealth of literary references. The bibliography and the chronological filmography are both useful, if somewhat dated. Neither was updated for the paperback edition.

5. Thomas P. Dunn, Richard D. Erlich (eds.): The Mechanical God: Machines in Science Fiction. Westport, Connecticut; London: Greenwood Press 1982.

This anthology includes essays on the machine and robot motifs in literature, music, and film. Particularly interesting essays are those by Donald Palumbo on sexual metaphor in science fiction films and Leonard G. Heldreth's study of mechanical war machines in literature and film. The bibliography on the machine motif in science fiction is outdated and has been superseded by the expanded book version (see 2).

6. Horst Albert Glaser, Wolfgang Kaempfer (eds.): Maschinenmenschen: Referate der Triester Tagung. Frankfurt am Main, Bern, New York: Lang 1988. (Akten internationaler Kongresse auf den Gebieten der Ästhetik und Literaturwissenschaft 6.)

Apart from essays on the history of literature and the arts, this publication includes an essay by Peter Gendolla on the mechanical man in cinema, which addresses such films as METROPOLIS, MODERN TIMES and WELT AM DRAHT.

7. Lucie Schauer (ed.): Maschinenmenschen. Katalog zur Ausstellung "Maschinenmenschen" des Neuen Berliner Kunstvereins in der Staatlichen Kunsthalle Berlin vom 17. Juni bis 23. Juli 1989. Berlin: Neuer Berliner Kunstverein 1989.

This exhibition catalogue does not contain any essays on film, but it does have a useful selected bibliography by Michael Glasmeier.

8. Rudolf Drux (ed.): Die Geschöpfe des Prometheus – Der künstliche Mensch von der Antike bis zur Gegenwart. Bielefeld: Kerber 1994.

This catalogue of the exhibition of the same name includes two essays on film. Eberhard Lämmert's essay addresses the theme of the machine-man in the theater of the 1920s, including an analysis of METROPOLIS. Inge Degenhardt analyzes the appeal of the artificial human being in film. The bibliography is slight.

9. Heidi J. Figueroa-Sarriera, Chris Hables Gray, Steven Mentor (eds.): The Cyborg Handbook. New York: Routledge 1995.

This handbook is one of the most comprehensive and indispensable anthologies on the subject and undoubtedly deserves to be called the standard work. The main focus is on the history of science, technology and the arts. Literature and film are marginal. Film-related contributions focus mainly on the actor Arnold Schwarzenegger and his role in the Terminator films.

10. Claudia Springer: Electronic Eros: Bodies and Desire in the Postindustrial Age. Austin, Texas: University of Texas Press / London: The Athlone Press 1996.

This book addresses the subject of the erotic relationship between humans and robots in fiction, film, television, and comics. Like Anne Balsamo in her book "Technologies of the Gendered Body" (see 19), Claudia Springer comes to the conclusion that the classical gender stereotypes are maintained in the portrayal of the relationship between humans and robots.

11. Richard van Dülmen (ed.): Erfindung des Menschen. Schöpfungsträume und Körperbilder 1500–2000. Vienna, Cologne, Weimar: Böhlau 1998.

This catalogue of the exhibition "Prometheus. Menschen. Bilder. Visionen" in Völklingen contains a number of essays on the history of the cult of the body beautiful, the subject of artificial beings, and cyberculture. Thomas Schlich's essay charts the development of the dream of creating an artificial human, from the Golem to the robot.

General studies on cinema

12. Janet Bergstrom, Elisabeth Lyon, Constance Penley, Lynn Spigel (eds.): Close Encounters: Film, Feminism, and Science Fiction. Minneapolis, Minnesota; Oxford: University of Minnesota Press 1991. (A Camera Obscura Book.)

This is an expanded book edition of a collection of essays published in the magazine "Camera Obscura." Raymond Bellour examines the motif of the ideal human in science, technology, art, and film, on the basis of Villiers de L'Isle-Adams' story "L'Eve future." Janet Bergstrom provides a feminist analysis of gender stereotypes in science fiction films, and Roger Dadoun looks at the motif of the robot in Metropolis – a subject that is also the focus of Enno Patalas' essay analyzing one specific scene from that film.

13. Nicholas Ruddick (ed.): State of the Fantastic: Studies in the Theory and Practise of Fantastic Literature and Film: Selected Essays from the Eleventh International Conference on the Fantastic in the Arts, 1990. Westport, Connecticut; London: Greenwood Press 1992. (Contributions to the Study of Science Fiction and Fantasy 50.)

This volume includes a number of essays on the robot and Golem motif in fantasy films. There is a particularly interesting contribution by J.P. Telotte, analyzing the revolt of the robots in such films as Westworld and Futureworld.

14. Ava Preacher Collins, Jim Collins, Hilary Radner (eds.): Film Theory Goes to the Movies. New York, London: Routledge 1993. (AFI Film Readers.)

The cyborg motif in literature and film is addressed in an essay by Forest Pyle, in which the author interprets the blurring of boundaries between organic and technical existence as the expression of a crisis of human self-understanding. This is particularly evident in Ridley Scott's Blade Runner and in the Terminator films.

15. Per Schelde: Androids, Humanoids, and other Science Fiction Monsters: Science and Soul in Science Fiction Films. New York: New York University Press 1993.

In the field of literary studies there is a long-standing debate as to whether the construction of robots and artificial beings is rooted in a primarily male desire to procreate, and create new life, without the involvement of women. Schelde seeks evidence for this theory in the science fiction film as well.

16. Thomas S. Frentz, Janice Hocker Rushing: Projecting the Shadow: The Cyborg Hero in American Film. Chicago, London: The University of Chicago Press 1995. (New Practices of Inquiry.)

This fascinating study takes as its starting point the archetypal myth of a young hero's rite of passage in which the struggle against evil helps him to become an adult. The modern hero uses technical aids, including the creation of robots and other artificial creatures. Dazzled by his own success, he loses sight of his true goal and the machine turns against its creator. This motif is examined by way of examples of the science fiction film.

17. Robert Arch Latham: Consuming Youth: Technologies of Desire and American Youth Culture. Stanford University, Ph.D. 1995. (Abstract in: Dissertation Abstracts International A 56, 1996, No. 10, p. 3777A)

In the nineteen-sixties and seventies a new youth culture oriented primarily towards technology and consumption became established in the USA. Latham's dissertation analyzes two cultural offshoots of this development: the vampire motif as an embodiment of the unquenchable and infinite desire to consume, and the cyborg motif as an expression of a technological fascination that oversteps all previous boundaries.

18. J.P. Telotte: Replications: A Robotic History of the Science Fiction Film. Chicago, Illinois; Urbana-Champaign, Illinois: University of Illinois Press 1995.

Telotte regards the history of the science fiction film as an expression of the post-modern fear of a loss of human identity when faced with the possibility of creating new life forms. The motif of the artificial being has a twofold function. On the one hand it is the expression of that fear (and a warning of the dangers of technological hubris), while on the other hand it is also the beginning of a new process of finding one's self.

19. Anne Balsamo: Technologies of the Gendered Body: Reading Cyborg Women. Durham, North Carolina; London: Duke University Press 1996.

The book delivers a feminist analysis of the body image in American popular culture of the nineteen-eighties and nineties, especially in literature, film, and television. The author seeks to prove that although the technological development of robots and cyberculture breaks down the borders between humans and machines, the gender stereotypes remain relatively stable (see 10).

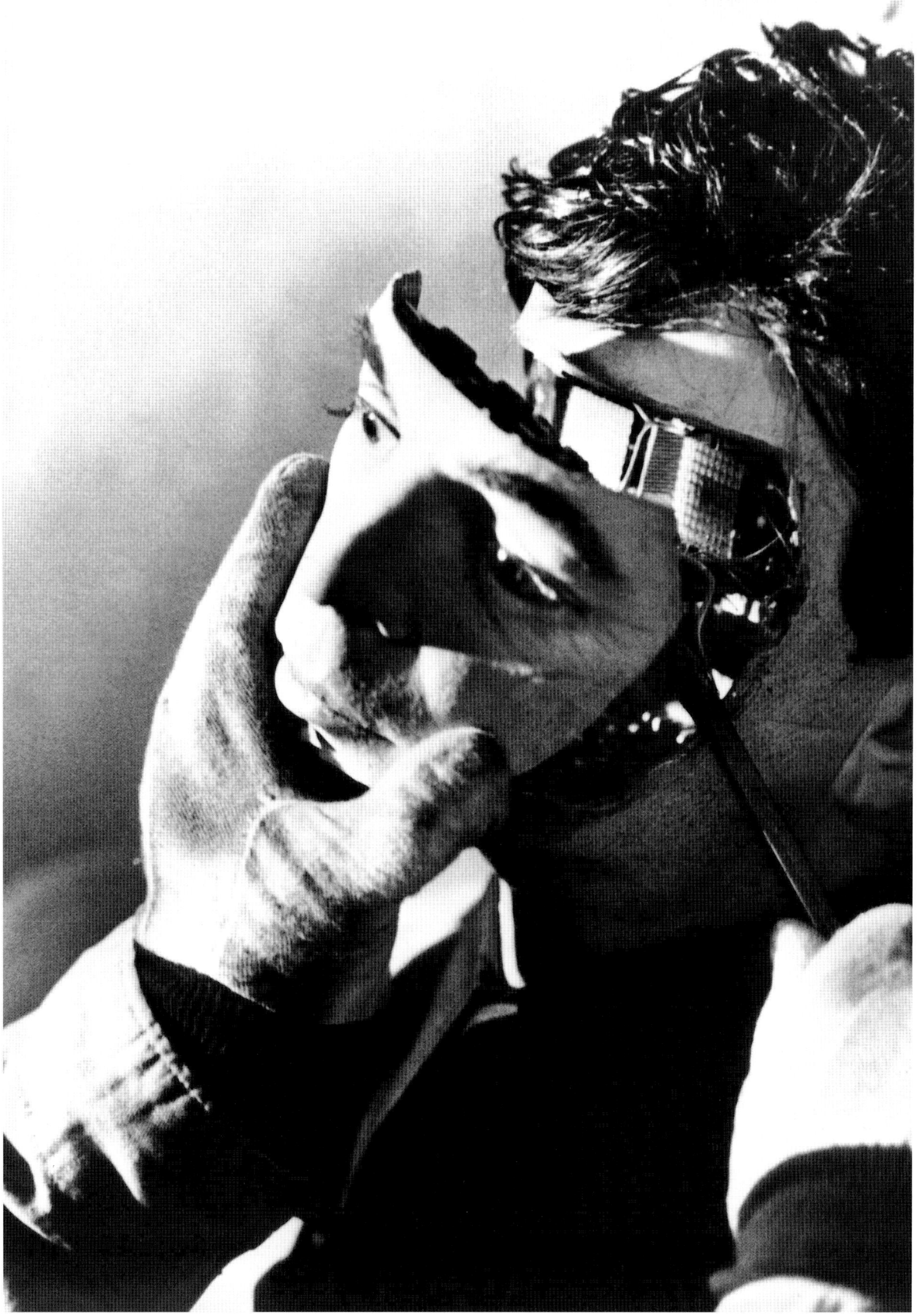

Studies on individual films

Much has been published on Fritz Lang's film METROPOLIS. Many of these publications address the motif of the robot in film. Yet until now, there had not been a comprehensive and consolidating monographic study of this topic. The same is true of the GOLEM films, with one exception:

20. Elfriede Ledig: Paul Wegeners Golem-Filme im Kontext fantastischer Literatur. Munich: Schaudig, Bauer, Ledig 1989, though its main focus is on literary studies.

For an analysis of the FRANKENSTEIN films, on the other hand, there are two useful monographic studies available:

21. Donald Glut (ed.): The Frankenstein Catalog: Being a comprehensive listing of novels, translations, adaptations, stories, critical works, popular articles, series, fumetti, verse, stage plays, films, cartoons, puppetry, radio & television programs, comics … Jefferson, North Carolina: McFarland 1984.

22. Stephen Jones: The Frankenstein Scrapbook: The Complete Movie Guide to the World's Most Famous Monster. Secaucus, New Jersey: Carol Publishing 1995.

An unusual interpretation of the FRANKENSTEIN motif can be found in Hans Schmid's essay in the anthology:

23. Cecilia Hausheer, Jutta Phillips-Krug (eds.): Frankensteins Kinder: Film und Medizin. Zürich: Museum für Gestaltung / Ostfildern-Ruit: Cantz 1997.
    Schmid regards the Frankenstein motif as a symbol of our modern grasp of reality, by which reality is no longer a given. Instead, we fragment the world into individual components and put them together again, with varying degrees of success, to create a new reality.

A number of monographic studies have been published on the TERMINATOR films, though they are generally of a popular nature or mere reiterations of the storyline. A laudable exception, albeit with a rather strenuous title, is:

24. Thomas Oberender: Zwischen Mensch und Maschine: Reflexionen über James Camerons Film Terminator 2 im Lichte der Philosophie von J.-F. Lyotard und über die Beziehung zwischen Narzismus und Video vor dem Hintergrund der Studentenrevolte. (Between Man and Machine: Reflections on James Cameron's Film Terminator 2 in the Light of the Philosophy of J.-F. Lyotard and on the Relationship between Narcissism and Video before the Background of the Student Revolts.) Siegen: Universität-Gesamthochschule Siegen 1993. (Massenmedien und Kommunikation 88.)

The fact that science fiction often has a political dimension is elucidated by Rob Wilson in his essay in the anthology:

25. Richard Burt (ed.): The Administration of Aesthetics: Censorship, Political Criticism, and the Public Sphere. Minneapolis, Minnesota: University of Minnesota Press 1994.
    Wilson persuasively interprets the ROBOCOP films by Paul Verhoeven and Irvin Kershner as the contradictory reflection of a post-industrial, post-national and post-democratic society.

Apart from METROPOLIS, Ridley Scott's BLADE RUNNER remains one of the most frequently debated and analyzed science fiction films, and this is reflected in the number of publications available on the subject. One that can be particularly recommended is:

26. Judith B. Kerman (ed.): Retrofitting Blade Runner: *Issues in Ridley Scott's* Blade Runner *and Philip K. Dick's Do Androids Dream of Electric Sheep? Bowling Green, Ohio: Bowling Green State University Popular Press 1991.*
    This collection of 19 essays examines the film from a number of angles, making this an excellent example of a well-structured and authoritative monographic study.

Even in the age of their technical reproducibility, works of art sometimes go missing. With this in mind, mention should be made of the following book:

27. Fritz Güttinger: Köpfen Sie mal ein Ei in Zeitlupe! Streifzüge durch die Welt des Stummfilms. Munich: Fink 1992.
    The author traces the lost robot film DIE GROSSE WETTE by Harry Piel (1915/16).

Artificial Humans
Biographical Notes

by Rolf Giesen

Alraune. German cinema took up this motif three times and devised an Alraune figure, embodied in 1927 and 1930 by Brigitte Helm and in 1952 by Hildegard Knef, that was based on the notorious novel of that title by Hanns Heinz Ewers (1911), which degraded Alraune to the quintessential embodiment of evil: "Whatever it touched turned to gold, where its gaze fell the wild senses laughed. Where its poisonous breath struck, however, all sin cried out, and out of the ground grazed by its airy feet grew Death's pale flowers."

Android. Frequently found in second-rate films: THE CREATION OF THE HUMANOIDS (1962), THE TIME TRAVELERS (1964), THE HUMAN DUPLICATORS (1964), DR GOLDFOOT AND THE BIKINI MACHINE (1965) and SCREAM AND SCREAM AGAIN (1969), THE QUESTOR TAPES (1973) as well as MILLENNIUM (1989). In ANDROID (1982) Klaus Kinski plays a scientist who has created artificial life on an abandoned space station. In Vittorio Cottafavi's Hercules muscleman epic ERCOLE ALLA CONQUISTA DI ATLANTIDE (1961), Queen Antinea of Atlantis breeds a blond Aryan "master race," with whose help she wants to subjugate the rest of the world. In EVE OF DESTRUCTION (1990), Renée Soutendijk creates an android fighting machine in her own image.

ANDROID
Don Opper

Artificial Intelligence. In his book "Eine schöne neue Welt?" (A Brave New World?, Düsseldorf: Econ 1994), Daniel Crevier sees an extraordinary threat emanating from AI: "The machines will someday become intellectually superior to us, and we will not be able to solve the problem by simply pulling the plug. (...) If machines acquire an intelligence that is superior to our own, there is no way we will be able to keep them in check. There have been countless cases in the history of mankind where a surrogate has set himself up as the actual sovereign of a country. The entire evolution of life on earth is nothing but a four-billion-year history of how descendants step into the footsteps of their parents. The relentless advance of AI forces us to ask the inevitable question: Are we about to create the next species of intelligent life on earth? (...) Can non-biological life reach a higher level of mental development than mankind?"

Ash. The science officer of the spaceship Nostromo in Ridley Scott's ALIEN (1979), played by Ian Holm, turns out in the course of the action to be a "damn robot."

Automaton. The first automaton in film history appeared in 1897 in Georges Méliès' film GUGUSSE ET L'AUTOMATE. In the British comedy THE PERFECT WOMAN (1949), a female automaton is the occasion for a lively story of mistaken identity. For Mikhail Romm's OBYKNOVENNYJ FAŠIZM (Ordinary Fascism, 1965), the distributor in Germany advertised the film with a poster showing an automaton with a clockwork.

Body Snatchers. In 1956 Don Siegel filmed Jack Finney's story of the alien Body Snatchers that slip into human bodies and take them over, under the title INVASION OF THE BODY SNATCHERS. Philip Kaufman returned to this material for a film in 1977. The scriptwriter Kevin Williamson used a similar motif in the film THE FACULTY (1998). Here, extraterrestrial parasites take possession of the bodies of the high school teachers.

C-3PO. Gold gleaming, butler-like robot from George Lucas' STAR WARS saga, modeled on Machine-Maria from METROPOLIS.

Cherry 2000. The love robot in the eponymous American film from 1988.

Clone. Genetic engineering is treated in such feature films as THE CLONES (1973), PARTS: THE CLONUS HORROR (1976), and EMBRYO (1976), in which Rock Hudson transforms an embryo into an adult woman. THE BOYS FROM BRAZIL (1978) and GATTACA (1997) both take up the topic of genetic engineering, as well. In THE CLONES OF BRUCE LEE (1980), a professor creates three Bruce Lee clones out of the dead master.

Cybernauts. Killer robots that gave three episodes of the popular British television series THE AVENGERS an 'uncanny' touch.

Cyborg. Michael Rennie as Garth A7 in CYBORG 2087 (1966). In the television series THE SIX MILLION DOLLAR MAN (1974–78) and THE BIONIC WOMAN (1976), human 'performance' is increased by means of medicine and electronics.

Daleks. Robots in a post-doomsday universe created by English film and television producers. Cinema versions included DR. WHO AND THE DALEKS (1965) and DALEKS – INVASION EARTH 2150 AD (1966).

Damned, The. The Hammer production THE DAMNED (1961), which Joseph Losey adapted from the novel "The Children of Light" by H.L. Lawrence, is about four girls and five boys who, like Kaspar Hauser, grow up in a subterranean prison at the foot of a cliff. They are deliberately exposed to radioactive radiation from birth on, so that they will be able to survive a possible nuclear war. Similarly, two further British productions centered around a group of cold-hearted, autistic (in this case alien-infiltrated) children: VILLAGE OF THE DAMNED (1960) and CHILDREN OF THE DAMNED (1963), based on the science fiction novel "The Midwich Cuckoos" by John Wyndham.

Data, Lt. Commander. The actor Brent Spiner, who plays the spacecraft android Data in the TV series STAR TREK: THE NEXT GENERATION (from 1987 on), reported that in the pilot episode he is called Pinocchio, which gave him a starting

Artificial Humans

MARY SHELLEY'S FRANKENSTEIN
Kenneth Branagh

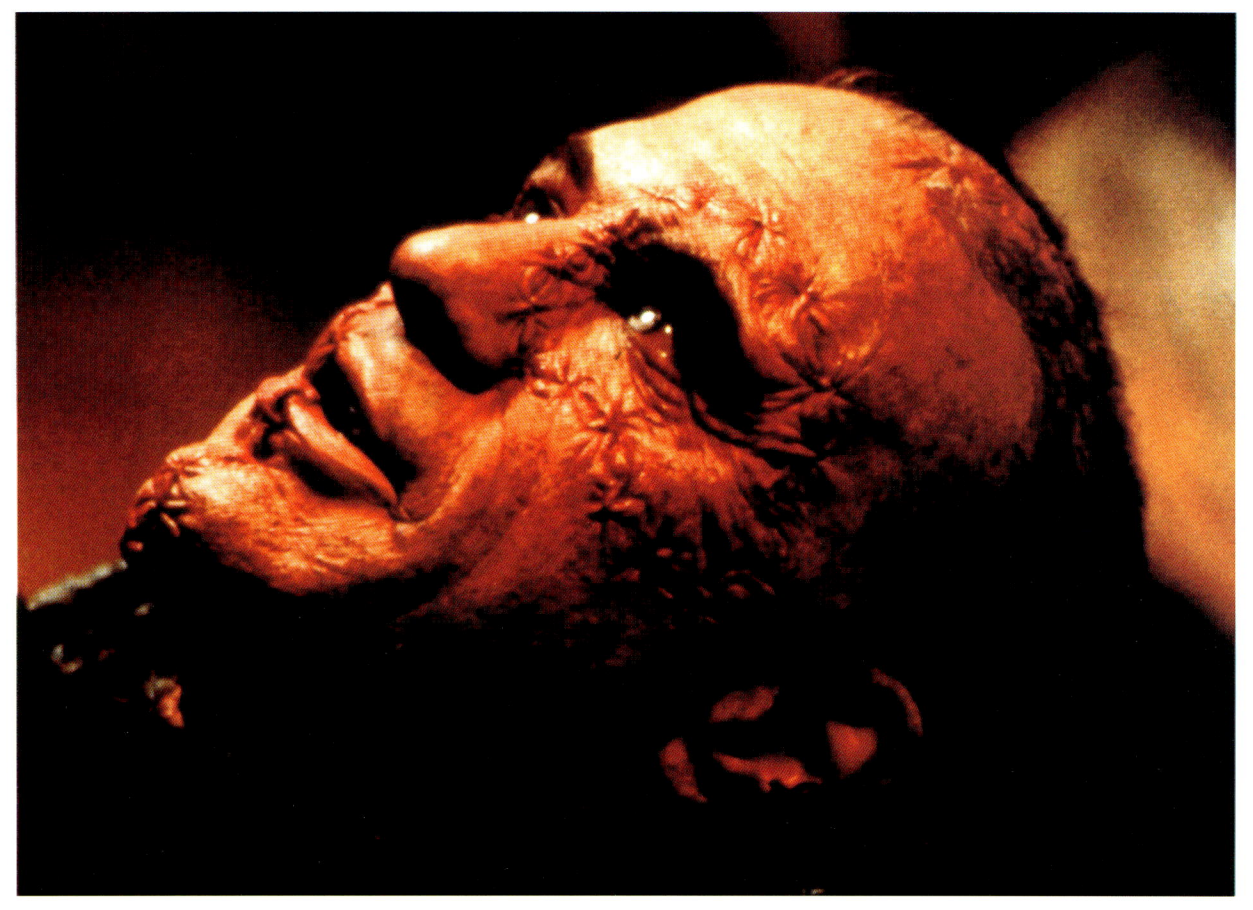

Robert De Niro

Artificial Humans

point for the conception of the role: he could mold the character of Data on the model of Pinocchio.

Dolls. Early cinematic examples include Méliès's Coppélia ou La Poupée animée (1900). In Ernst Lubitsch's Die Puppe (1919) a young man who is afraid of getting married orders a life-sized doll from a dollmaker. The dollmaker's daughter (played by Ossi Oswalda) has to take its place when the doll is broken. Murderous dolls are at the center of attention in the American film series Puppet Master (from 1989). Puppet animation represents a special section within the field of animation films: Aleksandr Ptuško and Novyi Gulliver (1935), Ferdinand Diehl and Die sieben Raben (1936/37), Jiří Trnka and Bajaja (1950), Karel Zeman as well as the Americans Willis O'Brien and Ray Harryhausen, who mixed animated models with live action.

Droids. Abbreviation for androids. Terminus technicus for robots in the Star Wars saga.

Drones. The little robots (drones) that look after the last Garden of Eden under the dome of a 21st century space ark in Douglas Trumbull's Silent Running (1971) have the Disney names of Donald Duck's nephews Huey, Dewey and Louie. The drones were played by leg-amputees.

Frankenstein. Three silent films avail themselves of this material: Frankenstein (1910) with Charles Ogle, Life Without Soul (1915) with Percy Darrell Standing and Il Mostro di Frankestein (1920) with Umberto Guarracino. They deal above all with the use of electricity as an agent of life-bringing energy, and accordingly, the electric apparatuses built by Kenneth Strickfaden are at the heart of the Frankenstein talking films that Universal produced with Boris Karloff and other actors as the monster, from 1931 on: "Your father was Frankenstein, but your mother was lightning," remarks Bela Lugosi to Lon Chaney Jr's monster in The Ghost of Frankenstein (1942). Starting in 1956, the British Hammer Films brought out a series of new Frankenstein films that concentrated on the creator (played by Peter Cushing) rather than the monster. Mel Brooks delivered his parody of the genre, Young Frankenstein, in 1974. One of the few films to treat the original subject matter sympathetically is Mary Shelley's Frankenstein (1994) by Kenneth Branagh.

Gog. In the Revelation of St. John the Divine, 20. 8, Gog and Magog are represented as the accomplices of Satan and of the enemies of God. In the film Gog, produced in 1954 by Ivan Tors, they are a pair of (non-humanoid) robots who are turned into crazy killer robots by an unknown power that infiltrates their subterranean research center.

Golem. The actor Paul Wegener directed the first three films about the clay colossus of the Talmudic legend: Der Golem (1914), which is apparently lost except for a few extant meters, Der Golem und die Tänzerin (The Golem and the Dancer, 1917) and, after World War I, Der Golem, wie er in die Welt kam (The Golem, How He Came into the World, 1920, with Carl Boese), in which Albert Steinrück plays Rabbi Loew. The Golem mask was designed by the sculptor Rudolf Belling. "The motif of the Golem, which flourished particularly in German Romanticism and was also taken up by Heine, Holitscher and Meyrink, underscores the relationship of Expressionism to the mind-set of this epoch and its fantastic stories about the unfathomable nature of the human soul, the power of fate, and the vulnerability of the creature in the face of an incomprehensible force." (Günther Dahlke, Günter Karl [eds.]: Deutsche Spielfilme von den Anfängen bis 1933. Ein Filmführer. Berlin/GDR: Henschel 1988) It is regarded as certain that the makers of the Frankenstein films at Universal knew Wegener's Golem. In addition to a French Golem version by Julien Duvivier (1935), there are also Czech films: Císařův Pekař and Pekařův Císař (both from 1951) as well as Slečna Golem (1972). In Peter Beauvais' German television movie Dreht Euch nicht um, der Golem geht rum! – oder das Zeitalter der Musse (1971), the evil-born Botho, a Golem figure, creates confusion in the 23rd century and poses a threat to the omnipotent cybernetic central brain.

Gort. Gigantic robot in the science fiction film The Day the Earth Stood Still (1951). In the utopian story on which the film is based, "Farewell to the Masters" by Harry Bates, the robot is called Gnut.

Hector. Robot from the film Saturn 3 (1980). Its brain is programmed directly through the brain of its constructor, who is a psychopath and murderer.

Homunculus. He first appeared as a film figure in the German film series Homunculus (1916). Here an artificial being created in the test-tube sets himself up as dictator over a weak and easily manipulated populace. In The Bride of Frankenstein (1935), Dr. Pretorius experiments with homunculi. For The Golden Voyage of Sinbad (1973), Ray Harryhausen animated a winged homunculus that a magician utilizes as a spy.

Kronos. Giant robot from the eponymous B-movie by Kurt Neumann (1957). Its designers used their creative imagination to design it in Cubist style.

Leloo. In a futuristic New York City nucleolab an alien warrior woman is reconstructed from 5000-year-old bone fragments. Milla Jovovich plays the role of Leloo in Luc Besson's film The Fifth Element (1997).

Machine-Woman Hel, also called: **Machine-Maria.** Android duplicate of the conciliator Maria (played by Brigitte Helm) created by the research scientist Rotwang in Fritz Lang's film Metropolis (modeled after E.T.A. Hoffmann's automaton Olimpia). The robot Maria is supposed to stir up the work force of the futuristic city. The figure was originally intended as a rebirth of Hel, the woman who had been taken away from Rotwang by Joh Fredersen, the ruler of Metropolis.

Majin. Gigantic Golem figure in three Japanese films produced by the Daiei film production company: Daimajin (1966), Daimajin Ikaru (1966) and Daimajin Gyakushu (1968).

Young Frankenstein
Peter Boyle

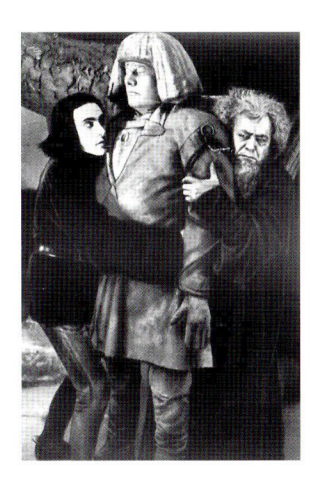

Der Golem, wie er in die Welt kam
Ernst Deutsch, Paul Wegener, Albert Steinrück

Artificial Humans

Maximilian. Caliban-like robot giant, companion of Dr. Hans Reinhardt (Maximilian Schell) in the Disney production THE BLACK HOLE (1979).

Mekagojira (Mechagodzilla). Robot counterfeit of the famous primeval monster Godzilla of Japanese cinema. Appeared in 1974 in the film GOJIRA TAI MEKAGOJIRA (Godzilla vs. the Cosmic Monster) for the first time.

Mogera. Mole-like giant robot in the Toho production CHIKYU BOEIGUN (1957), which might have been modeled on a Japanese Manga book from World War II: "Kagaku Senshi Nyu Yoku ni Shutsugen-su" (1943). It reappeared as Mobile Operations Godzilla Expert Robot Aero-Type in GOJIRA TAI SUPESU GOJIRA (Gojira vs. Space Godzilla, 1994). Skyscraper-high robot colossuses as expression of quasi puerile omnipotence and annihilation fantasies, controlled by specially trained "pilots," are also at the center of attention in both the Hong Kong production THE IRON MAN (1976) and the American film ROBOT JOX (1989) by Noah Gordon and animator Dave Allen.

Nija. In the Soviet film ČEREZ TERNII K ZVËZDAM (1980) by Richard Viktorov, Nija (played by Elena Metelkina) is an artificial creature subject to certain control impulses that has been created by the scientist Glan in order to counteract the ongoing destruction of the biosphere of his planet Dessa. With Nija's help he succeeds in overthrowing the dictator of Dessa, whose factories are poisoning the atmosphere.

Number 5. Robot developed by the military in John Badham's film SHORT CIRCUIT (1986). After being struck by lightning, it attains self-awareness and escapes from its pursuers; it also survives in the sequel SHORT CIRCUIT 2 (1988).

Pinocchio. Carlo Collodi's story of the wooden doll that wants to become a real boy has been a popular film subject since 1911, most successfully realized in Walt Disney's trick-film version of 1939/40. "After the performance of PINOCCHIO Collodi's nephew wanted to induce the Italian ministry to sue Disney, because the wooden rascal had become an 'American' boy." (Reinhold Reitberger: Walt Disney. Reinbek: Rowohlt 1979)

Replicants. The androids of the Nexus-6 series in Ridley Scott's cult film BLADE RUNNER (1982) arrive to take over power. In their external appearance they don't differ from normal people, are highly intelligent, and physically superior to any athlete. It comes to a showdown between the former cop Deckard and Batty, one of the replicants.

Robby. Isaac Asimov, pioneer of American science fiction, formulated the three "Laws of Robotics" that define the robot as a servant and should therefore prevent technology from getting out of control. They prescribe that a robot may not injure a human being, or, through inaction, allow a human being to come to harm; furthermore, a robot must obey the orders given it by human beings except where such orders would conflict with the first law; moreover, a robot must protect its own existence as long as such protection does not conflict with the first or second law. These postulates from Asimov's book "I, Robot" (published in 1950) were transformed into a film character most exemplarily in FORBIDDEN PLANET, an MGM production from 1956 for which special effects supervisor A. Arnold Gillespie designed the robot Robby in the form of a wandering oven – with a glass-dome as head. According to the screenplay, Robby, a mechanical version of the spirit Ariel from Shakespeare's drama "The Tempest," has mastered 188 languages and, if requested, can even reproduce alcohol. Robby also appears in other films: THE INVISIBLE BOY (1957), where a power-hungry computer wants to avail itself of Robby's services, and in certain episodes of the television series THE TWILIGHT ZONE (from 1959). John is the name of the Soviet counterpart of Robby in the film PLANETA BUR (1961).

Robocop. Cyborg cop, a synthesis of human being and machine. Paul Verhoeven's original movie from 1987 was followed by parts two and three as well as animated versions. Robot police also appear in the fully computerized underworld of THX 1138, staged by George Lucas in 1969.

Robot, Crow T. Robot from the American television series MYSTERY SCIENCE THEATER 3000 from 1988 that, together with its robot colleague Tom Servo, keeps a man company who has been banished to a space satellite. There they are constantly "bombarded" with trash movies. The three of them "pay tribute" to these works with sarcastic commentaries.

Robots. Many of the robots that appear in silent films (like THE AUTOMATIC MOTORIST, 1911), in cartoons (like MICKEY'S MECHANICAL MAN, 1933), in serials, and in more or less simple-minded science fiction movies are not without a certain unintentional humor: "These ghostly iron beings are gigantic toys that clank, squeak, purr and stamp their feet without actually producing anything, are destroyed in the end or destroy themselves and thus reduce the triumph of technology to absurdity." (Jürgen Menningen: Filmbuch Science Fiction. Cologne: Dumont Schauberg 1975) On television, robots appeared in series like LOST IN SPACE (1965–68) by Irwin Allen and the German TV series RAUMPATROUILLE (1966). In a futuristic Disneyland created by Michael Crichton (WESTWORLD, 1972), the robots suddenly flip out and start hunting down tourists for a change. In the film SLEEPER (1973), Woody Allen, who has been transported into a dictatorial future of the year 2173, parodies a robot.

R2-D2. Vacuum cleaner-sized robot from George Lucas' episode film STAR WARS (1976–1999). R2-D2 and its colleague C-3PO form a kind of Laurel & Hardy team. In EPISODE 1: THE PHANTOM MENACE (1999), the ten-year-old Anakin Skywalker is named as its designer.

Servo, Tom. Robot from the American television series MYSTERY SCIENCE THEATER 3000. For further information compare above under Robot, Crow T.

Stepford Wives, The. The (artificial) women of Stepford: Bryan Forbes filmed this American middle-class nightmare in 1975 after the eponymous novel by Ira Levin.

SHORT CIRCUIT
Ally Sheedy

The Black Hole

Artificial Humans

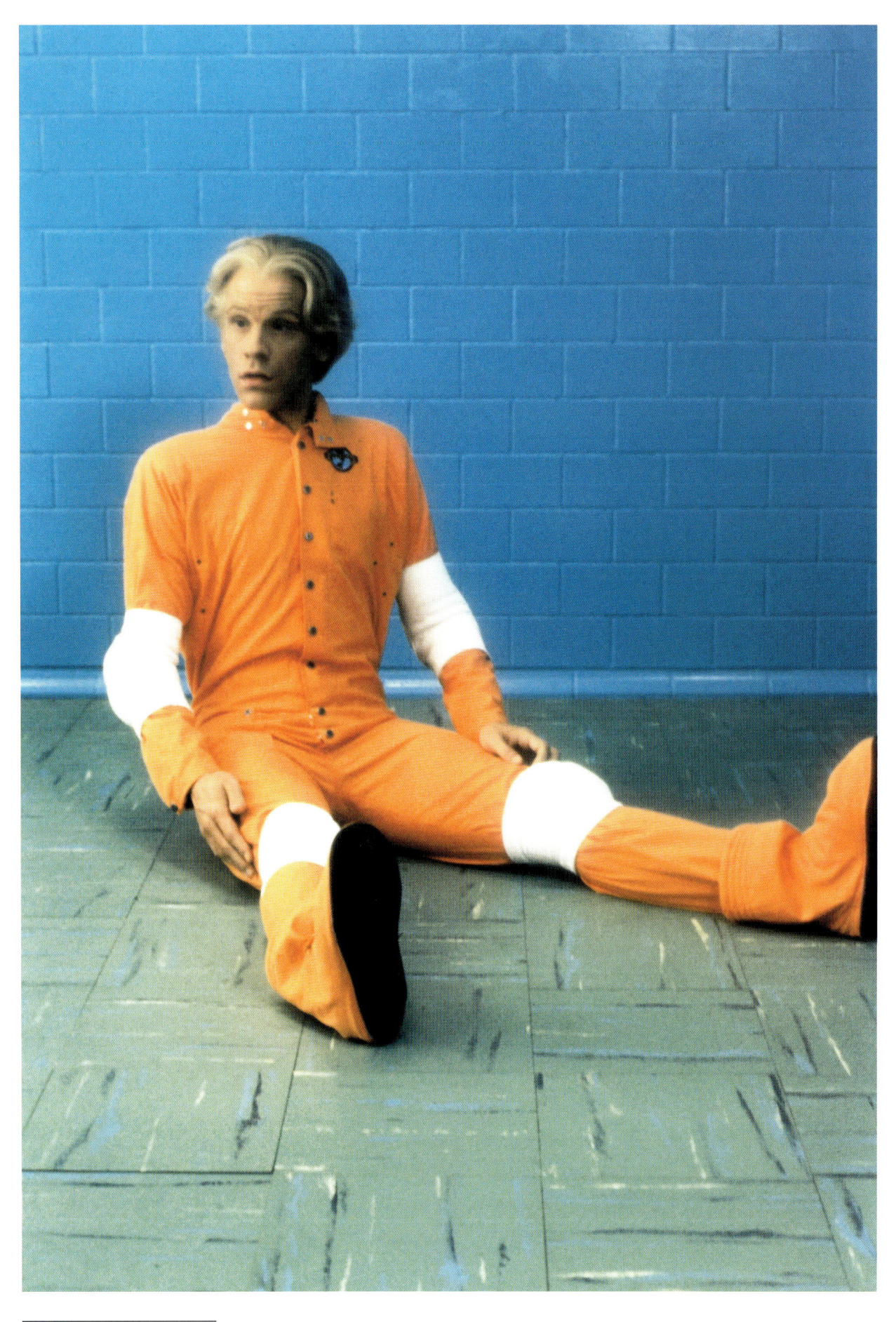

Artificial Humans

Making Mr. Right
John Malkovich

Talos. Bronze titan from Ray Harryhausen's Greek mythology adaptation JASON AND THE ARGONAUTS (1963) that grows to the size of the Colossus of Rhodes, comes alive, and then pursues the heroes of the Argonaut legend.

Terminator. Arnold Schwarzenegger as humanoid battle machine, robot of the type T-800: THE TERMINATOR (1984). In the better-known sequel TERMINATOR 2 – JUDGMENT DAY (1991), which was also directed by James Cameron, the T-800 is pursued by a newer T-1000 version, a terminator made of liquid steel that can "morph" (thanks to computer technology) into any form or shape it wants to.

Ultraman. Kaiju series launched in July 1966 by Tsuburaya Productions. Thanks to a Beta solar capsule left to him by an alien, Hayata, a member of the Science Patrol, is able to transform himself into the gigantic Ultraman, who fights all kinds of invaders and monsters by means of an energy ray. The film ULTRAMAN: TOWARDS THE FUTURE was realized as an Australian/Japanese co-production in 1990, followed by the Japanese-American partnership for the television series ULTRAMAN: THE ULTIMATE HERO in 1993.

Universal Soldier. In the eponymous movie from 1992, the musclemen Jean-Claude Van Damme and Dolph Lundgren play two soldiers who have been killed in the Vietnam War and are brought back to life by order of the U.S. Ministry of Defense and put to work combating terrorists. Roland Emmerich directed the comicbook-like orgy of violence, in the wake of TERMINATOR 2 and ROBOCOP.

Zylons. Family of robots from the film BATTLESTAR GALACTICA (1978).

Artificial Humans

Robocop
Peter Weller

Artificial Humans
A Glossary

by Rolf Giesen

Alraune. In the context of alchemistic experiments, not unlike the Homunculus myth, the figure of Alraune (or sometimes Alraun in the masculine form) was originally a goblin-like figure in popular mythology that takes its magic power from the root of the mandragora, or mandrake, which it is said to resemble. The little gallows creature is sometimes said to be engendered in a necrophile act of procreation, originating from the urine or sperm of a man immediately after he has been hanged dead.

Android. In contrast to genuine industrial robots, which are not necessarily anthropomorphous, androids are, in the tradition of living statues, human-like (from the Greek: andros – man, eides – having the form of).

Artificial Intelligence. In his book "AI. The Tumultuous History of the Search for Artificial Intelligence" (New York: BasicBooks 1993), Daniel Crevier sees an immense threat emanating from AI: "The machines will eventually excel us in intelligence, and it will become impossible for us to pull the plug on them. (...) When machines acquire an intelligence superior to our own, they will be impossible to keep at bay. Episodes where a deputy rises and becomes the effective ruler of a nation have happened countless times in history. The evolution of life on earth is itself nothing but a four-billion-year-long tale of offspring superseding parents. The unrelenting progress of AI forces us to ask the inevitable question: Are we creating the next species of intelligent life on earth? (...) Can nonbiological life achieve a higher spiritual evolution than humanity can?"

Automatons. Ancestors of the robot. The automatons came from the Arabian world to Europe. The 18th century, the Mechanical Age, saw man as a machine, a kind of bizarre mechanical toy. "The human automatons of Vaucanson, Jaquet-Droz, Kempelen and others fueled the dream of linear progress in the 18th century. They seemed to make it possible to see everything that is ideal and beautiful, such as music or thought, as a mere technical refinement of the material world." (Lienhard Wawrzyn: Der Automaten-Mensch. Berlin: Wagenbach 1976) The art of building automatons was firmly rooted in rationalism and philosophical materialism. Descartes, who was believed to have constructed automatons, saw the human body, analogous to a clock built of wheels and weights, as a kind of machine, to which he ascribed a soul, however, in contrast to the purely hydraulic systems of the animals.

Clones. "Clone" originally meant "twig" in Greek. Today, it refers to people, animals or cells whose genetic makeup is completely identical. Natural clones are, for example, identical twins; artificial clones originate through manipulation of egg or body cells. The nucleus of a body cell that contains all the genetic information is fused with an unfertilized egg cell from which the nucleus has been removed. The embryo that is formed is then implanted into the uterus of a surrogate mother. In 1997 the cloned sheep "Dolly" made headlines. Meanwhile, attempts by cyberneticians, biochemists, and gene technicians now aim at cloning a completely artificial human being whose physical and physiological reactions can be anticipated and influenced. Forerunners in this sector are found in the area of plastic surgery and the "spare parts store" of transplant surgery. The future belongs to gene manipulation, the goal of which, according to Dr. Domday of the Gene Center in Munich, is to "eliminate natural evolution." Aldous Huxley anticipated this in his novel "Brave New World." The future society he sketched in 1932 is determined by planned human procreation, whereby nothing is left to accident. Social problems are solved by eugenic, biological, chemical, and physical means. The test-tube babies are born in five different grades, from Alpha to Epsilon. From an article in the magazine "Dr. med. Mabuse": "Animals should soon be able to provide organs for people, the early diagnosis of human illnesses in the test tube is on the advance, and the decoding of the human genome will be completed in a few years. Even after 25 years of experience with genetic engineering, the evaluation of it still alternates between hope and horror." (January/February 1998) Visions of horror formulated in classical antiquity take shape in the human mind: hybrids of humans and animals, like the proverbial Chimera, a cross-breed of lion, goat and serpent, according to Homer. It seems possible that we will be able to produce genes synthetically one day or to put the genes of animals into the human genome. Scientists, philosophers and politicians demand that limits should be set where man deliberately sets out to change the hereditary factors of human beings by means of new biological methods. Unlike in the United States, there is an "Embryo Protection Law" in Germany that forbids the cloning of human beings.

Computer People. Virtual likenesses in 3-D animation. Animations of deceased stars like Marilyn Monroe and Humphrey Bogart are possible, but also synthetic beings *sui generis* like Lara Croft or The Mask.

Cyborg. Short for Cybernetic Organism. Man and technology join together to form a new organism. "Thad Starner is one of them. Since he got his first 'Wearable Computer' six years ago as a student at Massachusetts Institute of Technology (MIT) in Cambridge, USA, he is connected at every waking minute. During important conversations, he immediately takes notes with his one-handed keyboard, has the way to a new café displayed by means of GPS (Global Positioning System), knows an answer to almost every question within a few minutes. Starner is the latest step on the way to becoming a cyborg. (...) 'Wearable computers mean wearable intelligence,' says Professor Alex Pentland, academic head of the MIT Media Labs and leader of the 'Wearables' research group, explaining the concept behind the new technology. (...) Pentland's wearable computers possess all of the components of a normal PC. A

HOMUNCULUS
Friedrich Kühne (with glass ball), Albert Paul (right)

Ernst Ludwig, Albert Paul

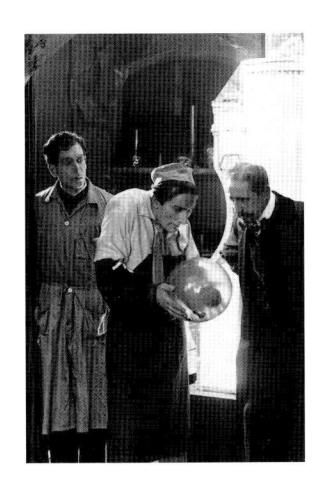

monitor as small as an ink cartridge sits on one of the sidepieces of the glasses and projects the picture via mirror onto the lens, which reflects it back onto the eye. The amazing thing is that the glasses don't weigh more than normal eyeglasses. The monitor can be plainly seen by the human eye and looks like a little blackboard seen from a distance of about two meters. 'Although I constantly alternate between the display and the real surroundings, it never gives me headaches,' says Starner." (Die Woche, June 4, 1999)

Dolls. Originally, they were replicas of human beings often used for cultic or magic rituals, as burial objects or as toys; now intended, in conservative socialization, primarily for young girls. We find dolls in Egypt, Mesopotamia, Greece, Rome, in the high cultures of antiquity as well as in the Orient. In puppet shows either hand puppets, puppets on a stick, or marionettes are used. "References from linguistic research confirm that the origins of puppet shows are to be found at the dawn of ancient world cultures, in the mythical realm of the cults of gods and idols." (Günter Böhmer: Puppentheater. Munich: Bruckmann 1977)

Frankenstein. Mary Wollstonecraft Shelley, daughter of the feminist Mary Wollstonecraft and wife of the poet Percy Bysshe Shelley, wrote her Gothic novel "Frankenstein, or The Modern Prometheus" (published in 1818) in 1816 at the age of 19. The Swiss Baron Victor Frankenstein creates new life not by means of magic practices, but by applying physical laws (even if he stays entirely within the tradition of individual alchemists). Then, however, he rejects the creature as if it were a changeling.

Golem. "Golem" originally comes from the Hebrew word for "embryo, or formless thing." In the 12th century the Golem was a being created through magical, cabalistic methods, unscientific processes. It is awakened to life and also destroyed again by means of a kind of password, as we would say today – through the power of the letters. The story of the Golem created by the High Rabbi Loew (1512–1609) first appeared in literary form in 19th century Prague: the clay colossus has been made in order to serve the Rabbi's people, but it rebels and has to be destroyed by its master. With the beginning of the Industrial Age, the diluted Golem myth was often thrown in together with the Frankensteins and robots of nascent science fiction.

Homunculus. Homunculi is the name Paracelsus gave to chemically generated miniature human beings. If the Golem myth is about the imitation of divine means of creation, the motif behind the Homunculus legend is the attempt to "perfect" the human being, the quest to achieve a new level in Goethe's sense.

Human Automaton. The human automaton is no longer a construct of wheels and feathers, but a citizen like us: "He has his feelings under control, prescribes his own pleasures and refuses to be nice except through polite phrases. He carefully organizes his time. If he visits friends, he knows in advance when he will arrive and when he will leave again." (Lienhard Wawrzyn: Der Automaten-Mensch. Berlin: Wagenbach 1976)

Hybrids. Sphinxes, centaurs, satyrs, chimeras, the Minotaur: originating from a caprice of the gods, they were a punishment for mankind. During the Moscow show trials, the chief prosecutor Vyshinsky called Bukharin "an accursed cross between fox and pig."

Industrial Robots. Introduced in the course of automation. Electronically controlled, programmed by a small computer or microprocessor, furnished with a number of possible movements, and equipped with pincers, tools and such things.

Living Statues. Pygmalion, "shocked at the vices Nature had given the female disposition," makes an ivory statue of a woman, "and the fire of the counterfeit creation burned in his breast" (Ovid). The living see themselves perpetuated in their image: the work of art, the statue, outlasts death and promises the longed-for eternal life.

Nanoworld. Ever greater miniaturizations are helping to accelerate the development of nanoelectronics. In the plans, among other developments, is a molecular data memory that can theoretically store thousands of gigabytes per square millimeter. The world of medicine is also on the way to being revolutionized through nanotechnology.

Olimpia. Automaton from E.T.A. Hoffmann's story "Der Sandmann" (The Sandman, 1817). Also appears in Léo Delibes's ballet "Coppélia" (1870) and in Jacques Offenbach's opera "Les Contes d'Hoffmann" (Tales of Hoffmann, 1880).

Robots. From the Czech "robota" – compulsory labor. Self-moving automatons. The first remote-controlled robot "Televox" was demonstrated in Pittsburgh by R.J. Wensley in 1927; in 1932 a corresponding model was introduced at the Chicago World's Fair; "Dynamo Joe," constructed in 1951 in Bristol, could ride a bicycle. Switzerland had its "Sabor" robot, particularly "Sabor V" (1960), and Japan its "Wabot-1" as of 1973. Autonomous robots have been in use now for a long time. They are automatons that learn and adapt, not machines that are controlled by inflexible programs or cybernetic systems. Robots equipped with artificial intelligence realize a target by carrying out a sequence of actions that are determined by environmental conditions registered via sensors; to a certain degree they perform physical or "mental" tasks independently. Robots with sensors and object-recognition systems have been constructed since 1968, those with the ability to learn since 1972. For Joachim Kalka the robot is characterized in the science fiction genre by means of the following unspoken analogies: the machine that has gotten out of control, the tool (not the worker!): the technology that is no longer clearly grasped and that suddenly turns into a puzzle. / the child, the servant, the watchdog. [compare the film title from 1909: THE ELECTRIC SERVANT] / the demon, the criminal, the wild animal: technology that gets out of control. / the rebellious slave. (see Kursbuch, No. 43, Berlin: Wagenbach 1976)

Artificial Humans

Die heiratsfähige Puppe
Dora Kaiser, Otto Wilhelm,
Frau Winterberg, Heinz Hanus

Die Puppe
Marga Köhler, Ossi Oswalda, Victor
Janson, Gerhard Ritterband

123

Artificial Humans

THX 1138

THX 1138
Robert Duvall

R.U.R. Rossum's Universal Robots. Stage play by the Czech author Karel Čapek (1890–1938) from the year 1920. Čapek derived the term "robot" from the Slavic word "robota." "While the term 'robot' now generally refers to automation predominantly by means of inorganic material, for Čapek it still meant beings that were produced from organic substances, namely from 'colloidal jelly.' The robots were manufactured mechanically in factories, however. 'What kind of worker in your opinion is the best one practically? ... the cheapest. The one with the fewest needs. Young Rossum has invented a worker with minimal needs. He had to simplify it. Discarded everything that didn't serve the work directly. With that he actually discarded the human being and created the robot... Robots are not people. They are mechanically more perfect than we are, have stunning intelligence, but they don't have a soul... the product of an engineer is technically more polished than a natural product.' (...) When the workers revolt against this and smash the robots into pieces, the governments give the automatons arms and teach them to kill and to wage war. Since they have enough robot soldiers, more and more wars are fought. Finally the robots rise up, destroy the people except for one, and set up their own rule." (Dieter Wuckel: Science Fiction. Eine illustrierte Literaturgeschichte. Hildesheim: Olms 1986) It can be assumed that the play that was presented in Germany in 1922 under the title "W.U.R. Werstands Universal Robots" served Fritz Lang and Thea von Harbou as a model for the machine beings in METROPOLIS. Čapek's play was filmed in 1935 in the USSR under the title GIBEL' SENSACII.

Artificial Humans

Tron

Addenda

Authors / Acknowledgements / Photos

Authors

Elisabeth Bronfen, born in 1958. Associate Professor of English and American Literature at the University of Zurich. Publications include: "Over her Dead Body: Death, Femininity and the Aesthetic" (1992), "The Knotted Subject: Hysteria and its Discontents" (1998) and "Heimweh. Illusionsspiele in Hollywood" (1999). Lives in Zurich.

Giorgio C. Buttazzo, born in 1960. Associate Professor of Computer Technology at the University of Pavia (Italy). Author and co-author of books about real time systems, numerous academic publications. Lives in Pisa.

Peter Gendolla, born in 1950. Professor of Literature, Art, New Media and Technologies at the Comprehensive University of Siegen. Publications include: "Anatomien der Puppe. Zur Geschichte des Maschinenmenschen bei Jean Paul, E.T.A. Hoffmann, Villiers de l'Isle Adam und Hans Bellmer" (1992), "MaschinenMenschen. Eine Bibliographie" (with Bernhard J. Dotzler and Jörgen Schäfer, 1992). Lives in Netphen.

Rolf Giesen, born in 1953. Film book author, designer of trick films (member of Visual Effects Society). Numerous film exhibitions. Publications include: "Kino wie es keiner mag" (1984), "Fernsehen wie es jeder hasst" (1987), "Alfred Hitchcock. Der Meister der Angst" (with Ronald M. Hahn, 1999). Lives in Berlin.

Ulrich Gutmair, born in 1968. Journalist. Writes for various daily newspapers and magazines on- and off-line and is part of the media arts collective convex tv. Lives in Berlin.

Klaus Kreimeier, born in 1938. Professor for Media Studies at the Comprehensive University of Siegen. Publications include: "Nadine Gordimer" (1991), "Die Ufa-Story", "Notizen im Zwielicht" (both in 1992), "Lob des Fernsehens" (1995). Lives in Pulheim-Dansweiler.

Holger Schnell, born in 1959. Freelance editor and journalist specializing in literature and art history, film history and theory, as well as the fantastic in literature and film. Lives in Berlin.

Georg Seeßlen, born in 1948. Journalist. Works for "Die Zeit", "Der Tagesspiegel", "Freitag", "Frankfurter Rundschau", "Konkret" and other publications. Author of numerous books, most recently "Quentin Tarantino" (with Robert Fischer and Peter Körte, 1999) and "Alfred Hitchcock" (with Lars-Olav Beier, 1999). Lives in Leinau/Allgäu and Borgo/Liguria.

Katharina Sykora, born in 1955. Professor of Art History of the Middle and Modern Periods specializing in gender-based research at the Ruhr University of Bochum. Recent publications include "Puppen Körper Automaten. Phantasmen der Moderne" (with Pia Müller-Tamm) and "Unheimliche Paarungen. Androidenfaszination und Geschlecht in der Fotografie" (both 1999). Lives in Berlin and Bochum.

Editors

Rolf Aurich, born in 1960. Editor at the Filmmuseum Berlin – Deutsche Kinemathek. Lives in Berlin.

Wolfgang Jacobsen, born in 1953. Film historian and head of the department Publications and Events at the Filmmuseum Berlin – Deutsche Kinemathek. Lives in Berlin.

Gabriele Jatho, born in 1959. Editor at the Filmmuseum Berlin – Deutsche Kinemathek. Lives in Berlin.

Translators

Stephen Locke, born in 1941 in New York. Freelance film journalist, editor, translator and press officer. Works for Internationale Filmfestspiele Berlin and Nordic Film Days Lübeck. Lives in Hamburg.

Ishbel Flett, born in 1958. Studied French, German and History of Art in Edinburgh. Freelance translator specializing in art and architecture. Lives in Frankfurt am Main.

Pauline Cumbers, born in 1949 in Dublin, Ireland. Studied German and French in Dublin. Freelance translator, specializing in the fields of art and photography. Lives in Frankfurt am Main.

Acknowledgements

Many people have provided generous support in approaching the topic of this retrospective through their advice and suggestions. The publishers would like to thank: Mareike Ahlborn (Oktagon. Architektur – Kunst – Medien, Cologne), Henning Aurich (Abbensen), Prof. APL. Dr. Dr. Udo Benzenhoefer (Medizinische Hochschule, Hanover), Knut Bergel (Eidos Interactive Deutschland, Hamburg), Volker Busch (Goldmann Verlag, Munich), Mr. Buschner (Landesbildstelle Berlin), Paolo Caneppele (Filmarchiv Austria, Vienna), Brigitte Capitain (Deutsches Filminstitut, Frankfurt am Main), Henrike Grohs (Haus der Kulturen der Welt, Berlin), Klaus Hoeppner (Berlin), Ute Klawitter (Bundesarchiv-Filmarchiv, Berlin), Rüdiger Koschnitzki (Deutsches Filminstitut, Frankfurt am Main), Joerg Kraut (Future Press, Hamburg), Günter Krenn (Filmarchiv Austria, Vienna), Ulrich Kriest (Weil im Schönbuch), Nicola Lepp (Deutsches Hygiene-Museum, Dresden), Klaus Lüchau (Munich), Jörg Magenau (Berlin), Helmut Merschmann (Berlin), Olaf Möller (Cologne), Schorsch Müller (Rosebud Entertainment, Berlin), Michaela Olbrich (FWU Institut für Film und Bild in Wissenschaft und Unterricht, Munich), Dr. Gorch Pieken (Deutsches Historisches Museum, Berlin), Gudrun Pukies (Institut für den Wissenschaftlichen Film, Göttingen), Yvonne Rehhahn (Berlin), Susanne Roeßiger (Deutsches Hygiene-Museum, Dresden), Dr. Rainer Rother (Deutsches Historisches Museum, Berlin), Hans-Joachim Schlegel (Berlin), Marion Schneider (Deutsches Hygiene-Museum, Dresden), Wilhelm Staudinger (Chaplin-Archiv, Frankfurt am Main), Winfried Sträter (DeutschlandRadio Berlin), Katharina Sykora (Berlin/Bochum), Tanja Witsch (VG Bild-Kunst, Bonn), Merten Worthmann (Hamburg).

We gratefully acknowledge the cooperation of the following individuals and organizations in making prints available for this series: Kevin Brownlow, Patrick Stanbury, Photoplay Productions; Elaine Burrows, National Film and Television Archive, London; Stefan Drößler, Filmmuseum München; Howard Green, Scott MacQueen, Walt Disney Company; Kiyo Joo, Gold View Company, Ltd; John Kirk, MGM Studios; Marion Koltai-Levine, FineLine Features; Richard May, Warner Bros./Turner Entertainment Corporation; Mario Musumeci, Cineteca Nazionale, Rome; Michael Schlesinger, Columbia Pictures; Edgar J. Sherick; Greg Forston, Palm Pictures; Gudrun Weiss, Friedrich-Wilhelm-Murnau-Stiftung, Wiesbaden; Ed Zeier, Universal Pictures; Paramount Pictures; First Run Features; Contemporary Films, London.

Photos

For their generous help in procuring photo material we would like to thank: André Chevalier, Cinémathèque Suisse, Lausanne; Beate Dannhorn, Deutsches Filmmuseum, Frankfurt am Main; Andreas Heese, Staatliche Museen zu Berlin – Preussischer Kulturbesitz, Kupferstichkabinett – Sammlung der Zeichnungen und Druckgraphik; Günter Krenn, Filmarchiv Austria, Vienna; Monika Krisch, Archiv für Kunst und Geschichte, Berlin; Tobias Lehmann, Archiv für Kunst und Geschichte, Berlin; Mr. Löher, Westfälisches Schulmuseum, Dortmund; André Mieles, Deutsches Filminstitut, Frankfurt am Main; Karen Müller-Kühne, Archiv für Kunst und Geschichte, Berlin; Hans-Peter Reichmann, Deutsches Filmmuseum, Frankfurt am Main; B.H. Wahl, Universal Pictures Germany, Hamburg.

Individual photo credits:
Archiv für Kunst und Geschichte, Berlin (11: p. 21; p. 56 above, center, bottom; p. 59 top; p. 80; p. 83; p. 88; p. 91 top; p. 92 bottom; p. 93 top); Cinémathèque Suisse, Lausanne (5); Deutsches Filminstitut, Frankfurt am Main (5); Deutsches Filmmuseum, Frankfurt am Main (20); Eidos Interactive Deutschland, Hamburg (1: p. 106/107); Filmarchiv Austria, Wien (3); Filmmuseum Berlin – Deutsche Kinemathek (47); Kobal Collection, London (15); Françoise Molinier, Saint Savin (3: p. 99); Staatliche Museen zu Berlin – Preußischer Kulturbesitz, Kupferstichkabinett – Sammlung der Zeichnungen und Druckgraphik (2: p. 78 left, photos: Jörg P. Anders); Ullstein Bilderdienst, Berlin (2: p. 97; p. 100); VG Bild-Kunst, Bonn (4: p. 98); Westfälisches Schulmuseum, (1: p. 42).